By the Numbers:
A Guide for Analyzing Race Data
from Vehicle Stops

Contents

Foreword vii
Acknowledgements xiii
Chapter 1: Introduction 1
Chapter 2: The Benchmarking Challenge 7
Chapter 3: Getting Started 35
Chapter 4: Data Analysis Guidelines for
    All Benchmarking Methods 49
Chapter 5: Benchmarking with Adjusted Census Data 75
Chapter 6: Benchmarking with DMV Data 113
Chapter 7: Benchmarking with Data from
    "Blind" Enforcement Mechanisms 123
Chapter 8: Benchmarking with Data for
    Matched Officers or Matched Groups of Officers 143
Chapter 9: Observation Benchmarking 161
Chapter 10: Other Benchmarking Methods 203
Chapter 11: .... forthcoming
Chapter 12: .... forthcoming
Chapter 13: .... forthcoming
Appendix A 263
Appendix B 289
Appendix C 291
Appendix D 295
Appendix E 301
References 307
About the Author 319
About the Office of Community
Oriented Policing Services (COPS) 321
About PERF 323
Related PERF Titles 325

Foreword

The term "racial profiling" emerged only in the late 1990s, but concerns about whether some police are racially biased in their decision making date back decades, arguably even centuries, in U.S. history. The tensions between police and minority residents are longstanding and their potency is reflected by the devastating riots of the 1950s and 1960s, as well as by urban unrest in more recent years in Los Angeles, Cincinnati, Miami and myriad other locations. The good news, however, is that the law enforcement field is more capable than ever of addressing this persistent issue. We have witnessed profound reforms in policing during the last few decades-including those linked to hiring, training, policies, and community partnerships. This "new age of policing"(characterized by openness, respect for human dignity, accountability, and outreach-provides a solid foundation and a great potential for unprecedented progress in addressing the perception and practice of racially biased policing.

And, indeed, law enforcement agencies across the country have been responding to the concerns raised by their residents about racial bias. A Police Executive Research Forum (PERF) 2001 publication, supported by the U.S. Department of Justice's Office of Community Oriented Policing Services (COPS Office), was developed to help them in those efforts. That document, *Racially Biased Policing: A Principled Response*, was the first major product of the PERF/COPS partnership on this critical topic. It outlined the major areas of intervention for agencies concerned about racially biased policing and the perceptions of its practice.[1] Chapters detailed approaches for agencies in supervision and accountability, policy, recruitment and hiring,

---

[1] This document can be downloaded from www.policeforum.org.

training and education, community outreach, and data collection. By choice or by mandate, many agencies have adopted this last response option(data collection. To collect data, line officers are asked to report information on vehicle and/or pedestrian stops. The information includes the race/ethnicity of the driver and other details about the stop (e.g., reasons for the stop, disposition of the stop, whether a search was conducted, outcome of the search). Data collection is meant to assist agency administrators and jurisdiction residents with determining whether racial bias influences police decisions to make stops. The chapter on data collection in the first document identified promising practices in terms of the types of stops to target for data collection and the data elements to collect. However, at that time, there had not yet emerged any promising approaches for analyzing and interpreting the data.

While the agencies that were the first to adopt data collection can be commended for their analysis efforts, PERF staff's review of early reports revealed that analyses were being conducted in a manner that did not reflect even minimal scientific standards and conclusions were being drawn that were wholly unsupported by the data. Back then, and even as this document goes to press, most agencies were and still are conducting "census benchmarking." In census benchmarking agencies compare the demographic profile of the drivers stopped by police to the demographic profile of the residents of the jurisdiction as determined by the U.S. Census. For a variety of reasons, such a comparison is of no scientific value for purposes of trying to measure racial bias in policing and, in fact, has very often resulted in misleading and unsupported findings.

Many agency executives and other stakeholders (e.g., concerned citizen leaders, civil rights leaders) have understood that the analyses of vehicle stop data is frequently wanting, but they have been frustrated by the lack of guidance in this area. Indeed, while people calling PERF and the COPS Office in the late 1990s and early 2000s inquired about the types of stops to target for data collection and the types of data to collect, by 2002 and into 2003 more calls were along the lines of, "We've collected the data; *now what do we do?*" The calls reflecting the most frustration have come from agencies that have been mandated by local or state legislation to collect data but have not been provided with the guidance or resources required to implement that charge effectively. These inquiries increased exponentially as more and more agencies voluntarily or through mandates adopted data collection. Pending state and federal legislation, if adopted, would further increase the number of agencies across the United States collecting data.

To meet the burgeoning needs of the police community, PERF and the COPS Office have partnered again, this time to provide the guidance that is needed to ensure the responsible analysis and interpretation of vehicle stop data. *By the Numbers* is a detailed "how to" guide for analyzing race data from vehicle stops. It provides a social science framework for understanding the challenges of trying to measure racial bias in policing and presents an array of methods for law enforcement professionals, researchers and other stakeholders to consider when interpreting the vehicle-stop data. The primary audience for this technical guide includes the people who will actually be conducting the analyses, though police professionals at all levels, policy makers and others have much to gain by reading the preliminary chapters. Following these introductory chapters, *By the Numbers* provides step-by-step guidance for implementing various benchmarking methods. A companion document, *Understanding Vehicle-Stop Race Data: A Stakeholders' Guide*, is specifically written for a broader audience-including police agency executives, concerned residents, advocacy groups, the media, and policy makers. It discusses the challenge of analyzing vehicle-stop data and summarizes the key contents of By the Numbers in a less technical fashion.[2]

---

[2] This guide can be downloaded from www.policeforum.org in the Spring of 2004.

By the Numbers does not recommend a "perfect method" that will allow an agency to simply, easily and definitively measure whether racial bias is manifested in police decisions. Such a method does not exist. The question of whether bias influences some officers when they stop drivers, like many other social science research questions in criminal justice and related fields, is impossible to answer with complete certainty. There are, however, some methodologies that are much stronger than others in their ability to answer the key research question—that is, we can have more confidence in the results. *By the Numbers* not only provides detailed guidance for implementing the various methods, but also includes assessments of each method's strengths and weaknesses. This information will help readers implement the strongest method that available resources will allow and ensure that the conclusions they draw from the chosen method are responsible.

While this technical document is meant to assist the individuals who are conducting the analyses, it is designed to serve many others. PERF and the COPS Office hope that this document will ensure that residents and other stakeholders receive responsible answers to their very real questions about racial bias. In addition, we hope that this document will assist policy makers who will make decisions regarding whether to mandate that agencies in their jurisdiction collect data. These men and women can now make this decision with an understanding of the challenges of measuring racial bias and the considerable resources required for the responsible implementation of a data collection mandate.

PERF and the COPS Office hope that this document will be of value to law enforcement practitioners. The vast majority of police officers in this country are principled, dedicated men and women who are committed to serving all citizens with equity and fairness. They now find themselves the "subjects" of study by virtue of voluntary or mandatory data collection. It is unjust to have their reputations tarnished by non-scientific analyses and we trust this document will help prevent this practice and, instead, ensure responsibly implemented and reported analyses of vehicle-stop data.

Beyond bringing value to individual audiences of concerned residents and law enforcement practitioners, we hope this document will facilitate stronger relationships between them. The issues related to racially biased policing and the perceptions of its practice cannot be addressed effectively by either group alone. To address this longstanding issue, residents, other stakeholders and police must join together to identify concerns about law enforcement practices and outline how they will be resolved. PERF and the COPS Office hope this document will substantially advance this important dialogue.

Carl Peed
Director, COPS Office

Chuck Wexler
Executive Director, PERF

Acknowledgements

On behalf of PERF, I convey great appreciation to Director Carl Peed, Deputy Director Pam Cammarata, and other leaders in the U.S. Department of Justice Office of Community Oriented Policing Services (COPS Office). They shared our belief that there was a significant need for this document and provided the necessary funding to bring it to fruition. I am particularly grateful for the very constructive guidance and unwavering support I received throughout this project from Tamara Clark Lucas, our COPS Office monitor.

An advisory board made up of both practitioners and social scientists met early on in the project to guide the content and form of this document. Many read chapters or sections as they were completed. Members of this board included Dr. Gary Cordner, Eastern Kentucky University; Dr. Scott Decker, University of Missouri, St. Louis; Assistant Chief John Diaz, Seattle (WA) Police Department; Captain Thomas Didone, Montgomery County (MD) Police Department; Dr. Don Faggiani, PERF; Dr. Amy Farrell, Northeastern University; Secretary Ed Flynn, Massachusetts Executive Office of Public Safety; Assistant Chief John Gallagher, Miami (FL) Police Department; Former Chief Mark Kroeker, Portland (OR) Police Bureau; Dr. John Lamberth, Lamberth Consulting; Dr. Catherine Lawson, State University of New York at Albany; Dr. Steve Mastrofski, George Mason University; Dr. Jack McDevitt, Northeastern University; Antony Pate, COSMOS Corporation; Assistant Deputy Superintendent Karen Rowan, Chicago (IL) Police Department; Professor Margo Schlanger, Harvard University; Dr. Ellen Scrivner, Former Deputy Director of the COPS Office; Dr. Deborah Thomas, University of Colorado at Denver; Dr. Sam Walker, University of Nebraska at Omaha; Dr. Charles Wellford,

University of Maryland; and Dr. Matt Zingraff, North Carolina State University.

A group of academics-most of them members of the advisory board-stand out for their contributions to the content of this report. They are the key social scientists around the country who are analyzing and interpreting police-citizen contact data for various law enforcement entities and who have been instrumental in advancing the methods used to assess racial bias. Members of this group were generous with their time and knowledge. They shared their draft and completed reports from their own research, responded to phone and email inquiries, served as a "sounding board" for particularly vexing issues, and reviewed critically the various chapters of this document that reported on their work and/or otherwise reflected most closely their experience and expertise. In alphabetical order, these people are

> Geoff Alpert, *University of South Carolina*
> Gary Cordner, *Eastern Kentucky University*
> Scott Decker, *University of Missouri at St. Louis*
> Robin Engle, *University of Cincinnati*
> Amy Farrell, *Northeastern University*
> David Harris, *University of Toledo*
> John Lamberth, *Lamberth Consulting*
> Catherine Lawson, *State University of New York at Albany*
> Jack McDevitt, *Northeastern University*
> Michael Smith, *Washington State University*
> Samuel Walker, *University of Nebraska at Omaha*
> Matthew Zingraff, *North Carolina State University*

It is no exaggeration to say that there would be no content for this document without their research efforts in the field and no summary of the promising approaches without their direct assistance in writing this document.

Appendix A was written by Karen Parker of the University of Florida and Appendix D was contributed by John Lamberth, David Harris, Jack McDevitt and Deborah Ramirez. Providing additional expert review of particular chapters or sections were Deputy Chief Michael Berkow of the Los Angeles Police Department; Jennifer Calnon of Pennsylvania State University; Jerry Clayton and Karl Lamberth of Lamberth Consulting; Mike Maltz of the University of Illinois at Chicago; Ken Novak of the University of Missouri, Kansas City; and Tim Oettmeier, Executive Assistant Chief of the Houston Police Department. Jerry Deichert at the University of Nebraska at Omaha provided expert advice on census data. To all of these people, I convey my sincere appreciation. And my thanks go as well to two "mystery reviewers" who provided very detailed and constructive feedback on many chapters but who prefer to remain anonymous. They know who they are.

I owe a tremendous debt to Barbara deBoinville who provided expert editing-ensuring that complicated, sometimes dense material was organized, accessible and clear. At PERF my thanks go to Executive Director Chuck Wexler who pushed me to complete the document while being completely supportive with the encouragement and resources I needed to do so. He also provided important insights related to the content. I'm grateful to Martha Plotkin and David Edelson who provided their usual high-quality, expert advice on the document's form and content and oversaw all aspects of Web and print publication. A colleague returning to PERF, Don Faggiani, reviewed various sections of the report and was on call day and night to provide advanced methodological guidance. Finally, special thanks to all of my staff in the Research Unit at PERF who are wonderful in many, many ways and, for this particular project, thoughtfully and patiently let me hole up without interruption for days at a time to write. This one's for you.

Lorie Fridell

Introduction

Law enforcement agencies across the country are attempting to address the issues of racially biased policing and the perceptions of its practice. Racially biased policing is here defined as the inappropriate consideration by law enforcement of race or ethnicity[1] in deciding with whom and how to intervene in an enforcement capacity.[2] Decades of profound reform reflected in community policing are threatened by perceptions of racially biased policing and its practice. This trust-shattering issue is placing at risk the partnerships with residents, particularly minority residents, that police have worked diligently to develop. At the same time, however, it is these very partnerships—if they are solid—that can provide the basis for effective reforms. In short, these partnerships with the community provide law enforcement agencies with the general capabilities and specific tools they need to address these critical issues.

In 2001 the Police Executive Research Forum (PERF), with funding from the U.S. Department of Justice, Office of

---

[1] Mirroring the U.S. Census we use "ethnicity" in this document to refer to whether a person is of Hispanic or non-Hispanic origin.

[2] For a discussion of the various policy options that, in effect, define "inappropriate," see the web site of the Police Executive Research Forum, www.policeforum.org.

Community Oriented Policing Services, published *Racially Biased Policing: A Principled Response*. This report (Fridell et al. 2001) outlined the various ways that law enforcement agencies can effectively address racially biased policing. Specifically, it discussed methods of reform and prevention in the areas of accountability and supervision, policies to address racially biased policing, recruitment and hiring, education and training, minority community outreach, and collection of data on police-citizen contacts.[3]

As part of their comprehensive response to the issues related to racially biased policing, many law enforcement agencies are collecting data on various types of police-citizen interactions, including information regarding the race and ethnicity of persons stopped by police. PERF's first report on racially biased policing (Fridell et al. 2001) discussed the pros and cons of data collection and provided guidance to agencies mandated or choosing to collect data regarding the types of activities to target (for example, traffic stops, investigative stops) and the specific data to collect (for example, date/time of stop, reasons for stop). The topic of this new report is the analysis and interpretation of the vehicle stop data collected by agency personnel.[4] One purpose is to describe the social science challenges associated with data collection initiatives so that agencies and other stakeholders can be made fully aware of both the potential and limitations of police-citizen contact data. The second purpose is to provide a "how to" guide for the analysis/interpretation of the data so that the jurisdictions that are collecting it can con-

---

[3] This report, funded by COPS Office Grant 1999-CK-WX-0076, is available in its entirety on the PERF web site at www.policeforum.org.

[4] The methods we describe pertain to the analysis of vehicle stops (not pedestrian stops) of all types. The term "vehicle stop" is used to denote any stop made by police of a person in a vehicle. The term "traffic stop" denotes a vehicle stop the stated purpose of which is to respond to a violation of traffic laws (including codes related to quality/maintenance of vehicles). The term "investigative (vehicle) stop" denotes police stops of people in vehicles when there is reasonable suspicion of criminal activity.

duct the most valid and responsible analyses possible with the resources they have. This report will be of greatest value to the people charged with analyzing the data. They include law enforcement agency research staff, outside social scientists, interest group members, or other stakeholders.[5]

A companion document entitled *Understanding Race Data from Vehicle Stops: A Stakeholder's Guide* (Fridell 2004) is geared more broadly for police practitioners; concerned residents; advocacy groups; the media; and local, state, and federal policy makers. Its purpose is to educate this wide audience about the potential and constraints associated with data collection efforts. It discusses the challenge of benchmarking, how to assess the quality of benchmarks, how to interpret results responsibly, and how to use the data for constructive dialogue and reform.[6]

Law enforcement agencies' documents reporting on the results of their data analysis efforts provided an important source of information for this report. In these documents PERF staff identified promising procedures and methodologies as well as common weaknesses and missteps.[7] Additionally, PERF staff relied upon the valuable expertise of an advisory board. Its

---

[5] For purposes of simplification, throughout this document we refer to the "agencies" or "agency researchers" conducting analyses, although we acknowledge that researchers outside or independent of the agency may be analyzing jurisdiction data.

[6] Many of the topics treated in the companion document are also covered in Chapter 2 of this report. A related resource, funded by the Office of Community Oriented Policing Services, is *How to Correctly Collect and Analyze Racial Profiling Data: Your Reputation Depends on It!* (McMahon et al. 2002). This document is available through the COPS Office web site at www.cops.usdoj.gov.

[7] The documents (for example, jurisdictions' reports of their results) that manifested weaknesses or missteps are not mentioned by name in this report. (The reader will always find references to strong studies and documents.) We saw no constructive purpose in publicly linking faulty work to specific agencies or researchers, most of whom generously provided PERF with their materials for review.

members—listed in the acknowledgments section—include the key social scientists around the country who are analyzing and interpreting police-citizen contact data, experienced law enforcement practitioners, and personnel within research units of law enforcement agencies. Members of this advisory board provided PERF with the documents they had written or commissioned on the methods and results of data analysis/interpretation. Board members helped define the contents of this report and reviewed early drafts. Therefore, the pronoun "we" is used throughout the report to acknowledge that its contents reflect this collective wisdom.

Chapter 2 describes the social science challenges associated with analyzing and interpreting the police-citizen contact data collected to measure racially biased policing; specifically, it explores the goal, the potential, and the limitations of what has come to be called "benchmarking" the data. Chapter 3, "Getting Started," explains the steps agencies should take when they initiate collection and analysis of police-citizen contact data, including how to develop a data collection plan, how and why to involve residents and police personnel from all levels of the agency, and how to select benchmarks. Chapter 4 examines issues that are relevant to all analysis efforts, regardless of their particular focus or the benchmarking method selected. Topics include reviewing data quality, selecting reference periods, and analyzing subsets of data.

Chapters 5 through 10 present information on methods that can be used to address the first of two research questions:

- Does a driver's race/ethnicity have an impact on vehicle stopping behavior by police?

In considering this question, a researcher is attempting to assess whether racially biased policing is manifested in the decisions of officers regarding whom to stop. In Chapter 11, we address the second research question:

- Does a driver's race/ethnicity have an impact on police behaviors/activities during the stop?

With regard to this research question, we describe how to assess the impact of race/ethnicity on the activities that occur after the stop is made. Most importantly, we discuss how to examine the disposition of the stop and search activity.

In Chapter 12 we suggest to the readers who are not advanced statisticians what calculations to use to measure disparity between racial/ethnic groups. In Chapter 13 we discuss how to use the results from data collection to achieve reform.

Chapters 1 through 3 present important information for all people who are stakeholders in the collection of police-citizen contact data; Chapter 13, on using the data for reform, is also geared toward this broad audience.[8] The material in between fills the need—identified by the Office of Community Oriented Policing Services and PERF—for very specific and technical information regarding how to analyze and interpret these data.

"Best practices" in analyzing and interpreting police-citizen contact data are continuing to evolve as social scientists make progress in this area. Because of these advances, PERF will retain a web site that will provide new resources and information as they become available.[9]

---

[8] The companion document, which is geared to a wide variety of stakeholders, conveys much of this material as well. It also summarizes material in Chapters 4 through 12 in a less technical fashion.

[9] See www.policeforum.org.

The Benchmarking Challenge

Jurisdictions collecting police-citizen contact data are calling upon social science to determine whether there is a cause-and-effect relationship between a driver's race/ethnicity and vehicle stopping behavior by police. In analyzing the data, researchers have attempted to develop comparison groups to produce a "benchmark" against which to measure their stop data. If an agency determines that, say, 25 percent of its vehicle stops are of racial/ethnic minorities, to what should this be compared? In other words, what percentage would indicate racially biased policing?" This is the question at the core of benchmarking. To determine an answer, researchers have compared the demographic profiles of people stopped by police to the demographic profiles of the residential population of the jurisdiction, to the demographic profiles of residents with a driver's license, and to the demographic profiles of people observed driving on jurisdiction roads—to name a few comparison groups.

THE OBJECTIVE OF BENCHMARKING

Before we discuss the various methods for benchmarking, it is constructive to consider our objectives when analyzing police-citizen contact data. Then we can outline how benchmarks vary in their ability to achieve these objectives. We start with two conceptual models. Figure 2.1 shows a model of the first research question: Does a driver's race/ethnicity have an impact on the decisions police make with regard to whom to stop? We want to know if X (driver race/ethnicity) has any causal impact on Y (police decisions to stop drivers). To determine causality, however, we must exclude or "control for" rival causal factors—factors other than the race/ethnicity of the driver—that could explain police stopping decisions (see the model in Figure 2.2). In attempting to test whether X causes Y, we need to rule out alternative hypotheses that A, B, C, and Z—either alone or together or in interaction with X—cause Y.

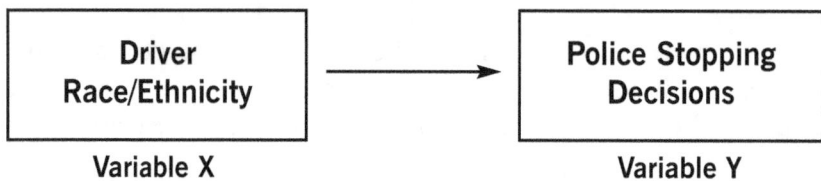

Figure 2.1. Model of First Research Question: Does Driver Race/Ethnicity Affect Vehicle Stopping Decisions Made by Police?

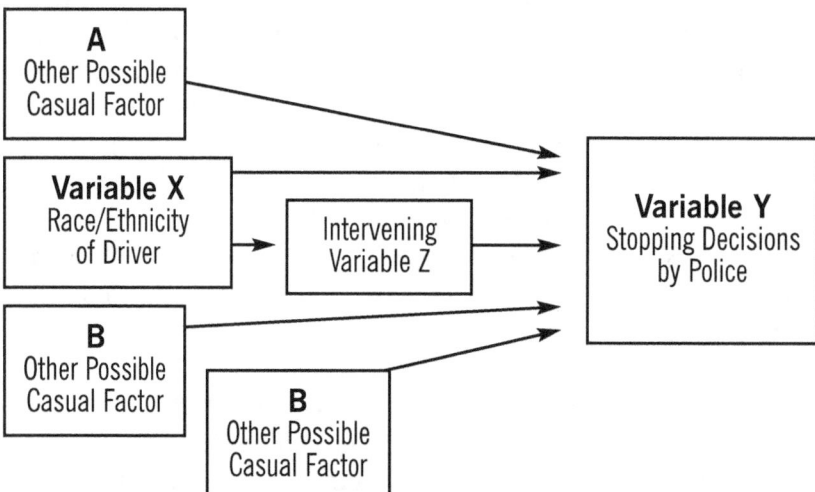

Figure 2.2. Model of Factors, Other than Bias, that Might Affect Stopping Decisions Made by Police

The following example clarifies why rival causal factors must be ruled out in any analysis of police-citizen contact data. Let us say that parents are concerned that the grading by math teachers at a high school reflects teachers' bias against females. The parents' allegation is that these math teachers believe boys are better than girls at math and that—consciously or unconsciously—these attitudes are reflected in the grades being given to the students.

Our basic conceptual model is that gender (X) has a causal impact on grades (Y). To test this scientifically, however, we cannot conduct analyses that consider only X and Y. We cannot, for instance, look only at the percent of females who got A's and B's and the percent of males who got A's and B's and draw any conclusions regarding teachers' gender bias. Instead, we must consider other factors that affect grading behavior. A key variable, of course, would be students' math performance. Our analyses must control for math performance (for example, scores on objective tests). In other words, our research design or statistical techniques must remove or "neutralize" the impact of performance on grades. If, after we have controlled for math performance, we still find that males get better math grades than do females, then we must seriously consider the possibility of gender bias by teachers.

Now let us return to the first research question concerning who is stopped by police. Police can have various legitimate reasons for deciding to stop a vehicle. These reasons are the rival causal factors that would become the A, B, and C of Figure 2.2. Let's again consider gender but in the context of analyzing police stopping behavior, not math grades.

The reports of most jurisdictions regarding their police-citizen contact data state that males are stopped by police more than females. For instance, a jurisdiction may find that 65 percent of its vehicle stops by police are of male drivers and 35 percent are of female drivers. Does this indicate gender bias on the part of the police? It is unclear from these data, but most of us are disinclined to jump to that conclusion because we can think of factors other than police bias that could account for the disproportionate stopping of male drivers. That is, alternative hypotheses for the data exist. One possibility is that men drive more than women (the quantity factor). Another possibility is that men violate traffic laws more often than women do (the quality factor). A third possibility is that more males than females drive in the areas where police stopping activity tends to occur (the location factor). We do not know if these possibilities are true, but we must consider these alternative explanations in our research design because it is logical to assume that

- people who drive more should be more at risk of being stopped by police,
- people who drive poorly should be more at risk of being stopped by police, and
- people who drive in locations where stopping activity by police is high should be more at risk of being stopped by police.

For the purposes of our example, the objective of benchmarking is to see if gender bias is at work. If we could develop a gender profile of the people who *should be* more at risk of being stopped by police, we could compare it to the gender profile of the people who *are* being stopped by police. That is, if we managed through our research design to determine that men *should comprise* 65 percent of the police stops because of their driving quantity, quality, and location, and if indeed they *do comprise* 65 percent of the police stops (based on the stop data collected), then we could conclude that gender bias was not affecting stopping behavior by police.

Benchmarking is the essential tool used by researchers in their quest to develop a racial/ethnic profile of the people who should be at risk of being stopped by police, assuming no bias. The variation in quality across benchmarks is directly related to how closely each benchmark represents the group of people who should be at risk of being stopped by police if no bias exists. The following example will help clarify what we mean by benchmark quality. If a researcher uses road-side observers to develop a demographic profile of drivers who violate traffic laws, the researcher has produced a benchmark that represents fairly well the group of people who should be at risk of being stopped by police if no bias exists. On the other hand, if that same researcher used instead U.S. Decennial Census data to develop a demographic profile of people who live in the jurisdiction, the researcher has produced a benchmark that does not represent well the people at risk of being stopped by police if no bias exists. The next section on the bias hypothesis and the alternative hypotheses expands upon this discussion of benchmark quality. As we will demonstrate in this report, the variation in quality across benchmarks is great.

THE BIAS HYPOTHESIS AND THE ALTERNATIVE HYPOTHESES

Here we introduce the alternative hypotheses (hypotheses other than the one that reflects the possibility of police bias). Law enforcement agencies should consider these hypotheses when analyzing the police-citizen contact data they have been mandated to collect or have voluntarily collected to measure whether racially biased policing exists in their jurisdiction. The hypotheses reflect drivers' driving quantity, quality, and location—the factors that could legitimately influence whom police stop. This list of hypotheses will become a tool in the chapters ahead for evaluating each benchmarking method. We will indicate which of the alternative hypotheses are adequately addressed in each benchmark.

Again we want to know what the demographic profile of drivers stopped by police would look like assuming no bias. Starting at the very basics to make our point, we might ask why—in a jurisdiction made up of Caucasians, African Americans, Hispanics, and Asians—the police do not report that 25 percent of their traffic stops are of Caucasians, 25 percent are of African Americans, 25 percent are of Hispanics, and

25 percent are of Asians? One hypothesis is that *police are racially/ethnically biased in their decisions regarding whom to stop.* Competing alternative hypotheses are as follows:

- racial/ethnic groups are not equally represented as residents in the jurisdiction
- racial/ethnic groups are not equally represented as drivers on jurisdiction roads
- racial/ethnic groups are not equivalent in the nature and extent of their traffic law-violating behavior
- racial/ethnic groups are not equally represented as drivers on roads where stopping activity by police is high.

In order to draw valid conclusions regarding whether racial bias is occurring, we would need to rule out all other possible, legitimate explanations for disparity. Ideally, our analysis and interpretation of stop data would encompass all of the factors reflected in those alternative hypotheses.

If we address the second hypothesis—*racial/ethnic groups are not equally represented as drivers on jurisdiction roads*—we need not concern ourselves with the first hypothesis—*racial/ethnic groups are not equally represented as residents in the jurisdiction.* That is, for purposes of identifying who is at risk of being stopped by police in a vehicle, if we know who is driving on jurisdiction roads, we do not need to know who lives in that jurisdiction. Similarly, addressing the third hypothesis—*racial/ethnic groups are not equivalent in the nature and extent of their traffic law-violating behavior*—arguably negates the need to address the first two. It can be argued that knowing who is engaging in law-violating behavior negates the need to know who is on the road. Police are not told to pull over "people on the road" but rather "people who are violating laws." The fourth hypothesis—*racial/ethnic groups are not equally represented as drivers on roads where stopping activity by police is high*—stands alone and must be addressed independently of the other three. Each will be discussed below.

Research has shed light on the alternative hypotheses. This information is important because it shows us that we cannot ignore these hypotheses and presume no differences exist between racial/ethnic groups. (That is, we cannot presume the null hypothesis.) For each of the hypotheses, there is evidence that differences do exist between groups, or at least there is insufficient information to prove to any acceptable degree of certainty that no differences exist. Unless research shows there are no differences between groups as pertains to these hypotheses, we must assume that there are differences. Again this requires researchers to use methods that consider the factors encompassed in the alternative hypotheses or, at the very least, interpret their results responsibly in light of any deficiencies in their chosen methodology.

Hypothesis 1: Racial/ethnic groups are not equally represented as residents in the jurisdiction.

The demographic profile of people who live in a jurisdiction will affect the demographic profile of the people who are driving on the jurisdiction's roads. Thus, the above hypothesis is indirectly related to the "quantity" factor, and we need to include it in anticipation of our later discussion of census benchmarking (a comparison of the demographic profile of people stopped by police to the demographic profile of jurisdiction residents as measured by the U.S. Census Bureau). That racial/ethnic groups are not equally represented among residents in jurisdictions is, of course, quite obvious to all. According to the 2000 Decennial Census, 75.1 percent of the U.S. population is White, 12.3 percent is Black or African American,[1] and 3.6 percent is Asian; 9.0 percent of the population self-identify as being of more than one race. Just over 12 percent (12.5 percent) of U.S. residents (of all races) are of Hispanic origin. Although figures for different jurisdictions will deviate from this breakdown of the total U.S. population, we can

---

[1] African American and Black are used interchangeably for the purposes of this document.

confidently state that no jurisdiction has equal representation in its population of racial/ethnic groups.

Hypothesis 2: Racial/ethnic groups are not equally represented as drivers on jurisdiction roads.
Not only are racial/ethnic groups not equally represented among residents in the jurisdiction (the alternative hypothesis mentioned first), but their representation as residents might not match their representation as drivers using jurisdiction roads. This might be because of (1) racial/ethnic differences in driving quantity and/or (2) racial/ethnic differences in the population of people who do not live in the jurisdiction but drive in it. This is relevant to the analysis of vehicle stops by police. If one demographic group has more presence on the road than another, it should be more at risk of being stopped.

Driving Quantity
There is evidence that racial/ethnic groups differ in the amount of their driving. National data from the U.S. Decennial Census and from the National Household Transportation Survey (NHTS) indicate that racial/ethnic minorities are under-represented as drivers relative to their residential populations.[2] The U.S. Decennial Census provides data on the percent of households that do not own vehicles, an indirect measure of driving quantity. In his comprehensive report on commuting patterns based on 1990 Census data, Pisarski (1996, xv) reports that "on average, more than 30 percent of Black households do not own vehicles, and in central cities the number is over 37 percent."[3]

---

[2] The National Household Transportation Survey (previously called the Nationwide Personal Transportation Survey and the American Travel Survey) is conducted by the U.S. Department of Transportation. See www.bts.gov/nhts.

[3] Some cities have "extraordinary levels of Black households without vehicles" (Pisarski 1996, 36). In New York, 61 percent of Black households are without vehicles. The corresponding figures for Philadelphia, Chicago, and Washington, D.C., are 47 percent, 43 percent, and 43 percent, respectively.

Nationally, 19 percent of Hispanic households do not own vehicles; in central cities that number rises to 27 percent. In contrast, just under 9 percent of White non-Hispanic households are without vehicles, with a corresponding figure of 15 percent for central cities (Pisarski 1996, 36).

Vehicle ownership is an indirect measure of driving quantity. Information from the National Household Transportation Survey provides more direct measures of driving quantity. Its data indicate that nonminorities drive more than minorities. For instance, the 1995 NHTS indicated that African Americans average fewer "trips per day" (including fewer vehicle trips) than do Caucasians and that Hispanics are twice as likely as non-Hispanics to use public transportation (instead of privately owned vehicles).

While the 2000 Census data on vehicle ownership and NHTS data on driving quantity both imply that minorities are under-represented as drivers relative to their representation in the U.S. population, other research reminds us that this is not going to be true in all places at all times. For instance, research conducted by the United Kingdom's Home Office (MVA and Miller 2000) found that minorities were over-represented as drivers relative to their representation in the residential populations in the areas studied.[4] In Sacramento, California, Howard Greenwald compared the demographic profiles of drivers at various intersections (using observation) to the demographic profiles of residents in the same areas (using census data); he found over-representation of minorities as drivers in some areas and under-representation of minority drivers in others (Greenwald 2001). These two small-scale studies, although of less weight than the large-scale research findings of the NHTS and U.S. Census, nonetheless support our simple point: jurisdiction-level studies of racially biased policing must consider

---

[4] The Home Office of the United Kingdom is the government department responsible for promoting safe communities. Its closest equivalent in the United States is the National Institute of Justice.

the possibility that racial/ethnic groups are not equally represented as drivers on jurisdiction roads because of differences in their quantity of driving.

The need to consider the extent to which the various racial/ethnic groups are driving on the roads becomes more clear in the context of a recommendation that we will make repeatedly throughout this report—namely that researchers should conduct analyses for geographic "subareas" of the jurisdictions they are studying. Researchers are cautioned not to conduct a single analysis for the entire jurisdiction but numerous analyses within the various subareas. Within this context, it becomes more obvious why researchers should consider the extent to which each racial/ethnic group is driving on the particular roads of a subarea. Whereas it may be true (as the various large-scale studies described above indicate) that for the jurisdiction as a whole, minority representation on the roads is less than for Caucasians, this certainly will not be true for all subareas. Indeed, in some areas, minorities will be the predominant group on the roads.

Driving by Nonresidents

There is another reason—other than differences in driving quantity of jurisdiction residents—that racial/ethnic groups may not be equally represented as drivers on jurisdiction roads (and why their representation on the roads may not reflect their representation as residents). Racial/ethnic groups may not be equally represented among the *nonresidents* who drive in the jurisdiction; that is, racial/ethnic groups may not be equally represented among the people who live outside of the jurisdiction but drive into it.[5] The extent to which nonresidents drive with-

---

[5] In its first annual report regarding police-citizen contact data, the Denver Police Department (Thomas 2002) revealed that 62.5 percent of the Whites stopped in their vehicles by police were nonresidents compared to 32.8 percent of the Blacks who were stopped and 35.2 percent of the Hispanics who were stopped.

in the jurisdictions that are collecting police-citizen contact data will vary greatly, as might the demographic profile of those drivers. The influx of nonresident drivers will be particularly significant in the big cities that draw commuters in from surrounding jurisdictions, especially the suburbs, during the daytime hours.[6] Additionally, nonresidents will drive into the "target jurisdiction" (the jurisdiction that is the subject of police-citizen contact data analysis) to shop, seek entertainment, vacation, travel on to another jurisdiction, and for other reasons. These nonresident drivers will affect the demographic profile of drivers on the roads of the target jurisdiction.

Clearly, the hypothesis that *racial/ethnic groups are not equally represented as drivers on jurisdiction roads* is a viable alternative hypothesis that should be accounted for in the analysis of police-citizen contact data. This report will describe how law enforcement agencies can incorporate this alternative hypothesis into their study design.

Hypothesis 3: Racial/ethnic groups are not equivalent in the nature and extent of their traffic law-violating behavior.

Driving behavior is a critical component of any model that seeks to explain decisions by police to stop drivers. Indeed, police are asked to make driving behavior a key part of these decisions, and therefore we must recognize this variable in our methodology unless we are quite confident that there are no differences across racial/ethnic groups. Excluding driving behavior from the model is equivalent to excluding math performance from the earlier analysis that tested gender bias in math teachers.

---

[6] In 1993, 43 percent of the traffic tickets given in Seattle were given to nonresidents (Scales 2001). The Denver Police Department (Thomas 2001) reported that from June 2001 through May 2002 (the reference period for its second summary report) over one-half of its traffic stops were of nonresidents. In Louisville (Edwards et al. 2002a) and Iowa City (Edwards et al. 2002b), fewer than two-thirds of all drivers stopped were city residents.

It is possible, according to this hypothesis, that vehicle stopping behavior by police may not be equivalent across racial/ethnic groups because racial/ethnic groups violate traffic laws at different rates or at different levels of seriousness. These possibilities must be recognized. Concerned stakeholders have questioned the inclusion in our analysis of the third hypothesis (*racial/ethnic groups are not equivalent in the nature and extent of their traffic law-violating behavior*). They have asked the author whether the unstated implication is that minorities violate more. Indeed, no direction is implied by its inclusion. Minorities may violate traffic laws with less frequency than do majority populations. (In fact, this could be the case in light of minorities' concern about racial profiling and the increased attention they perceive they get from police.) If minorities do violate less, then it is important that this information be incorporated into the analysis to appropriately determine the rate at which they should be stopped by police in light of their driving quality. Driving behavior cannot be removed from our analysis unless there is clear evidence in support of the null hypothesis (no differences between racial/ethnic groups exist). The following information calls the null hypothesis into question.

Information on the Equivalence of Driving Behavior
The scarcity of large-scale quality research on driving behavior and race/ethnicity does not negate the importance and viability of this alternative hypothesis. In fact, it does just the opposite: what is important for our purposes is the absence of sufficient research to *rule out* the possibility of racial/ethnic differences in the nature and extent of law-violating behavior. Again, even if we had national data pointing to equivalent driving behavior or pointing to one particular direction or the other, we could not presume that those results were applicable to all times and all places.

The information on the equivalence of driving behavior across racial/ethnic groups is limited and mixed. There is research in the transportation field, albeit not substantial, indicating some differences across racial groups with regard to certain traffic violations. For instance, Feest (1968) found that Whites were more likely than minorities not to stop at stop signs. Other researchers analyzing police-citizen contact data have produced information indicating other differences in violating behavior across racial/ethnic groups. For instance, Lange, Blackman, and Johnson (2001) found that along segments of the New Jersey turnpike where the speed limit was 65 miles per hour rather than 55 miles per hour, African Americans were disproportionately represented among the few speeders.[7] In contrast, Lamberth (1996a, 1996b) conducted research in New Jersey and Maryland and found no differences in the demographics of speeders versus nonspeeders. He reports that all racial/ethnic groups were speeding in high, and similar, proportions.[8]

In citing these mixed findings, we are not trying to argue that there are differences in violating behavior across racial/ethnic groups. Quite the contrary: we do not know whether differences exist or not. Because the research does not allow us to rule out the possibility of differences in driving quality across racial/ethnic groups, we contend that research analyzing police-citizen contact data should address the alternative hypothesis that *racial/ethnic groups are not equivalent in the nature and extent of their traffic law-violating behavior.*[9]

Youthfulness and Driving Behavior
Youthfulness has been linked to law-violating behavior. If a racial/ethnic group has proportionately more young people than

---

[7] This study was criticized for various aspects of its methodology and the high proportion of missing data produced by those methods.

[8] These studies defined speeding so broadly (1 mile per hour over the speed limit in Maryland and 5 miles per hour over the speed limit in New Jersey) that speeders included most drivers. This broad definition reduced the researcher's ability to detect any existing, finer distinctions in driving behavior across groups.

[9] A challenge to this view is presented in Appendix D in the context of discussing the observation method of benchmarking.

another, age becomes an important "intervening variable"[10] in the analysis model. (It is a potential "Variable Z" in Figure 2.2.) We must consider whether the breakdown of age groups in a jurisdiction (or in the subareas being analyzed) varies across racial/ethnic groups. For example, if 30 percent of the minority population of an area is young (24 years of age or less) and only 20 percent of the Caucasian population is young, this phenomenon would lead to more drivers who violate the law in the minority population than in the nonminority population, assuming the link between poor driving and age.

An example using (extreme) hypothetical data will convey the potential impact of this circumstance (unequal proportions of young people within racial/ethnic groups) on police-citizen contact data being analyzed to measure racially biased policing. Table 2.1 shows the representation of Caucasian and minority drivers on the road and among those stopped by police in hypothetical Jurisdiction Q. There were 1,000 Caucasian drivers and 1,000 minority drivers on the road during the data collection period. That is, Caucasians and minorities each made up 50 percent of the driving population. Among the Caucasian drivers, 300 or 30 percent were between the ages of 15 and 24, and 700 or 70 percent were 25 or older. (We use age 15 as the lower cut-off point to include only people of driving age.) The corresponding percentages for the minority group of drivers were 60 percent and 40 percent. That is, 600 of the drivers were between the ages of 15 and 24, and 400 were 25 years of age or older.

The police in hypothetical Jurisdiction Q are completely devoid of racial/ethnic bias, and they legitimately stop, as a result of the drivers' poorer quality driving, two times as many drivers between the ages of 15 and 24 as drivers 25 years of age and older. (To make our point, we assume equivalence of driving behavior across racial/ethnic groups.) Twenty percent of the young

---

[10] We use the term "intervening variable" to refer to a variable (measured or unmeasured) that is linked causally to one or more other variables in an equation or model.

Table 2.1. Representation of Caucasian and Minority Drivers in the Driving Population and Population of Stopped Drivers, by Age, Hypothetical Jurisdiction Q

Age Group	Caucasians (n=1,000)		
	Number of Drivers	Percent Stopped	Number Stopped
15-24	300	20%	60
25+	700	10%	70
Total	1,000	13%	130
Percentage of all stops: 45.61%			
Age Group	Minorities (n=1,000)		
	Number of Drivers	Percent Stopped	Number Stopped
15-24	600	20%	120
25+	400	10%	40
Total	1,000	16%	160
Percentage of all stops: 56.14%			

Caucasians were stopped (0.2 x 300 = 60), and 20 percent of the young minorities were stopped (0.2 x 600 = 120). They stopped 10 percent of the Caucasian drivers age 25 or above (producing 70 stops) and 10 percent of the minority drivers age 25 or above (producing 40 stops). The effect of the differential representation of young people among the minority drivers can be seen when we look at the overall representation of Caucasians and minorities among the drivers stopped by police (Figure 2.3). Caucasians made up 50 percent of the drivers (1,000 of the total 2,000) and only 46 percent of the stops. Minorities made up the other 50 percent of the drivers but 56 percent of the stops. Even though racial bias is not manifested by the police (equivalent stopping behavior across racial/ethnic groups), our data indicate (falsely) that disparity exists. If the researcher for Jurisdiction Q did not, as we did, analyze the data within age groups to confirm a lack of disparity, the researcher would have mistakenly concluded that there was disparity across racial groups. The disproportionate representation of youth in the minority population and the increased likelihood of young people being stopped by police produced the misleading results shown in Figure 2.3: minorities appeared to be over-represented among people stopped relative to minorities' representation in the driving population.

In sum, the strongest research methodologies will address the alternative hypothesis that *racial/ethnic groups are not equivalent in the nature and extent of their traffic law-violating behavior.* Theoretically, driving behavior is quite relevant to decisions by police to stop drivers, and the research that has been conducted on the relationship between driving quality and race/ethnicity is not sufficient for us to assume no differences across groups. Complicating matters as pertains to this "quality of driving" factor is the link between age and driving behavior. In the chapters that follow, we convey various benchmarking methods, including those that take into consideration driving quality. We also provide guidance to analysts on how to consider a potential "intervening variable": age.

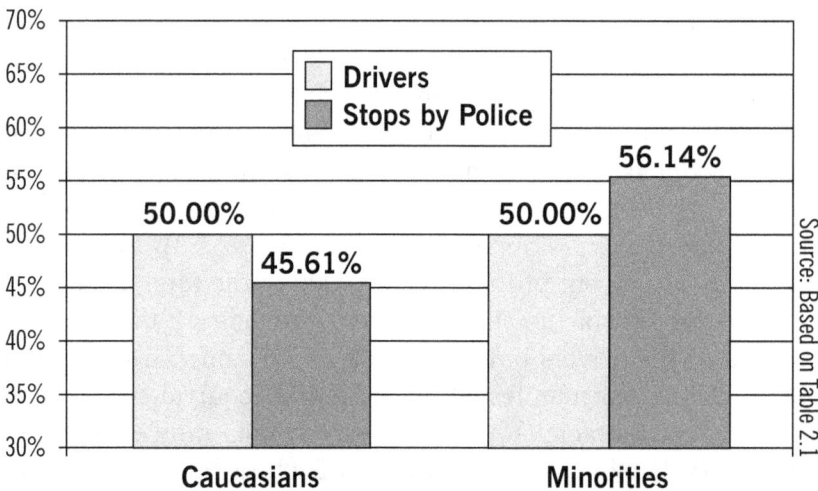

Figure 2.3. False Indication of Racial/Ethnic Bias Based on Age Differences of Drivers in Hypothetical Jurisdiction Q

Hypothesis 4: Racial/ethnic groups are not equally represented as drivers on roads where stopping activity by police is high.

The law enforcement activities of police are not the same in all areas at all times. Indeed, the level of vehicle stops by police may vary quite legitimately from area to area.[11] People who drive in areas where stopping activity by police is high are at greater risk of being stopped than are their counterparts who drive in areas with low stopping activity. This difference could affect efforts to assess racially biased policing if law enforcement activities vary across geographic areas where the demographic composition also varies. If variations in police stopping activity are not considered in analyses of police-citizen contact data, results that indicate disparity may reflect not racial/ethnic bias, but very legitimate variations in police practices.[12]

A hypothetical example, analogous to the earlier example that focused on differences in age demographics across racial/ethnic groups, illustrates how misleading indicators of racial/ethnic disparity can easily emerge. This example also highlights the need for researchers to conduct analyses within subareas of the jurisdiction under study. Table 2.2 shows the racial/ethnic profile of driving-age residents and the racial/ethnic profile of the drivers stopped in hypothetical Jurisdiction R (composed of Area A and Area B). There are an equal number of people of driving age in each area (1,000 each), but Area A is predominantly Caucasian (80 percent of driving-age residents)

---

[11] Heavy levels of police deployment will not necessarily coincide with high levels of vehicle stops for traffic violations. In fact, in some high-crime areas where police deployment is likely to be correspondingly high, traffic enforcement may be a low priority in light of the more critical problems that need to be addressed.

[12] These variations in police activities across areas within a jurisdiction would not be legitimate if the differential enforcement were based on inappropriate factors such as racial/ethnic bias. To discern whether bias is a factor, the researcher could assess whether legitimate factors (such as calls for service, traffic accidents) adequately predict levels of law enforcement activities.

and Area B is predominantly composed of minorities (80 percent of driving-age residents). In each area, the demographic profile of the drivers stopped by police matches the demographic profile of the driving-age adults in the area. That is, in Area A, 80 percent of the residents are Caucasians, and 20 percent are minorities; similarly, 80 percent of the drivers stopped by police are Caucasians and 20 percent are minorities. (We use this particular benchmark, residential population, for purposes of making our point—not to promote it as a method.)

Table 2.2. Representation of Caucasian and Minority Drivers in the Driving Population and Population of Stopped Drivers, by Subarea, Hypothetical Jurisdiction R

Types of Drivers	Area A			
	No. of Driving-Age Residents	Percent of Residents	No. of Stops	Percent of Stops
Caucasians	800	80%	80	80%
Minorities	200	20%	20	20%
Total	1,000	100%	100	100%

Types of Drivers	Area B			
	No. of Driving-Age Residents	Percent of Residents	No. of Stops	Percent of Stops
Caucasians	200	20%	40	20%
Minorities	800	80%	160	80%
Total	1,000	100%	200	100%

Types of Drivers	Total Jurisdiction			
	No. of Driving-Age Residents	Percent of Residents	No. of Stops	Percent of Stops
Caucasians	1,000	50%	120	40%
Minorities	1,000	50%	180	60%
Total	2,000	100%	300	100%

In Area B, like Area A, the demographic profile of the drivers stopped by police matches the demographic profile of the residents. In short, the results as analyzed within Area A and Area B indicate no disparity. Note, however, that more traffic stops are made in Area B than in Area A. The reason for the greater traffic enforcement within Area B in hypothetical Jurisdiction R is the occurrence of many accidents there, prompting concerned citizens to request that local law enforcement crack down on speeders. Because of this heightened traffic enforcement—legitimate in our example—twice as many stops are made in Area B (200 stops) than in Area A (100 stops). If the researcher had not controlled for police activity within the two areas but instead had presented data for the whole jurisdiction, a false disparity would have become evident. The researcher would have reported disproportionate representation of minorities among drivers stopped by police (see the Total Jurisdiction results of Table 2.2). When the absolute numbers of stops across areas are summed, and the demographic profile of the drivers who are stopped is compared to the demographic profile of the residential population, these misleading indications of disparity emerge. Those misleading data, graphed in Figure 2.4, show that minorities comprise 50 percent of the jurisdiction population but 60 percent of all stops. These would be the misleading results *even if* officers' decisions to stop were devoid of bias, and the increased traffic enforcement activity in Area B was completely legitimate.

In sum, it is appropriate to assume that people who drive in areas where stopping activity by police is high are at greater risk of being stopped than those who drive in areas where stopping activity is low. The nature and extent of policing activities may legitimately vary across geographic areas where the demographic composition also varies. Because of these possibilities, the methods used to analyze police-citizen contact data should reflect consideration of the hypothesis that *racial/ethnic groups are not equally represented as drivers on roads where stopping activity by police is high*. Because law enforcement agencies

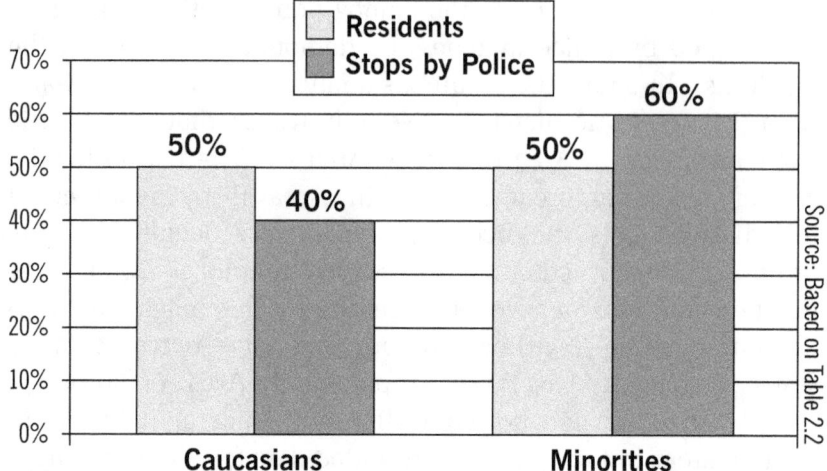

Figure 2.3. False Indication of Racial/Ethnic Bias Based on Differential Stopping Activity by Police Across Subareas in Hypothetical Jurisdiction R

cannot feel confident about the null hypothesis (there are no differences), they should take into account differential stopping activity by police across geographic areas when they analyze police-citizen contact data. In the chapters that follow, we discuss how researchers can recognize this alternative hypothesis. The example given here supports our recommendation that law enforcement agencies conduct analyses within geographic subareas of their jurisdiction and that they select those subareas in a way that allows researchers to hold constant (or "control for") the exposure of drivers to stopping activity by police.

SUMMARY OF THE BENCHMARKING CHALLENGE

The researcher developing a "benchmark" for police-citizen contact data is trying to determine the demographics (particularly the racial/ethnic composition) of the drivers who are at risk of being stopped, assuming no bias by police. We identified the key factors that influence this risk: driving quantity, driving quality, and the location of driving vis-a-vis levels of stopping activity by police. In order to determine whether there is a cause-and-effect relationship between the race/ethnicity of drivers and police stopping behavior, we must be able to show that this relationship exists even when the other factors are considered. To test the hypothesis that driver race/ethnicity has an impact on stopping behavior by police, the alternative hypotheses that reflect the factors that increase the risk of being stopped must be ruled out. The alternative hypotheses are

- racial/ethnic groups are not equally represented as residents in the jurisdiction,
- racial/ethnic groups are not equally represented as drivers on jurisdiction roads,
- racial/ethnic groups are not equivalent in the nature and extent of their traffic law-violating behavior, and
- racial/ethnic groups are not equally represented as drivers on roads where stopping activity by police is high.

It is not difficult to measure whether there is disparity between racial/ethnic groups in terms of stops made by police; the difficulty comes in identifying the causes for disparity. The alternative hypotheses present potential causes that need to be ruled out before a researcher can claim that the identified disparity is likely the result of police bias. After controlling for driving quantity, driving quality, and driving location (as pertains to levels of police stopping activity), a researcher who finds that minorities are disproportionately represented among drivers stopped by police can conclude with reasonable confidence that the disparity reflects police bias in their decision making. If no disparity was found, the researcher can fairly confidently conclude that bias was not a part of police decision making. If, on the other hand, the researcher finds disparity in the results after controlling for only driving quantity and driving location, he or she can report that disparity exists and that the results can be explained either by police bias or differential driving quality. That is, the researcher could not pinpoint a single cause (for example, bias) but must report that two possible explanations for the disparity remain.

Even results showing no disparity would need to be qualified if all factors were not controlled for. If, for instance, results indicated no disparity in stops, but driving quality had not been considered, the researcher cannot rule out the possibility of racial/ethnic bias in stopping behavior. We explore this possibility further in our discussion below of "masking."

A benchmark's value depends on the extent to which it addresses the alternative hypotheses. The higher the quality of the benchmark, the more confidence a researcher can have in the results. The need to rule out alternative hypotheses shows how much more complex benchmarking is than many have previously thought. When researchers attempt to interpret police-citizen contact data, they are, in effect, trying to look inside the heads of officers to discern their decision-making processes. Even a research model that incorporates the factors above does not begin to do justice to the complexity of these decisions. This caveat, however, is not unique to the analysis or interpretation of police-citizen contact data but is applicable to virtually all efforts by social scientists to measure human behavior and interaction.

THE PROBLEM OF INCONCLUSIVE RESULTS: A CENSUS BENCHMARKING EXAMPLE

In this section we use the census benchmarking method of analyzing police-citizen contact data to illustrate how researchers' failure to address the alternative hypotheses can lead to inconclusive results. In census benchmarking, a jurisdiction compares the demographic profile of the drivers stopped by police to the demographic profile of the residents of the jurisdiction as measured by the U.S. Decennial Census. Regardless of the results of this comparison (minorities are over-represented, minorities are under-represented, minorities are proportionately represented), *researchers can draw no definitive conclusions regarding racially biased policing.*

As an example, suppose that a law enforcement agency finds that minorities are over-represented among drivers stopped by police relative to minorities' representation among jurisdiction residents. The racial/ethnic disparities manifested in this comparison might reflect racially biased policing, or they might reflect variation in the demographic profiles of (1) drivers on jurisdiction roads, (2) traffic law violators, or (3) drivers driving in locations where stopping activity by police is high. Our comparison of stop data to census data has indicated disparity, but the *causes* of that disparity have not been identified. We know that we have "disparate impact" (using the social science rather than the legal definition of the phrase), but we do not know if we have unjustified disparate impact in the form of racially biased policing. Because of these limitations, no conclusions can be drawn with regard to the existence or absence of racially biased policing.

Census benchmarking (assuming no adjustments of the census data)[13] takes into consideration only one of the four alternative hypotheses presented in this chapter—the hypothesis that *racial/ethnic groups are not equally represented as residents in the jurisdiction.*[14] Census benchmarking does not address hypotheses related to demographic variations across driving quantity, quality, or location. Nevertheless, stakeholders (for example, public officials, law enforcement executives, civil rights group representatives) often draw inappropriate conclusions about the results. Some of those inappropriate conclusions are represented in the benchmarking "myths" to which we turn next.

---

[13] Chapter 5 discusses ways that census data are being adjusted by researchers in an attempt to encompass factors related to several, additional alternative hypotheses.

[14] A common criticism of census data is the systematic undercounting of certain racial and ethnic groups. For the 2000 Census, the Census Bureau estimates that for one minority group—non-Hispanic Blacks—the percent undercount is statistically different from zero. The Bureau estimates a 1.84 percent undercount. See www.census.gov/dmd/www/ace2.html.

BENCHMARKING MYTHS
Myth 1: No racial/ethnic disparity means no racially biased policing.

As noted in the preceding example, the results produced by unadjusted census benchmarking, regardless of whether they showed under-representation, over-representation, or proportionate representation of minorities among the persons stopped by police, cannot enable researchers to draw sound conclusions about racially biased policing. This important truth has been contradicted in a few reports. Although the authors of these reports correctly acknowledge that their benchmarking method (census benchmarking) cannot produce conclusions regarding *the existence* of racially biased policing (because the alternative hypotheses have not been ruled out), they argue that it can prove *the absence* of racially biased policing. A finding of disproportionately high minority representation among persons stopped does not prove racially biased policing, they say, but a finding of disproportionately low minority representation or proportionate minority representation does prove that racially biased policing does not exist. This argument—that a method is valid for one result although not for another—is not true.

The adequacy of a law enforcement agency's benchmark is the same for all results. The researchers who put forth the argument that, regardless of benchmark quality, a showing of no disparity means no racially biased policing fail to recognize that an inadequate benchmark can "mask" (or hide) disparity. The following example shows how.

Let us say that a jurisdiction uses census benchmarking and finds that the demographic profile of residents matches perfectly the demographic profile of people stopped by police. It is still possible that policing in the jurisdiction is racially biased. If minorities are on the road in, or violating at, proportions less than their residential representation, the fact that they are stopped proportionate to their residential representation indicates disparity, and it may indicate racially biased policing. Indeed, the existence of racially biased policing may be masked by flaws inherent in the benchmark. Hypothetical data on the representation of minorities and nonminorities among jurisdiction residents, traffic violators, and people stopped for traffic violations are presented in Figure 2.5. It shows that 25 percent of the residents are racial/ethnic minorities as are 25 percent of the people who are stopped by police for traffic violations. This is the type of finding (a finding of no disparity) that some mistakenly have argued indicates an absence of racially biased policing.

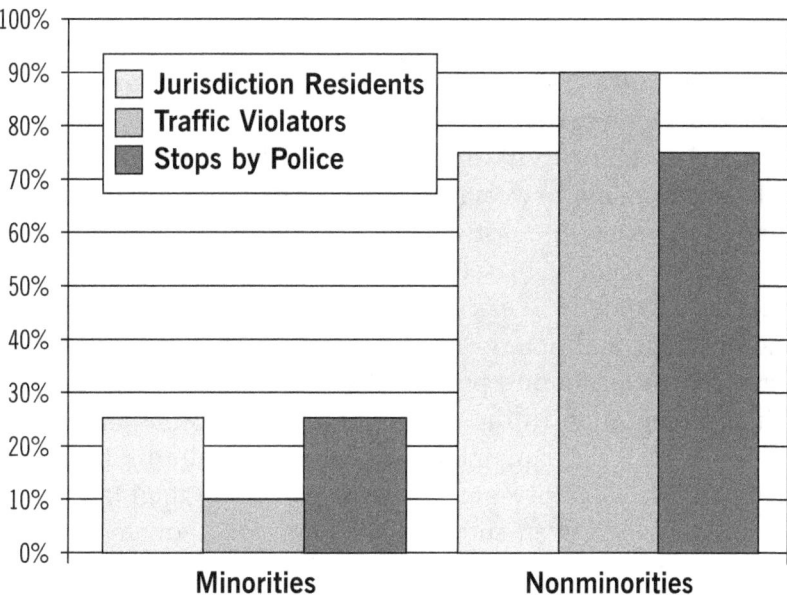

Figure 2.5. Racially Biased Policing Masked in Hypothetical Jurisdiction S

The figure also shows the proportion of minorities and nonminorities who are *traffic violators* (information that would not be available to the researcher who conducted only census benchmarking), and this information indicates that minorities are over-represented among the drivers who are stopped. If minorities comprise only 10 percent of the traffic violators (that is, 10 percent of the population *legitimately at risk of being stopped by police*), but 25 percent of the population that *is stopped by police*, racial bias is indicated. The key here is that the researcher conducting census benchmarking would not have had the information (on violating behavior) necessary to interpret either results that showed disparity or results that showed no disparity.

Researchers who are assessing police-citizen contact data should remember that (1) a weak benchmark is weak for all results, and (2) their benchmarking method can mask racially biased policing.

Myth 2: Results from a weak methodology become more worthy over time.

It is not true that results from a weak methodology, or benchmark, can become a worthy baseline for interpreting data in subsequent years—at least not for the purpose of assessing the existence of racially biased policing. An example will help explicate this myth. Let's say that a jurisdiction uses census benchmarking and determines that racial/ethnic minorities are over-represented among people stopped by police relative to their representation in the residential population as measured by the census. As explained above, these results indicate the existence of a disparity but not its cause. The temptation for stakeholders, and even some researchers, is to equate the disparity with racially biased policing and to desire a reduction in that disparity in subsequent years. That is, they might acknowledge that their benchmark is weak, but claim nonetheless that the results produced during the first year of analysis can be used to assess and evaluate change in subsequent years. This is not true. Because of the weak methods used, the researcher cannot equate the disparity with racially biased policing and therefore should not presume that a reduction in disparity the following year would be desirable and that it would indicate reduced bias. The disparity may reflect wholly legitimate factors at work. If that is the case (which cannot be known with some benchmarking methods), then a reduction in disparity is not a legitimate goal.

Similarly, a jurisdiction that finds no disparity as a result of its census benchmarking analysis the first year and does find disparity the second year should not blame the police department. Again, because of the methods used, this disparity cannot be equated with police bias. In sum, a benchmark that cannot pinpoint cause cannot produce explanations of cause over time.

Myth 3: Results from a weak methodology become strong if replicated in multiple geographic areas.

A police department that conducts census benchmarking within multiple subareas of the city (say, within each police district) and finds no evidence of racial/ethnic disparity in each one can easily believe the myth stated above. The police spokesperson might acknowledge the weaknesses of census benchmarking but discount those weaknesses and claim that because the results are consistent throughout the city, this proves policing in the city is not racially biased. Such a claim would be in error. The results from a weak methodology are not validated if the results are consistent across multiple geographic areas.

If a methodology can measure only disparity and not the cause of that disparity, that limitation persists even when the methodology is used over and over again in multiple areas. In a contrasting example, a researcher may find disparity in all or most of the subareas within a jurisdiction. Again, however, multiple measures of disparity do not accumulate to provide a cause for that disparity; they continue to represent only multiple measures of disparity.

CONCLUSION

In this chapter we discussed the challenge of benchmarking—the process of developing a demographic profile of drivers at risk of being stopped by police, assuming no bias. We pinpointed the factors that should legitimately increase or decrease the likelihood of being stopped and framed those factors in the form of "alternative hypotheses" to the "bias hypothesis." To assess whether there is differential stopping by police of demographic groups, we test the hypothesis that police are biased in their decision making and do so by ruling out the alternative hypotheses. The strength of a benchmark depends on the degree to which it encompasses the factors associated with the alternative hypotheses. In Chapters 5 through 10 we discuss the major benchmarking methods: adjusted census benchmarking, benchmarking based on a comparison of licensed drivers and drivers stopped by police, benchmarking based on blind versus not-blind enforcement, internal benchmarking, and observation-based benchmarking. The framework of alternative hypotheses is used to convey the strength of the benchmark and, relatedly, to make recommendations regarding how the results of the police-citizen contact data analysis can be responsibly conveyed. However, before we turn to these various benchmarking methods, we discuss how agencies mandated or choosing to collect data initiate collection (Chapter 3) and prepare the data for analysis (Chapter 4).

Getting Started

This chapter describes the preliminary steps associated with collecting police-citizen contact data and explains how and why a jurisdiction might involve residents, police personnel from all levels of the department, and independent social scientists in these efforts. Additionally, we discuss factors that a law enforcement agency should consider before choosing a benchmark for analyzing its data.

Any law enforcement agency that is planning to collect data needs to address the following questions:

- On what law enforcement activities should the agency collect data?
- What information should the agency collect regarding those activities?
- How should the agency analyze and interpret the data?

Building upon the work of Ramirez, McDevitt, and Farrell (2000), Fridell et al. (2001, Chap. 8) discuss the options available to agencies regarding the first two questions. For instance, the 2001 report reviews the considerations for deciding whether to collect data on traffic stops only, all vehicle stops, or all detentions (including pedestrian stops). Also discussed are the data elements that agencies should consider for inclusion in their protocol (for example, the date, time, and reason for the vehicle stop; the race, ethnicity, age, and gender of the person stopped; information regarding stop dispositions and search activity). We do not repeat those discussions here. Agencies in the first stages of planning data collection will find these previously published sources helpful. (Again, the Fridell 2001 document can be downloaded from www.policeforum.org.) It also may be constructive for them to contact peer agencies and request to review their "forms."[1] Be sure to ask relevant personnel what, in hindsight, they would change about their forms.

DEVELOPING THE DATA COLLECTION PROTOCOL: TWO RECOMMENDATIONS

We offer two important recommendations related to developing the data collection protocol. First, plans for how an agency will analyze its data should be developed, if feasible, at the same time the decision makers develop the overall data collection strategy. Uninformed or after-the-fact decisions in these matters can lead to unnecessary tensions between residents (particularly racial/ethnic minority residents) and policy makers and/or between police officers and policy makers. Both jurisdiction residents and officers have a strong stake in the highest quality analyses of the data. Officers, in particular, can be legitimately skeptical of—even strongly opposed to—data collection efforts if they lack assurances that the data will be analyzed using the best social science methods available or, at least, responsibly interpreted. An early designation of the method of analysis and a commitment to responsible interpretation can mitigate these concerns. In the same vein, it is important for the agency to confirm early on that sufficient resources are available to meet

---

[1] Not all agencies are using paper forms to collect their data. Some agencies ask their officers to submit data by using handheld or in-car computers; in other agencies, officers verbally submit the stop information over the radio. The word "forms" used throughout this report denotes all methods of data submission.

its objectives. Otherwise, an agency may make a significant investment in a data collection system only to find out that analyses of the quality it desires cannot be implemented. Some of the methods that can be chosen to analyze police-citizen contact data rely on particular data elements in the forms that officers complete. This is another reason for early planning.

Second, we strongly advise that, in identifying which activities a jurisdiction will target for data collection, the decision makers select all traffic stops, all vehicle stops, and/or all investigative stops and not a subset of any of these categories as defined by their outcomes.[2]

Some agencies (indeed, some states) are collecting and analyzing data only from the traffic stops that *result in citations*. (That is, instead of collecting and analyzing data from all traffic stops, these jurisdictions are focusing on a subset of traffic stops as defined by the outcome, a citation.) This common practice is convenient because it does not add paperwork for the officers (relying, as it does, on existing, albeit possibly modified, forms), but the practice is not recommended. The resulting data exclude stops by police that may be at heightened risk of being racially motivated. A data collection system based on citation stops alone excludes stops of law-violating drivers who should have received a citation but did not, and it may include law-abiding drivers who should not have been stopped in the first place. The "selection" by police of the fortunate drivers or illegitimately stopped drivers could be based on their race/ethnicity, and thus by excluding drivers who do not receive citations, a jurisdiction severely jeopardizes its ability to assess the existence of racially biased policing, regardless of the strength of the benchmark used. The

---

[2] As explained in Chapter 1, "vehicle stop" denotes any stop made by police of a person in a vehicle; "traffic stop" denotes a vehicle stop the stated purpose of which is to respond to a violation of traffic laws (including codes related to quality/maintenance of vehicles); and "investigative (vehicle) stop" denotes police stops of people in vehicles when there is at least reasonable suspicion of criminal activity.

researcher could, with these limited data, identify bias where none exists or conclude there is no bias when, in fact, there is.

This faulty methodology is analogous to assessing the impact of race on prison sentences by focusing only on those who are in prison. For example, by examining only the racial makeup of the prison population and comparing length of prison sentences across races, a jurisdiction will be unable to reach sound conclusions. It must also assess whether or not there are racial differences with regard to who gets sentenced to prison (versus sentenced to jail or to probation, for example).

If a jurisdiction is collecting data only on subsets of stops, it needs to include a strongly stated caveat regarding the stops that are excluded from its research. This limitation on the data concerning who is stopped will also affect the analysis of post-stop activities and outcomes. This is because some people who were stopped by police—some of whom were searched and maybe even detained for long periods of time—will not be included in the data set being analyzed.

INVOLVING RESIDENTS AND POLICE PERSONNEL IN PLANNING DATA COLLECTION AND ANALYSIS

It is advantageous for jurisdictions to involve residents and a cross-section of law enforcement agency employees in planning how the data will be collected and analyzed. (Regarding the latter, we note that even if a jurisdiction did not involve residents and police in planning the data collection system, it could still involve them in discussions about the data's analysis and interpretation.)

Police personnel—particularly line personnel—can bring valuable information and an important perspective to the table. These agency representatives have a critical stake in ensuring a high-quality initiative, and they should have the opportunity to raise any of their concerns about the integrity and fairness of the data collection and analysis system. Employees' involvement can also facilitate "buy in" by the line officers upon whom the agency will rely to collect the data.

Law enforcement agencies' involvement of residents (particularly minority residents) in data collection planning can improve police-citizen relations, enhance the credibility of the research efforts, and increase the likelihood that the community will view the outcome as legitimate.[3] Involving jurisdiction residents in discussions regarding data analysis/interpretation has the additional advantage of educating a core group of residents about the complexities and constraints of the process. These residents can serve as important voices affirming the integrity of the analysis and the sound interpretation of the results when reports are released to the public.

In the interest of responsible social science, the caveats associated with various benchmarking methods should be included in jurisdiction reports. The caveats should convey why the results may not provide definitive proof of racially biased policing or its absence in the jurisdiction. Coming only from the police department spokesperson, these caveats may be interpreted by skeptical residents as defensive excuses for why results showing disparity (if they do) are not proof of racial bias. Although the use of independent social scientists to conduct analyses will add credibility to these caveats, the additional voices of respected residents who understand the methodological constraints will increase the likelihood that the results and the conclusions drawn from them will be viewed as legitimate by the general public and the media. "If the community understands benchmarks and the variables that skew aggregate data there is less likelihood the information will be misinterpreted and misused," writes McMahon et al. (2002, 94). One way to facilitate the understanding of data analyses on the part of citizens is to set up a local racial profiling task force or advisory committee.

---

[3] See Farrell, McDevitt, and Buerger (2002) for a discussion of how police-community task forces can be used to oversee the data collection system and to otherwise address the issue of racially biased policing in a jurisdiction.

As recommended in PERF's first report on the topic of racially biased policing, these task forces should be composed of fifteen to twenty-five people with representatives from both the department and the community (Fridell et al. 2001, Chap. 7). In selecting community members, decision makers should focus on those people who are most concerned about racial bias by police. The task force should include representatives from the jurisdiction's various minority groups and representatives from civil rights groups. Consideration should be given to media representatives as well because these professionals will be in the important position of conveying the results to jurisdiction residents. Police personnel selected for the task force should represent all departmental levels, particularly patrol.

Citizens and police can bring knowledge to the discussions that is of value in planning the data analyses and understanding the results. What they know about the jurisdiction's characteristics, residents, and police activities can be of great help to the researchers charged with actually implementing the analysis plan. For instance, their knowledge of jurisdiction roads may be helpful to a researcher trying to choose representative intersections where observers will document the race/ethnicity of drivers. (See discussion of the observation method of benchmarking in Chapter 9.) Or their knowledge that a particular high-minority downtown entertainment area draws large numbers of white suburbanites on Saturday nights can be helpful to a researcher seeking to understand the results for that area.

PARTNERING WITH SOCIAL SCIENTISTS

If resources allow, an agency should consider obtaining the assistance of independent social scientists for analyzing its police-citizen contact data. There are two major reasons for partnering with social scientists:

- Partnering with an individual or a team external to the agency can add credibility to the process and thus to the results.

- The skills of trained social scientists can supplement the internal resources available for research.

Data collection to assess racially biased policing is both a social science and a political endeavor. Thus, an agency must attend to both social science and political objectives in developing and implementing an analysis plan. An agency could use internal staff to conduct a high-quality analysis but lose in the political arena because the jurisdiction's residents did not consider the internally conducted analysis to be credible.

Many law enforcement agencies (especially small and medium-sized ones) do not have the in-house expertise to analyze and interpret police-citizen contact data. A social science partner may be essential to supplement agency resources and perform these functions. The analyst(s) should be trained in social science methods and have general knowledge of law enforcement; they also should have demonstrated knowledge of the specific issues associated with analyzing police-citizen contact data (Fridell et al. 2001, Chap. 8). Ideally, this "demonstrated knowledge" would come from having conducted similar analyses for other jurisdictions. Capable analysts are most likely to be associated with a college or university or with an independent research firm. The individual social scientist or the research team will play a major role in educating jurisdiction residents about the various methods that can be used for analysis and the strengths and weaknesses of each.

Importantly, the social scientist(s) become "partners" with the agency or, preferably, with the jurisdiction task force in the data collection/analysis effort. They are not just handed the data to analyze as they see fit in the privacy of their university or agency offices. The analysis plan should be agreed upon by all parties and the social scientists should communicate with their agency and/or task force partners throughout their work. The researchers should share preliminary results, soliciting perspectives from their police and resident partners who likely have superior knowledge regarding local conditions that may be pertinent to the interpretation of the data.

SELECTING BENCHMARKS

In subsequent chapters we describe the various benchmarks that law enforcement agencies can use to analyze and interpret vehicle stop data. These benchmarks vary considerably in terms of their ability to address the alternative hypotheses discussed in Chapter 2. In deciding which benchmark(s) to use, decision makers should consider the following factors: the level of measurement precision they desire, the financial and personnel resources that are available, the data elements that must be collected, and the availability of other data that may be required for using a particular benchmark. Later chapters describe for each benchmarking method its level of precision, required agency resources, required data elements, and requirements in terms of information from outside sources.

Level of Measurement Precision Desired

The higher the quality of the benchmark, the greater the ability of the researcher to "measure" and draw conclusions regarding racially biased policing. High-quality analysis can provide meaningful information not only on whether the problem exists and, if so, to what degree, but also on the nature of the problem and the specifics of its manifestation (in terms of particular geographic areas, shifts, or officers). However, the institution conducting the analysis need not pick one of the most precise methodologies (coming as these do with generally higher complications and sometimes higher costs) in order to make its data collection system successful and constructive. The keys to success for an agency picking a benchmark are (1) responsible interpretation and (2) constructive discussion with stakeholders concerning benchmark weaknesses.

For each benchmark described in later chapters, we provide information related to the strength of the conclusions being drawn. (This will be conveyed in terms of the extent to which each benchmark encompasses the alternative hypotheses.) Reports will need to include this information to ensure responsible interpretation of the data. Imperfect data can still provide a solid base for constructive dialogue between police and citizens. Results showing "disparity" that cannot be linked to a particular "cause" (such as bias) can still lead to a meaningful discussion of possible causes and desirable reforms. Importantly, these discussions can lead to the collection of other forms of "data," including that which comes from an open and frank sharing of concerns by citizens.[4] Commenting on the value of police-citizen contact data for facilitating police-citizen dialogue, Farrell, McDevitt, and Buerger (2002, 365) report: "The most effective and productive use of racial profiling data is not its ability to determine if racial profiling exists but rather its ability to provide concrete information to ground police-community discussions about patterns of stops, searches, and arrests throughout local communities."

REQUIRED AGENCY RESOURCES

In selecting a benchmark for analyzing police-citizen contact data, an agency should consider not only the level of measurement precision it desires but also the resources it has available. Not surprisingly, the most effective benchmarks usually (but not necessarily) require the most resources in terms of finances and personnel. An agency will want to select the most effective method given its resources and objectives.[5]

Data Elements

The use of some benchmarks is dependent on the inclusion of particular elements on the data collection form. If the agency is

---

[4] Fridell et al. (2001, Chap. 7) promotes police-resident discussions of racially biased policing and perceptions of its practice. A video and accompanying guide, funded by the Office of Community Oriented Policing Services in the U.S. Department of Justice, was developed to facilitate and structure these dialogues. This video and guide can be ordered through the PERF web site, www.policeforum.org.

[5] We do not have reliable information regarding the costs that are associated with the various benchmarks. Many jurisdictions seeking to hire outside analysts issue requests for proposals and then review the proposals, balancing strength of methodology and resources required.

in the early stages of developing the data collection protocol, decisions regarding how to analyze/interpret the data should be made in conjunction with decisions about the content of the form (that is, what data elements to include). If an agency has already developed the form, decision makers will need to ensure that the method selected for analysis/interpretation is supported by available data. As an example, we describe in Chapter 7 how some jurisdictions have compared the demographic profiles of drivers stopped for speeding by police unaided by radar to the demographic profiles of drivers stopped because of radar measurements of their speed. (The radar stops are conducted in a manner so that the radar operator cannot discern the driver's race/ethnicity.) To make such a comparison, the jurisdiction must be able to identify, from data on the forms, which stops were conducted with and without radar.

For all benchmarking methods we advocate analyses within specific geographic subareas. Therefore, the location of the stop is an important data element to include on the police-citizen contact data form. For purposes of reviewing and monitoring data for quality, a unique identifier (number) on the form also is helpful. Most advantageous is an incident number or similar identifier that corresponds to information about the event that is contained in other data sets, such as computer-aided-dispatch (CAD) data and citation data.

The Availability of Other Data
Some benchmarking methods are dependent upon the availability of information from outside sources. An example is a method that compares the demographic profile of drivers who are identified as traffic violators by enforcement cameras (cameras that are used at controlled jurisdictions to detect and ticket red-light violators or speeders) to the demographic profile of drivers who are identified as traffic violators by officers on patrol in the same area as the cameras. This method would, of course, be available only to jurisdictions that have enforcement cameras in place and are able to identify through the license

plate number (or photos) the race/ethnicity of the violators (or at least the race/ethnicity of the vehicle owners when the license plate number is used).

Other Considerations

A jurisdiction may decide to use multiple benchmarks. For example, it might implement "internal" benchmarking and some "external" method as well. Internal benchmarking is a strong benchmark for identifying which police officers, units, or shifts may be stopping minorities at higher rates than their "similarly situated" counterpart officers, units, or shifts. A drawback to internal benchmarking, however, is that it only compares parts of the law enforcement agency to itself. For this reason, the agency might choose—in addition—to compare the agency's performance to some outside benchmark, such as that provided by the blind versus not-blind enforcement method, or the observation method. Thus, a jurisdiction might implement both internal benchmarking and some external method as well.

An agency might also decide to implement a relatively simple benchmark (for example, adjusted census benchmarking) in all the subareas of its jurisdiction and then invest in a more complicated and more effective benchmark (for example, the observation methodology described in Chapter 9) in those subareas identified by the simpler benchmark as having the greatest racial/ethnic disparities.

INFORMING THE PUBLIC OF
DATA COLLECTION EFFORTS

Some law enforcement executives, when announcing their data collection efforts, have referred to the initiative as an opportunity to "prove" that policing in their jurisdiction is not racially biased. This is inappropriately and unnecessarily defensive. First of all, such a prediction of research results is *inappropriate*. While a particular executive might be justified in having confidence that racially biased policing is neither systematic nor widespread within his or her jurisdiction, the executive is naïve to claim absolutely that it never occurs. Such a statement is almost certain to offend racial/ethnic minorities who perceive otherwise. Our society has serious racial/ethnic biases, and the police profession—like every other profession—hires from a population with these prejudices. Even in a department in which racial bias is neither systematic nor widespread, it is likely that it occurs in some places, at some times, committed by some individual officers. Finally, such a strong claim (the police executive's use of the word "prove") implies that police-citizen contact data can provide definitive answers—which they cannot. As is true of social science in general, even strong methods will not provide definitive proof of the existence or lack of racially biased policing.

A claim of innocence even before the data are collected and analyzed is also *unnecessary*. An executive can reasonably assert that the agency is undertaking data collection in a sincere effort to determine whether or not a problem of racial/ethnic bias exists and, if it does, will implement corrective and preventive actions.

That said, we are not advocating that agencies wait until the data are collected and analyzed to implement remedial actions. In a perfect world (where social science could quickly and definitively answer all the questions we pose), agencies would first analyze the problem and then, based on that analysis, develop appropriate responses (policies, training, outreach) to promote reform. In the context of our imperfect world (where data collection takes time and social science cannot provide definitive results), agencies should not make data collection showing racial disparity the minimum requirement for implementing reforms to address this critical issue. In fact, while the practice of data collection as a response to racially biased policing has had important benefits, a negative side effect, arguably, is the inherent implications that (1) some agencies are "guilty" of racial bias and others are not and (2) agencies shown to be "guilty" are the ones that should implement reforms. All agencies committed to democratic policing, not only agencies "proven guilty" of bias through data collection, need to implement reforms.[6]

CONCLUSION

In this chapter we reviewed important considerations in developing the data form and deciding which types of activities to target for data collection. We encourage the involvement of residents and police personnel from all levels in making decisions regarding the data collection system, and we discussed the circumstances in which agencies might want to involve independent social scientists. The selection of benchmarks should be based on considerations of measurement precision, resources, existing data elements, and the availability of other data. A police executive announcing data collection plans to the public should not claim innocence before the fact. Indeed, like society at large, an agency is rarely bias free. Neither should that agency executive await the results of data collection—whatever they might be—to implement reforms to address the long-standing, widespread issues of racially biased policing and the perceptions of its practice.

---

[6] Various responses to racially biased policing are set forth in Fridell et al. (2001).

Data Analysis Guidelines for All Benchmarking Methods

Law enforcement agencies, regardless of the benchmarking method they choose for evaluating whether policing in their jurisdiction is racially biased, should follow certain guidelines on the analysis of police-citizen contact data. This chapter presents these guidelines. The information will be most useful for researchers who are handling the data. It will also be useful to the police executives and other policy makers who will oversee or hire the social scientists and assess their competencies.

We start by explaining how the data that have been collected from officers can be checked for quality, an important first step in any type of social science research and not unique to the analysis of police-citizen contact data. We also discuss "reference periods," the length of time that agencies should collect data before they begin analyzing it. As we explain, it is advisable for agencies to conduct some analyses on portions or "subsets" of their full data set. Subsets based on the type of stop (proactive or reactive), whether the officer could discern the driver's race/ethnicity before the stop, and the geographic location of the stop are recommended. The final section of the chapter explains the need for comparability of the stop data and benchmarking data in any analysis, or what we call "matching the numerator and the denominator."

REVIEW OF DATA QUALITY

All good social science involves a careful review of data to check for and, if possible, correct errors before analysis of the data begins. Once data collection is under way, we recommend that agencies "audit" the incoming data from officers for quality. The purpose of these audits is to ascertain whether line personnel in the police department are submitting data collection forms for each and every targeted stop and filling out the forms fully and accurately.[1] Even if the data collection has been under way for a while, a "data review/monitoring system" can be added.

Although there is no cost-effective way to ensure that the data are 100 percent accurate, the methods described below can help the researchers check for and enhance the quality of their data. Quality data are a prerequisite for quality research. A review/monitoring system also has other benefits. If officers know that the data they gather are being inspected for comprehensiveness and quality, they may be more diligent in their data collection efforts and more committed to data quality. Internal monitoring also may remove the necessity of external monitoring. The research team at Northeastern University's Institute on Race and Justice describes internal monitoring as that which is conducted by the agency and runs "concurrently with the data collection" (Farrell 2003a). External monitoring occurs when outside stakeholders challenge the agency's data quality,[2] and as a result monitoring is conducted by independent researchers.

---

[1] As noted in Chapter 3, not all agencies use paper forms to collect their data. Some officers submit data by using handheld or in-car computers, or they relay information on vehicle stops over the radio.

[2] For example, in Providence, Rhode Island, the American Civil Liberties Union (ACLU) sued the City of Providence for noncompliance with state data collection mandates. The ACLU alleged that the police made many stops for which they did not submit data collection cards (Rhode Island Affiliate, American Civil Liberties Union v. Providence Police Department, Rhode Island Superior Court C.A. 01-5900 combined with Whitehouse v. City of Providence, C.A. 01-5884).

Checking for Submission of Data Forms for All Targeted Stops

A range of methods from simple to complex can be used to ascertain whether forms are received by the agency for each and every stop targeted for data collection (for example, for all vehicle stops, for all traffic stops). Not surprisingly, the more complex methods are the most effective.

The data collection forms can be cross-checked with other agency data—for example, citation data, computer-aided-dispatch (CAD) data—to ensure that the required forms are submitted for all targeted stops. The simplest cross-check is to compare aggregate numbers across data sets. For instance, an agency might compare (1) the total number of police-citizen contact forms that indicated citations were issued to (2) other agency records regarding the number of citations issued.[3] Similarly, police-citizen contact form totals or subtotals can be matched to records of officers' calls to their communications or dispatch center regarding stops. If an agency can count (using, for instance, CAD data) the number of times officers reported they were making a vehicle stop or traffic stop, it can compare these totals to the total number of forms submitted for stops during the same period of time. Again, in these two examples, the researcher is comparing totals of some type of stop across data sets. If, for example, the number of traffic stops according to the CAD data is significantly larger than the number of traffic stops according to police-citizen contact forms, the researcher can conclude that forms are not being submitted by officers for all of the targeted activities.

The preceding comparison of totals has a drawback: a problem can be detected, but the specific nature of the problem cannot be

---

[3] This comparison presents a potential complication. The citation total will likely reflect all citations, including multiple citations for a single incident. In contrast, the total for the police-citizen contact forms will likely reflect all the incidents involving the issuance of one or more citations and may not indicate the total number of citations issued. In short, this comparison may be precluded if one measure is of citations and one measure is of incidents in which citations were issued.

identified. The law enforcement agency cannot tell from the comparison of totals the nature of the stops for which forms were not submitted and/or which specific officers or units or shifts were undersubmitting data. This more detailed information can be gleaned from review/monitoring methods that actually match incidents across data sets. Therefore, some researchers are checking on a stop-by-stop basis whether a form was submitted. Again, this requires having another source of data within the agency regarding stops that are made. Referring back to CAD data, researchers can match—on an incident-by-incident basis—the stops included in the CAD data and the stops recorded on a police-citizen contact form.

This process is greatly facilitated if the law enforcement agency sets up an efficient way to link the incidents within the two data sets. For example, agencies require officers to call dispatch when they are stopping a vehicle for either traffic or investigative purposes. Some agencies number all of their police-citizen contact forms and then require the officer to provide the dispatch center with the number on the police-citizen contact form that will be filled out for that event. The system can be set up so that dispatch cannot close the call until that number is obtained.[4] With this information, agencies can then cross-check dispatch records with the submitted forms for police-citizen contacts to ensure that each stop corresponds with a form.[5] Cross-checking

---

[4] Without numbers that linked call-in data and police-citizen contact forms, the Northeastern University team working in Providence (Farrell 2003a) had to try to match stops as recorded by dispatch to police-citizen contact forms by referencing such information as officer identification, stop location, date, and time. This very time-consuming process is more error prone than a method that links data for stops through a numbering system.

[5] The Northeastern University team (Farrell 2003b; McDevitt 2003) reports that this method has the potential for both positive and negative indirect outcomes. On the one hand, linking these call-ins to the police-citizen contact form may lead some officers to not report all of their stops to dispatch—an omission that has safety ramifications. On the other hand, it is possible that linking the forms to the dispatch system may improve compliance with call-in rules.

can be conducted on the population of forms, or random checks can be conducted. An agency might choose to compare aggregate numbers as described above and then implement the stop-by-stop audit if discrepancies are found between totals produced by the sources being compared.

In another method for making stop-by-stop comparisons, an agency could check to be sure that each citation issued by its personnel was matched to a corresponding police-citizen contact form filled out by the officer. Again, this process would be greatly facilitated by a numbering system that links citations to police-citizen contact forms. This comparison using two sources of citation data (the citations themselves and the subset of police-citizen contact forms that indicate citations were issued) is not as strong as the method described above because that method audits all stops whereas this method focuses only on those stops that resulted in citations. This, however, is still a viable data review/monitoring method if the agency does not have the resources to conduct the broader analysis.

Although not practical for most departments, the creative method used by the Northeastern University team in Providence for reviewing and monitoring data is noteworthy. To assess the extent to which vehicle stops resulted in police-citizen contact forms, the team reviewed in-car videotapes to identify when stops were made by officers and then checked to see that a form for each of those stops had been submitted. The team's assessment was limited because videotapes were not made for each and every stop. Moreover, the team had to use information from the video regarding the date, time, location, and nature of the stop to match the event to the corresponding form. This matching process was very labor intensive.

In sum, to check for comprehensive data submission, agencies should try to identify a second source of data that tracks some or all of the stops that are targeted for data collection. That second source of data may be CAD data, citation data, written warning data, videotapes, or other departmental data. The agency can compare aggregate totals from the two data sets to see whether, for instance, there are as many police-citizen contact forms as there are stops, or it can compare the two data sources on a stop-by-stop basis. The latter method, which has the added advantage of identifying the source of any problems, can lead to interventions to improve data quality. The results of these assessments should be included in the agency's report on its overall analysis of police-citizen contact data.

It is difficult to set a precise cut-off point that would indicate a positive outcome of an audit. The extent to which two data sets will show correspondence will depend, in part, on the quality of the data base selected for the comparison. Thus, while we cannot state with any level of confidence a lower level at which the results are unacceptable, we can say that a correspondence of 90 percent or more between the two sources of information is quite acceptable. That is, the results can be considered positive for the agency if the data review/monitoring methods show that 90 percent or more of the stops identified through the CAD system have a corresponding police-citizen contact form.

Checking for Missing Data or Errors
In addition to checking to ensure that forms are being submitted for all of the stops targeted for data collection, the researchers should review the data that are submitted to detect missing or potentially erroneous data. This review should occur early on (during the first two months that officers are collecting the data) so that remedial measures can be implemented. If this review identifies significant amounts of missing data for particular variables or large numbers of apparent errors on forms, the agency can use this information to implement corrective measures (for example, education of officers) early in the data collection process.

Some computer systems can prevent errors at the time of data entry by using "error traps." In computerized data entry programs, programmers can build checks into the software so that data for particular items that are clearly erroneous or missing will be identified immediately. This type of preventive measure can be implemented in conjunction with an automatic system for data entry (such as scantron), but it is most valuable if it is linked to systems in which an officer personally enters the data directly into a mobile digital terminal (MDT) or other computer. For instance, if an officer on the MDT enters an "8" in a field that offers only options 1, 2, 3, 4, and 5, the computer will immediately reject the entry and ask for a correct input. If the data on the incident or date of birth of the driver is illogical, the officer will be immediately notified of this and can make corrections on the spot. To avoid "missing data," the system can be set up so that the officer cannot "close" the form until all fields are completed. Because of these capabilities, an "error trap" system linked to officer data entry allows for errors to be caught and corrected immediately by the officer.

If a jurisdiction does not have the means of instituting a computerized data entry system with these features, it will need to assess the existence of missing data in other ways. For instance, it could run frequencies for all variables.[6] As a rule of thumb, if more than 10 percent of the forms have missing data on a particular variable, corrective action should be taken (for example, communication to all officers through, for instance,

---

[6] When running these frequencies, law enforcement agencies should not mistake data that are truly "not applicable" for "missing data." Blanks on a form may mean an answer was "not applicable," or blanks may mean "missing data." Confusion of the two possibilities is most likely to occur with regard to items that officers are supposed to complete only in certain circumstances. For instance, an officer would provide information on "authority to search" or "results of search" only if a search was, in fact, conducted during the stop. If the researcher's data does not, for these items, distinguish between "not applicable" blanks and "missing data" blanks, the researcher should run the frequencies for these secondary questions (the ones that are answered only in some circumstances) for the subset of data that represents the circumstances in which the secondary questions should be answered. For instance, if the item should have a response only if a search was conducted, run the frequencies for the secondary items only for the forms that indicate searches were conducted.

roll call).⁷ Extensive missing data might prompt an agency to measure the extent of missing data for each officer to determine whether individual officers need specific corrective feedback.

Forms should also be reviewed to identify another consistent problem: multiple responses where single responses are required. (Ideally, an "error trap" system could also prevent such entries.) For instance, if an agency instructs officers to check off only a single disposition for a stop (for example, the most severe disposition, such as arrest), the audit system should identify consistent double responses (two dispositions are marked). How this is achieved will depend on the type of data processing system or software being used. A high proportion of double responses where single ones are called for should, again, prompt the agency to take remedial action and give officers feedback.

A researcher should try to detect errors in the data, but this objective will never be fully achieved. It is impossible to detect all errors merely by reviewing the data that have been submitted. For example, a review of the data is unlikely to detect that the correct disposition of a traffic stop was a warning when the officer erroneously indicates on the form that a citation was given. Certain types of errors, however, can be detected by running cross-tabulations.⁸ For instance, the analyst can cross-tabulate "reason for the stop" with "disposition" to see if the dispositions are logical in light of the reasons. If a number of incident forms indicate *arrests* for *seat belt violations*, further inquiry would be advisable. Similarly, cross-tabulating "search results" (positive or negative) with "what was recovered" might

---

⁷ It is possible that a high level of missing data is because the item is faulty in some way, making it difficult for officers to answer. Discussions with individual officers or groups of officers could identify these problems.

⁸ A cross-tabulation shows the frequency of values for one variable within the values for another variable. Said another way, a cross-tabulation is a table that "contains counts of the number of times various combinations of values of two variables occur" (Norusis n.d., 125).

indicate some incidents where the officer indicated "negative results" (that is, nothing was found) and yet also indicated something was recovered. This illogical combination of results signals that at least one of the entries is incorrect.

Table 4.1 indicates that in six incidents an officer reported on the form that a search produced "negative results" (that is, no seizable materials were recovered) but also reported that something was recovered. These conflicting data indicate errors in filling out the forms.

Table 4.1. Crosstabulation Indicating Erroneous Data

What Was Recovered	Number of Incidents When the Result of the Search Was	
	Negative (No Seizable Materials)	Positive (Seizable Materials)
Currency	0	452
Weapon	5	233
Stolen Property	0	108
Illegal Drugs	0	76
Other	1	89

In addition to cross-tabulating results, an agency can detect erroneous data by conducting follow-up checks on the facts associated with stops. As discussed below, it can obtain information from the people who were stopped by police.

Checking for Misstatements of Facts

Sometimes in social science research, the participants make errors intentionally rather than inadvertently. When collecting police-citizen contact data, we must consider the possibility that some officers may not merely forget to complete items or commit other unintentional errors; they may input incorrect data on purpose. To try to identify intentional data distortions, an agency should begin by identifying the elements in the data collection protocol for which officers, trying to "look good," might submit incorrect data. Examples include data on race/ethnicity of the person stopped, the length of the stop, and whether the person's racial/ethnic characteristics were observable before the stop.

There are no highly effective ways to identify these data distortions. In fact, the way many agencies are measuring race/ethnicity (observations by officers) precludes a valid cross-check of this variable against official records, such as Department of Motor Vehicle (DMV) records. Consistent with the recommendations of most social scientists, many agencies measure race/ethnicity based on the officer's perception of the subject's characteristics when the officer makes the stop.[9] Officer perceptions—not the official DMV designation of race—is what is important in determining if officer bias was at play. This method assumes that the officer's perceptions will not always match the person's race/ethnicity as listed on his/her driver's license. If these perceptions were cross-checked against DMV records, we would expect some level of discrepancy, and we do not know how much that should be. Consequently, the cross-check is of little use.

One police-citizen task force for a jurisdiction proposed cross-checking the race/ethnicity data, not against DMV records, but against the driver's self-report of race/ethnicity on a "tear-off" portion on the data collection card. Officers would give the drivers they stopped the tear-off portion to fill out and return to the department (by mail or fax), and they would complete the other portion of the card. The two forms—one for the police officer to submit and one for the citizen to submit—were to have a common identifier contained in a bar code. The person who was stopped was asked to self-identify age and gender as well as race/ethnicity. The problem with this proposal—and maybe the reason the task force decided not to implement it—is that the offi-

---

[9] For a discussion of measuring race/ethnicity, see Fridell et al. (2001, Chap. 8).

cer's perceptions will be wrong some proportion of the time, yet researchers could not know how much legitimate discrepancy to anticipate. Because of this unknown, it would have been very difficult to interpret the results of the comparison of the driver self-report data to the officer perception data.

The information contained in the mail-in "tear-off" card could be used for other types of data checks.[10] Individuals could be asked to provide information about how the officer treated them, what type of vehicle they were driving, whether they were given a ticket/citation, and other aspects of the incident. This information could be used to compare the driver's version of the incident with the officer's version. For instance, driver and officer information could be compared with regard to the length of stop, whether a search was conducted, and whether the driver provided consent to search. A variation on this theme involves conducting follow-up calls to a random subset of stopped individuals to ask about the incident. Again, however, some legitimate but unknown amount of discrepancy is to be expected between the citizen and officer versions if only because of differing perceptions or faulty memories.

The team analyzing police-citizen contact data for the Miami-Dade Police Department, headed by Geoff Alpert, developed a way to cross-check the race/ethnicity information. These researchers selected a random sample of stops for a random sample of officers and compared the race/ethnicity data that the officers had inserted on their forms to the DMV-computerized driver's license pictures of the people stopped.[11] A panel of citizens reviewed the pictures and the race/ethnicity

---

[10] Departments should not expect a very high response rate (maybe 30 percent or less); further, the citizens who respond may be systematically different from those who do not. For instance, the more dissatisfied motorists may be more inclined to return their cards.

[11] Note that this method requires that the driver's license number of the person stopped be included on the form. Some civil rights groups are opposed to having such identifying information appear on the data collection forms.

designation on the forms to see if the officers' stated perceptions were reasonable ones. Another way to implement this system would be to cross-check the contact form designation of race/ethnicity against the DMV designation of race/ethnicity and then have a panel review the photographs of only those drivers (or a random sample of those drivers) whose race/ethnicity data do not match across the two sources of information (Canter 2003).[12]

For some information included on the form, the analyst can compare data across similarly situated officers to identify "outliers" (officers whose data are very different from the data submitted by their peers). This process could be used to assess whether any officers are systematically over-reporting that "the citizen's characteristics were *not observable* before the stop," even when the characteristics are frequently visible. An analyst might compare the frequencies with which officers on the same shift indicate "characteristics not observable."[13] If most officers on one shift indicate "characteristics not observable" 30 to 40 percent of the time and one officer indicates "characteristics not observable" 70 percent of the time, further inquiry would be warranted. Within-shift comparisons could be used for other variables as well.

Removing Duplicate Data on Incidents

As part of checking the data for quality, analysts may need to develop a method for identifying duplicate entries. The researcher should ensure that information on a particular stop is not entered more than once in the data set. Whether this step is necessary will depend on the way the data are entered; specifically, some data input methods may be more likely to produce duplicate entries than others.

---

[12] It's important to note that how a person looked to the police officer from his/her vantage point may be very different from the way the person looked in the DMV photo.

[13] Of course, the ability to discern the race/ethnicity of a driver is affected by the time of day. A comparison within shifts takes this into account.

REFERENCE PERIOD FOR ANALYSIS OF DATA

A key question for most social science studies is "How much data should be collected before analyses are initiated?" We recommend that analysis be based upon the stops occurring within a full twelve-month period, if feasible. This reference period length will lessen the impact on the data of special events or circumstances, it will eliminate seasonal effects (since all seasons will be included), and it will increase the reliability of the data. A twelve-month reference period, however, may not be economically feasible or politically viable. Regarding the latter, residents may not expect to wait more than one year for the results of the analysis. If researchers choose a reference period of less than one year (for example, six months), they should include in the report a caveat that the results do not necessarily generalize to the rest of the year for which data were not analyzed.

It is advisable to delay the start of the reference period for the analysis until officers have become accustomed to the data collection process. (That is, the first one or two months of data collection should not be included in the analysis.) As noted above, these first few months of data should be reviewed to identify problems (such as large amounts of missing data on particular variables), and these problems should be resolved through communications with officers or other retraining. Once the problems appear to be resolved, the reference period should begin.

REASONS FOR ANALYZING SUBSETS OF DATA

For many reasons, it is appropriate for agencies to analyze subsets of their police-citizen contact data. In this section we describe why a researcher might choose not to analyze all of the data submitted during the reference period but only a portion and how and why a researcher might conduct separate, multiple analyses using subsets of the data. For example, the researcher might choose to analyze for his or her report only proactive stops; then the researcher might choose to conduct separate analyses of these data within geographic subareas of the jurisdiction. Below we discuss subsets based on (1) whether stops are proactive or reactive, (2) whether the officer could discern the driver's race/ethnicity, (3) whether the driver appears in the database once or multiple times, (4) geographic location of the stops, and (5) whether the stops are for traffic violations or for the purpose of investigating crime. As we explain, some subsets are advisable for the analysis of "who is stopped" but may not be an advisable subset for analyzing poststop data.

Type of Stop: Proactive or Reactive

In analyzing police-citizen contact data, researchers are attempting to find out whether or not individual officers are making decisions to stop drivers based on racial/ethnic bias or based only on legitimate factors that might, and indeed should, affect their law enforcement behavior. Therefore, analyses of "who is stopped" should legitimately focus on those incidents where officers have discretion in making this decision (proactive stops) and exclude stops where officers have little choice in the matter (reactive stops). The latter include stops such as those in response to automobile accidents and stops at driving checkpoints.[14]

Some agencies have designed their data collection process to target only proactive stops, and in such circumstances there is no relevant subset of data to identify. Agencies, however, that are mandated to collect or voluntarily collect data on both proactive and reactive stops should include only "proactive stops" in their assessment of "who is stopped."[15] Of course, selection of this subset requires relevant information on the

---

[14] This holds for stops at checkpoints that are conducted in accordance with constitutional requirements concerning equitable treatment of all drivers, and officers exercise very little discretion.

[15] Both proactive and reactive stops should be included in the analysis of poststop variables (for example, length of stop, whether a search is conducted). Although officers had little discretion deciding whom to stop in reactive situations, they regain their discretion in deciding how to proceed once the stop is made.

form. The Police Executive Research Forum's model protocol (Fridell et al. 2001, 126–128) advocates the inclusion on the data collection form of an item where officers can specify whether the stop was "reactive" (for example, a stop in response to a call for service or a stop necessitated by a special detail such as a roadblock) or "self-initiated" (for example, a proactive vehicle stop). An agency might also be able to identify proactive stops based on its "reason for a stop" data, assuming the options can be separated easily into proactive (for example, a moving violation) and reactive (for example, an accident) groups.

Prestop Observability of the Driver's Race/Ethnicity
"Was the driver's race/ethnicity observable by police before the stop?" The answer to this question has significant relevance to an assessment of whether or not stopping decisions are based on race/ethnicity and identifies another legitimate subset for analyses of "who is stopped." Therefore, it makes social science sense—at least in the abstract—to exclude those incidents in which the officers could not discern (at the time the decision was made to stop the vehicle) the driver's racial/ethnic characteristics.[16]

The decision, however, to exclude data for stops for which officers said they could not discern the driver's racial/ethnic characteristics can have negative effects, political as well as statistical. In some jurisdictions, concerned citizens have questioned the inclusion of this variable on police-citizen contact data forms because they doubt the validity of officers' responses. Mistrustful of the data submitted for this variable, they will likely be skeptical of a decision to exclude all data for "not observable characteristics" stops. Another potential drawback is that the exclusion of stops for which officers report that they could not discern the race/ethnicity of the driver may reduce the size of the data set

---

[16] Both "observable characteristics" stops and "not observable characteristics" stops (like proactive and reactive stops) should be included in the analysis of poststop factors.

dramatically.[17] We recommend that, if politically and numerically feasible, agencies include in their analysis of data regarding "who is stopped" only those stops for which the driver's racial/ethnic characteristics can be discerned.[18]

Number of Same-Driver Stops during the Reference Period

Some individuals will be represented more than once in an agency's police-citizen contact data because they were stopped by police two or more times during the reference period. (Hereafter we refer to these people as "multiple stoppees.") A potential subset of data would include all vehicle stops minus the multiple stops of the multiple stoppees.[19] Most departments, however, will be unable to identify the multiple stops of these drivers. The ability to remove multiple stoppees from the data set requires information identifying the driver, such as a name or driver's license.[20] Further, not all social scientists and other stakeholders agree that the incidents associated with multiple stoppees should be removed. We report the various views below.

Some commentators and researchers have argued that multiple stoppees should, if possible, be identified and treated dif-

---

[17] In its report on the first six months of police-citizen contact data in 2002, the Denver Police Department reported that officers could discern race/ethnicity in 77 percent of the pedestrian stops but only 8 percent of the traffic stops (Thomas 2002, 16).

[18] Another alternative is to use the stops for which characteristics were not observable as a benchmark for stops in which they were observable. We describe the Rand Corporation's exploration of this method in Chapter 7.

[19] Ideally, this subset would include one of the stops of the multiple stoppee–either the first stop or, better yet, one stop that is randomly selected from among his/her stops.

[20] In some jurisdictions that developed new forms for data collection (as opposed to adopting existing forms, such as citations), civil rights spokespersons considered it inappropriate to include driver identifying information on the data collection forms.

ferently because inclusion of their data distort the analyses: multiple stoppees are represented more than once in the stop data collected by police but may be represented only once in the comparison group (benchmark) against which the demographics of the stoppees will be assessed. This is particularly relevant, they argue, when the demographics of the drivers stopped are compared with the demographics of the people who live in the jurisdiction.[21] By way of example, suppose that 100 African Americans live in the small area where data are being collected, and 50 traffic stops were of African Americans during the reference period. Researchers who advocate identifying and separating multiple stoppees from the data set argue that it would be misleading, in this example, to report that one of every two African Americans were stopped. Conceivably—and we use an extreme example for purposes of making the point—only one individual in the area was stopped fifty times. There is no one "right" answer to the issue of whether multiple stoppees should be included in the data. Certainly, the point these experts make is a valid one that is mathematically grounded and relevant to various research questions. (And, indeed, it may be interesting and enlightening for a jurisdiction to assess the extent to which multiple stoppees are represented in their police-citizen contact data.[22]) However, the consensus of our advisory board is that, in light of the research question underlying data collection efforts, the identification of people who are represented more than once in the data is not required. Further, the incidents involving multiple stoppees should absolutely *not* be removed from the data for an agency's general overall analysis.

---

[21] A valid argument made by one advisory board member was that "multiple stoppees" should be removed from data that will be benchmarked against the census data. The argument is that if the person can be represented only once in the benchmark data, the person should be represented only once in the stop data. This reflects a concept referred to later in the chapter as "matching the numerator and the denominator."

[22] See, for instance, Eck, Liu, and Bostaph (2003).

The research question in the overall analysis is *What is the nature and extent of racially biased policing?* Racially biased policing might manifest itself as the illegitimate one-time stops of fifty minority individuals during the reference period or the illegitimate stopping of ten individuals five times each. To remove from the data the second, third, fourth, etc., stops of the "multiple stoppees" would seem to imply that those incidents could not reflect racially biased policing. They could. Regardless of whether the fifty stops represent fifty or ten individuals, these data can be benchmarked, and conclusions can be drawn in accordance with the strength of the benchmark.

Geographic Location of Stop
In Chapter 2, to address the alternative hypothesis that *racial/ethnic groups are not equally represented as drivers on jurisdiction roads where stopping activity by police is high*, we recommended that agencies analyze data for geographic subareas of the jurisdiction. That is, instead of conducting a single comparison of the demographics produced by a jurisdiction-level benchmark (the demographics of all driving-age residents of the jurisdiction in the case of census benchmarking) and the demographics of all persons stopped, agencies should conduct separate comparisons of benchmark and stop data within smaller geographic areas of the jurisdiction.[23] These subareas become subsets of the analyses.

Analyses within subareas are preferable to single, jurisdiction-level analyses because racial/ethnic disparities might be very strong in some specific areas but go undetected in the aggregate, jurisdiction-level results. Subarea analysis can also "control for" the volume of stopping activity by police. Some areas may have many more stops per capita than others because these areas have a high rate of calls for service or a large volume of accidents. As suggested earlier, the race/ethnicity of the resident population in these high-activity and low-activity areas

---

[23] While there is no "rule of thumb" for how many subareas should be analyzed, most jurisdictions could reasonably develop between four and fifteen.

may vary considerably. The greater vehicle stop activity in Area A than in Area B, for example, won't affect an agency's analysis if it compares the demographics of residents to the demographics of people stopped within A and within B separately.[24]

To conduct the analyses within subareas of the jurisdiction, the agency must be able to link the stop data to these specific areas. This could be accomplished in various ways. The agency could collect information on the data collection form that provides a link to the subareas (either the officer's district/beat assignment recorded on the form or the officer's ID, which can be linked to geographic assignment), or the agency could collect detailed location information on the forms and use geo-coding capabilities to link stop location to identified geographic subareas. (Project advisors report that information on the actual location of the stop is preferable to information on officer assignment for linking stop data to subareas of the jurisdiction.)

When dividing up the jurisdiction into smaller geographic subareas for analyses, the agency should consider two factors. The first is the level of vehicle stopping activity by police. Each subarea selected should be fairly homogeneous with regard to the level of vehicle stop activity. In other words, neighborhoods with a high level of vehicle stop activity should not be combined with adjoining neighborhoods characterized by low levels of activity to form one subarea.[25] The second factor concerns each

---

[24] In some circumstances, the researcher may be able to weight the results (for instance on the basis of police stop volume) for the subareas and produce an overall jurisdiction result. If the researcher is not familiar with the criteria and procedures for weighting data, s/he should confer with a social scientist.

[25] There is always a tradeoff between size of subarea and precision of the findings. An area that is relatively small will have a homogeneous population composition but may not produce enough data for a reliable analysis. Conversely, a large area will have sufficient data but may combine areas with relatively different population compositions. Each subarea should have sufficient numbers of stops during the reference period to produce reliable data, but this requirement should be balanced against population composition considerations. In addition, there is no need for all subareas to be of the same size.

subarea's demographics in terms of proportion of ethnic/racial minorities.[26] Neighborhoods with a high proportion of racial/ethnic minorities should not be combined with adjoining neighborhoods characterized by a low proportion of minorities to form a geographic subarea.[27] Summarizing these recommendations, we describe an ideal situation as one in which a police department's geographic areas (districts) correspond to areas within the jurisdiction that are each homogeneous in terms of vehicle stop activity by police and level of minority representation.

Type of Stop: Traffic or Investigative

Should agencies collecting data on all vehicle stops analyze traffic and investigative stops together as a group or separately?[28] (As noted in Chapter 1, the term "traffic stop" refers to a vehicle stop the stated purpose of which is to respond to a violation of traffic laws, including codes related to quality/maintenance of the vehicle. The term "investigative stop"—in a vehicle context—denotes police stops of people in vehicles when there is a reasonable suspicion of criminal activity.) In addressing the question stated above, we will make distinctions between what is theoretically appropriate and what is practical in terms of measurement capa-

---

[26] Available information for making these distinctions will probably pertain to area residents (for instance, via the census), although information on the demographics of people driving (not living) in the various areas is most relevant.

[27] Smith et al. (2003, Chap. 2) discussed "spatial heterogeneity" in the distribution of minority drivers and speeders and in the distribution of patrol. These North Carolina researchers measured the impact of spatial heterogeneity and showed empirically the value of small geographic units of analysis. Based on research on the North Carolina State Highway Patrol (NCSHP), their report cautioned against large geographic units of analysis: "comparison of rates at the level of county or district ...will be prone to biased estimates in the face of a mismatch [between] where drivers drive and where the NCSHP monitors vehicles" (p. 99).

[28] This discussion is not relevant to agencies that are collecting data only on traffic stops.

bilities. At a theoretical level, traffic stops and investigative stops should be analyzed separately and alternative hypotheses developed for both categories. The factors that put a person at legitimate risk of being stopped by police for a traffic violation are different from the factors that put a person at legitimate risk of being stopped by police for purposes of investigating criminal activity.

The police-citizen contact data that are collected, however, do not enable agencies to distinguish between the stops made for the purpose of enforcing traffic laws and those made for the purpose of investigating crime. Police can and do stop vehicles on the basis of legitimate traffic violations but *for the purpose of* investigating crime. In most agencies these "pretext stops"—as they are called—will be coded as traffic stops, even though at their core they are investigative stops.[29] Therefore, we recommend that all vehicle stops—those for traffic and for investigative purposes—be analyzed together because the theoretical ideal is quite difficult to achieve. It is important to note, however, that this necessary, practical resolution does reduce the precision of the analyses that will be conducted. This is clear when you consider that the higher quality benchmarks that we describe in this report attempt to measure who is violating *traffic laws* and not *criminal laws*.[30] That is, the stop data for the

---

[29] Forms could be developed to produce information that would help researchers to identify pretext stops. For instance, the team at Northeastern University uses two items on the data collection form for Rhode Island that, together, can help to identify pretext stops. This team (see Farrell et al. 2003) had officers code not only the reason for the traffic stop, but also the legal authority for the stop. Thus, an officer might indicate that the legal authority or "basis" for a stop was, for instance, an equipment violation, but that the "reason" was to investigate possible criminal activity. This seems to be a viable model, but it's possible that officers are not always clear about what their own motives are and/or they may be reticent for various reasons to indicate when their stops are pretextual.

[30] Related to this, our relevant alternative hypothesis refers to the possibility that racial/ethnic groups are not equivalent in the nature and extent of their traffic law-violating behavior.

analysis encompass suspected violations of both traffic and criminal laws, while the benchmarks focus on the former.

Note that the quandary posed by pretext stops impacts only agencies' ability to determine which stops that were coded in their data as "traffic" were, in fact, "traffic" and not "investigative." The converse is not true. Agencies can be confident that the stops coded investigative stops are truly investigative stops and not a "ruse" for catching a traffic violator. Although we recommend that agencies analyze all vehicle stops for their major analyses, we include a section in Chapter 10 regarding how crime data might be used to benchmark a subset of only investigative stops.

Subset Summary

When analyzing "who is stopped," agencies should include data on proactive stops where the stopped driver's racial/ethnic characteristics were observable before the stop.[31] Proactive stops are those in which the officer exercises discretion in the choice of whom to stop. To select a subset of data on proactive stops, an agency must use a data collection form that enables officers to specify this type of stop. Selecting for analysis only those stops for which the driver's characteristics are observable reduces the size of the data set; it also is controversial. Citizens have questioned the validity of officers' responses. Use of this subset is advisable if both political and numerical obstacles can be overcome. Analyses should not be conducted for the jurisdiction as a whole but rather for individual geographic subareas.

This chapter has also discussed the pros and cons of other subsets. We recommend including the data on "multiple stoppees" in an agency's general analyses, but the extent to which they are represented in the database might provide for an

---

[31] Data on poststop activities should include both proactive and reactive stops and both "observable characteristics" and "not observable characteristics" stops.

interesting separate inquiry. Finally, all vehicle stops—both traffic and investigative—can be analyzed as a single group.

MATCHING THE NUMERATOR AND THE DENOMINATOR

Social scientists analyzing police-citizen contact data to measure racially biased policing emphasize the importance of "matching the numerator and the denominator." In their specialized lingo, the "numerator" refers to the data collected on stops by the police, and the "denominator" refers to the data collected to produce the benchmark. To "match the numerator and the denominator" means the researcher should adjust the stop data to correspond to any limiting parameters of the benchmark or vice versa.

For example, the researcher conducting census benchmarking adjusted for vehicle ownership should include in his or her analysis only the stops by police involving drivers who are residents of the jurisdiction. In this method of analysis, the researcher adjusts the census data on the demographics of residents to take into consideration who, among those residents, owns a vehicle. That is, the researcher compares the racial/ethnic profile of the people stopped by police to the racial/ethnic profile of people who live in the jurisdiction who have access to vehicles as measured by the U.S. Census. The "numerator" is the stop data collected by police, and the "denominator" is the adjusted U.S. Census data. The denominator in this situation is restricted: it only includes people who live inside the jurisdiction. This parameter on the denominator must be applied to the numerator data. That is, the researcher must compare the census data only to the stops by police of residents. The researcher must select out of the numerator data all of the stops of drivers who do not live inside the jurisdiction. Nonresidents of the jurisdiction are excluded from the denominator, and therefore they must be similarly excluded from the numerator.

In this example there was an inherent limitation on the denominator. Here we consider an adjusted census benchmarking example with an inherent limitation on the numerator (the stop data). Only people of driving age will be included in the numerator. With very few exceptions (we hope so few we can reasonably ignore them), the drivers stopped by police will be of legal driving age (in many jurisdictions it is 15 or 16 years of age and older). Because only people of driving age will be represented in the numerator, the researcher must also limit the denominator data to people of driving age. Thus, in the example of census benchmarking, the researcher will not calculate the race/ethnicity of all residents of the jurisdiction but only of those residents who are of driving age (for example, age 15 and older).

"Matching the numerator and the denominator" applies to other benchmarks as well. For instance, in the observation method described in Chapter 9, researchers collect data from the field (for example, from intersections in the jurisdiction) regarding the race/ethnicity of drivers. Placed at various locations, the observers count the drivers in the various race/ethnicity categories. This process produces a racial/ethnic profile of drivers around that intersection that can be compared to the people who are stopped by police. Since the denominator (observation data) pertains only to a certain area of the city (a single intersection), the relevant analysis will only include police stops in that area. Using this method (described more fully below), the researcher will compare the demographics of the people who are observed driving through Intersection A to the demographics of the people stopped by police in and around Intersection A. (This type of analysis will be conducted separately for each intersection.)

"Matching the numerator and the denominator" applies to the time period during which the data are collected as well. In this observation methodology example, if the observation data are collected during January through May 2002, the analysis will involve only those police stops that occurred during that same (or reasonably similar) time period. If the researchers collected observation data only during daylight hours because of visibility issues, then the analysis should include in the numerator only those stops that occurred during daylight hours.

We have described just a few examples of "matching the numerator and the denominator." Within each chapter on the various benchmarking methods, our recommendations for conducting the analysis of police-citizen contact data will reflect this important rule.

CONCLUSION

This chapter reviewed issues related to data analysis that apply to all benchmarking methods: the need for data monitoring/review for quality, the choice of a reference period, reasons for analyzing subsets of data, and the process of "matching the numerator and the denominator." These issues, for the most part, cut across all benchmarking methods. In the next six chapters, we describe the various benchmarks that can be used to analyze either traffic stop data or vehicle stop data. (The latter includes both traffic and investigative stops of people in vehicles.) For each method, we describe

- the data elements and external information that are required for its use;
- how to implement it; and
- its strengths and weaknesses, particularly in terms of the extent to which the method addresses the alternative hypotheses set forth in Chapter 2.

Benchmarking with Adjusted Census Data

In census benchmarking law enforcement agencies compare the demographic profile of drivers stopped by police to the demographic profile of jurisdiction residents as measured by the U.S. Census Bureau. A straight comparison between the demographics of these two groups is called "unadjusted" census benchmarking. The weaknesses of this method in ruling out alternative hypotheses were discussed in Chapter 2. Most jurisdictions appear to be benchmarking their police-citizen contact data against unadjusted census data. We reach this conclusion based on the large number of jurisdiction reports that PERF staff collected for this project. Many of the agencies that submitted completed reports to PERF are the ones that were on the forefront of addressing racially biased policing—responding when very few models, if any, were available to guide them in their analysis and interpretation of police-citizen contact data. All too often an agency must undertake data analyses using the finite resources at hand, and unadjusted census benchmarking is the simplest and least costly benchmarking method. That said, we do not recommend unadjusted census benchmarking. Agencies that must rely on census methods should use one of the various adjustment techniques described in this chapter.

In "adjusted" census benchmarking researchers adjust the census data by incorporating into their benchmarking method information pertaining to one or more of the alternative hypotheses (such as quantity of driving).[1] For example, researchers may adjust the census data on the demographics of residents to take into consideration who, among those residents, owns a vehicle. This adjustment reflects the fact that not every resident owns a vehicle, and people without vehicles are clearly at less risk of being stopped in vehicles by police. Census benchmarking with this adjustment is a stronger method than unadjusted census benchmarking for assessing the nature and extent of racially biased policing.

ASSESSING RESOURCES REQUIRED

To implement benchmarking with adjusted census data, agencies need the 2000 Decennial Census data for their jurisdiction. This information can be downloaded from the U.S. Census Bureau web site. Appendix A provides comprehensive information regarding how researchers can access and use census data. They will need measures of race and ethnicity on the data collection forms[2] that match the census measures of race and ethnicity or measures of race and ethnicity into which the census measures can be transformed. To conduct high-quality benchmarking, the agency should solicit information on the form regarding the location of the stop for purposes of conducting analyses within the various subareas of the jurisdiction (see Chapter 4). Some procedures require additional information resources (for instance, age of the driver, driver's jurisdiction of residence); these resources are described within each subsection.

---

[1] Quantity of driving, quality of driving, and location of driving are three factors that can legitimately influence police decisions about whom to stop (see Chapter 2), and these factors are reflected in the alternative hypotheses that a researcher must account for before the bias hypothesis can be tested.

[2] As explained in Chapter 3, not all agencies are using paper forms to collect their data. Some officers submit data by using handheld devices or in-car computers; others verbally submit the stop information over the radio.

MEASURING RACE/ETHNICITY

Figure 5.1 presents census items measuring ethnicity and race. Some agencies will need to transform the census data on the race and ethnicity of jurisdiction residents to match the measurement of race/ethnicity on their own data collection forms. As indicated in the figure, the U.S. Census Bureau treats race and ethnicity separately; in addition to the census questionnaire item assessing race, an item pertaining to Hispanic origin is included. Agencies that similarly have separate questions for race and ethnicity on their data collection forms need not transform the census data to match the structure of their own data. (Ideally, an agency will choose a benchmarking method and then devise its form. If an agency knows that it will be census benchmarking, it should make race and ethnicity separate items on the form so that it will not need to transform the census data.)

→ NOTE: Please answer BOTH Questions 5 and 6.

5. **Is this person Spanish/Hispanic/Latino?** Mark ☒ the *"No"* box if *not* Spanish/Hispanic/Latino.
   - ❏ **No**, not Spanish/Hispanic/Latino
   - ❏ Yes, Mexican, Mexican Am., Chicano
   - ❏ Yes, other Spanish/Hispanic/Latino—Print group.
   - ❏ Yes, Puerto Rican
   - ❏ Yes, Cuban

6. **What is this person's race?** Mark ☒ **one or more races** to indicate what this person considers himself/herself to be.
   - ❏ White
   - ❏ Black, African Am., or Negro
   - ❏ American Indian or Alaska Native—Print name of enrolled or principal tribe.

   - ❏ Asian Indian   ❏ Japanese   ❏ Native Hawaiian
   - ❏ Chinese   ❏ Korean   ❏ Guamanian or Chamorro
   - ❏ Filipino   ❏ Vietnamese   ❏ Samoan
   - ❏ Other Asian—Print race.   ❏ Other Pacific Islander—Print race.

   - ❏ Some other race—Print race.

Source: U.S. Census Bureau, Census 2000 questionnaire.

Figure 5.1.   U.S. Census Questions on Race/Ethnicity

Agencies that do not treat race and ethnicity as separate items likely have forms that reflect one of the following. First, the agency may include ethnicity (that is, Hispanic origin) within a single race/ethnicity variable. For instance, its form might include Caucasian, African American, Hispanic, Asian, and Other. To match this single-variable structure, the agency must transform the two-variable census data (see Appendix B). Second, an agency may measure race with a single variable and disregard entirely the driver's ethnicity. Its police-citizen contact data form will not have a separate question on ethnicity, nor will it include ethnicity in the race variable. If the agency does not measure ethnicity at all, it would use the race information provided by the U.S. Census to compare the *racial* profile of people stopped to the *racial* profile of jurisdiction residents. This agency's analysis—quite unfortunately—would not address ethnic bias.

If police stops of certain race groups are few, researchers should combine these categories. For example, if the racial category "American Indian and Alaska Native" comprises a small percentage of stops by police and a small percentage of jurisdiction residents, researchers might reasonably include this group in the category for "Other" race. Analyses using small numbers are unreliable. We recommend that a racial group be included in "Other" if the group represents less than 5 percent of the stops or less than 5 percent of the residential population.

Finally, a transformation of census data to match agency data may be needed because of the "two or more race" category adopted by the U.S. Census Bureau. If the 2000 Decennial Census shows that 4 percent or more of the jurisdiction's population identifies itself as "two or more races," it may be advisable to transform that 4 percent into more detailed race/ethnicity information using instructions provided by the Office of Management and Budget.[3]

---

[3] See Office of Management and Budget Bulletin No. 00-02 available at www.whitehouse.gov/omb/bulletins/b00-02.html.

CONSIDERING AGE

The purpose of benchmarking vehicle stops is to develop a population of people *at risk* of being stopped. Therefore, when developing the racial/ethnic profile of residents from the census data, agencies should, when possible, use only residents of driving age. The researcher should develop the demographic profile of residents using only people who are legally able to drive in the jurisdiction. A jurisdiction within a state where juveniles can drive (either accompanied or unaccompanied) at age 15 would compare the race/ethnicity of the drivers stopped by police to the race/ethnicity of residents 15 years of age and older.[4]

The researcher using adjusted census benchmarking also should consider the potential intervening variable of age (see discussion in Chapter 2) when possible.[5] The researcher would start by assessing whether the various racial/ethnic groups within the subarea being analyzed are equivalent in terms of their age demographics. What percentage of residents for each racial/ethnic group are in the 15-to-24 age group, and what percentage are 25 and older?[6] If racial/ethnic groups in the subarea

---

[4] A researcher might also exclude the residential population that is 85 and older on the presumption that these persons usually are not driving on jurisdiction roads. For the same reason, the research might eliminate from the denominator people living in institutions, such as prisons or nursing homes.

[5] It is not possible to make a meaningful adjustment for vehicle access within age groups. This is because the census information on households does not include information on the age of the household members. Therefore, using this method, a researcher is unable to control for the potential intervening variable of age.

[6] As explained in Chapter 2, young drivers are thought to be especially prone to driving violations. The Advisory Board for this project defined young drivers as those 24 years of age or younger.

are fairly equivalent in terms of age,[7] the researcher may proceed without analyzing the data within age groups. If they are not equivalent, analyses should be conducted within age groups. This means that all of the analysis would be conducted two times: once to analyze the data for the 15-to-24 age group and once for the 25 and older age group.

ADJUSTING CENSUS DATA ON JURISDICTION RESIDENTS TO ACCOUNT FOR VEHICLE ACCESS

Innovative researchers have strengthened census-based methods by incorporating into their benchmarks information that reflects the alternative hypothesis that *racial/ethnic groups are not equally represented as drivers on jurisdiction roads*. Here we describe how to incorporate information regarding vehicle access as a proxy for driving quantity. In the section entitled "Adjusting Census Data on Jurisdiction Residents to Account for the Influx of Nonresident Drivers," we take into account the drivers on jurisdiction roads who come from neighboring jurisdictions.[8]

Harris (1999) was among the first to adjust census data on residential population using data from another source on vehicle access. He realized this adjustment was needed because (1) people without access to vehicles are clearly less at risk of being stopped by police while driving than are people with access to

---

[7] Lack of age equivalence may be defined as a greater than 10 percent absolute difference between any two categories of race in the proportion of residents who are between the legal driving age and age 24. Take, for example, a subarea of analysis where 15-to-24 year-olds represent 24 percent of the Caucasians, 35 percent of the African Americans, 30 percent of the Asians, and 20 percent of persons of "Other" races. The 35 percent figure for the African Americans is more than 10 percent greater than the Caucasian group (35−24=11) and the "Other" group (35−20=15). Therefore, analysis within age groups for that subarea is required. (The importance of analyzing data within subareas was discussed in Chapter 4 and is discussed again later in this chapter.)

[8] In Chapter 10 we describe how Gary Cordner and his team "adjusted" census data with crime data to account for the 25 percent of traffic stops estimated to be pretext stops (stops based on traffic violations, that are, in fact, motivated by suspicions of criminal activity on the part of the officers).

vehicles, and (2) the proportion of households without access to vehicles varies across racial/ethnic groups. In his analysis of data for four Ohio cities, Harris used data from the National Personal Transportation Survey (NPTS)—now called the National Household Transportation Survey (NHTS)—to adjust the census data. Using the most recent NPTS data at the time (1990 data), Harris determined that 21 percent of African American households nationwide do not own vehicles. He then adjusted census data on the percentage of African Americans in the four cities under study to account for vehicle access. In a hypothetical case, if African Americans comprise 18 percent of the target jurisdiction population, a researcher using Harris's method would multiply 18 percent by 0.21 to get 3.78 percent and then subtract 3.78 percent from 18 percent to get the benchmark population for African Americans with access to vehicles (14.22 percent).

The NHTS reports the percentage of vehicle-less households for racial/ethnic groups for the entire United States. Making adjustments using local data rather than national data is preferable because the proportion of households without vehicles across racial/ethnic groups varies by jurisdiction (see, for example, Pisarski 1996). Local data are available through the U.S. Census Bureau. The U.S. Census Bureau data on vehicle-less households are preferable to the NHTS data because they are available at the jurisdiction level and for smaller geographic units as well (for example, census-defined blocks, block groups, tracts).

To adjust census data to account for vehicle access, a researcher would subtract from the census population data for each racial/ethnic group in the jurisdiction the estimated number of people within each of those groups who do not have access to vehicles.[9] To do this, the researcher would obtain the census information for the jurisdiction on vehicle-less households by race and ethnicity. It is advisable to conduct these

---

[9] Harris (1999) suggests that further adjustments could be made on the basis of "private vehicle trips per day." The NHTS reports this information by racial groups.

adjustments within small geographic subareas of the jurisdiction,[10] exclude stop data for nonresidents, and transform the information on number of *households* without vehicles into information on the number of *individuals* without vehicles. These processes are described below.

Conducting Analyses within Subareas of the Jurisdiction
Instead of conducting a single analysis comparing the race/ethnicity of all drivers stopped by police to the race/ethnicity of the residents of the entire jurisdiction, agencies should conduct analyses for each geographic subarea. Within each of these subareas, the researcher should compare the stop data and the census data. In Chapter 4 we explained how this strengthened the analysis, and how those subareas should be selected. Once logical subareas of the jurisdiction are defined, the researcher can link those areas to the corresponding census areas.[11] For instance, one subarea (Area B) could encompass three census tracts; when developing the demographic residential profile for Area B, the researcher would use the census data for those three tracts.

Following this important recommendation for law enforcement agencies—separate analyses for subareas—will produce many results for a jurisdiction instead of the one result that would be produced if the census data and stop data were compared for the jurisdiction as a whole.

Excluding Stop Data for Nonresidents
The agency should compare the racial/ethnic profile of jurisdiction residents to the profile of *residents* stopped by police. (We return later to the issue of whether these drivers should be residents of the jurisdiction or of the jurisdiction subarea under

---

[10] Note that vehicle ownership is available by race and ethnicity down to the census-tract level.

[11] The census areas should be census tracts rather than blocks or block groups because some census information required for the analysis is available only for tracts and not for those smaller geographic units.

analysis.) The recommendation that researchers compare against census data only data on residents stopped by police represents the rule of benchmarking called "matching the numerator and the denominator" (see Chapter 4). The "numerator" refers to the data collected on stops made by the police. The "denominator" is the benchmark information. To "match the numerator and the denominator," the researcher must match the numerator to any limiting parameters of the benchmark (or adjust the denominator to match any parameters of the numerator). In this case the benchmark is U.S. Census data, and it encompasses only jurisdiction residents. Therefore, the researcher must impose the same parameter on the numerator by including in the analyses only the police stops that were of residents.

To follow this recommendation, an agency must be able to identify from the police-citizen contact data who is and who is not a jurisdiction resident. It should then exclude the stop data for the nonresidents. It will be possible for an agency to exclude nonresidents if its data collection form includes (1) an item "jurisdiction resident or not," (2) an item requesting the stopped driver's address, (3) an item requesting the stopped driver's zip code, or (4) information, such as a driver's license number, that can be linked to another source that provides information on residency.

Now we return to this question: Should the numerator include any jurisdiction resident who was stopped in the subarea (labeled Area A in our discussion) or only the residents of the particular subarea being analyzed? An example may clarify this point. We have recommended that analyses be conducted within subareas of the jurisdiction. At its purest form, matching the numerator and the denominator within Area A would mean comparing the demographic profile of the residents of Area A (census data) to the demographic profile of the residents of Area A who were stopped by police in Area A. That is, the stop data included in this analysis would be for drivers who (1) lived in Area A and (2) were stopped in Area A.

This "purist" approach has the considerable drawback of excluding from the analysis all of the residents of the jurisdiction who were stopped outside of the subarea within which they reside. It also may reduce considerably the sample size, and this limits the reliability of the findings. Furthermore, a researcher may be unable to determine in which subarea of the city the driver lives. For these reasons, we recommend that researchers compare against the census data for the driving-age population in a subarea the stop data that meet the following criteria: (1) the stops occurred in the subarea and (2) the stops were of jurisdiction (not necessarily subarea) residents.

Transforming Household-Level Data into Individual-Level Data

The census data that researchers will use to estimate the race/ethnicity of the residents in the jurisdiction have *individuals* as the unit of analysis; a hypothetical jurisdiction might be comprised of 112,492 Caucasians, 14,942 African Americans, 5,492 Asians, and 1,492 individuals of other races. In contrast, the census data on vehicle access show *households* as the unit of analysis; in that same jurisdiction, there might be 2,250 Caucasian households without vehicles, 1,400 African American households without vehicles, and so forth. Households can be, and usually are, comprised of more than one individual.

Since we cannot subtract apples (households) from oranges (individuals) and because an agency's stop data (or "numerator") is comprised of individuals, the household-level information must be converted into individual-level information. This conversion is shown in Table 5.1 for hypothetical Area A.

According to the census, there are 15,142 residents in this subarea—9,492 of whom are Caucasian, 3,667 of whom are African American, 1,294 of whom are Asian, and 689 of whom are of another race, categorized in the table as "Other" (see Column A).[12]

---

[12] Very unfortunately, we cannot use residents who are of driving age in Column A. This is because Column D—average number of individuals per household—represents all residents regardless of age. As a result, Column A should include residents of all ages.

Table 5.1. Census Data Adjusted for Vehicle Ownership, Hypothetical Area A

	A	B	C	D	E	F	G
Race	Number of Residents	% of Total Residents	No. of Households without Vehicles	No. of Individuals Per Household (average)	No. of Individuals without Vehicles	No. of Individuals with Vehicles	% Individuals with Vehicles
					C × D	A − E	
Caucasians	9,492	62.69%	407	2.1	854.7	8,637	67.43%
African Americans	3,667	24.22%	459	2.8	1285.2	2,382	18.59%
Asians	1,294	8.55%	50	2.6	130.0	1,164	9.09%
Other	689	4.55%	27	2.3	62.1	627	4.89%
TOTAL	15,142	100.00%				12,810	100.00%

Note: Area A is one subarea of a hypothetical jurisdiction. Three adjoining census tracts were combined to produce this subarea. The unadjusted census data are presented in Column B; the adjusted census data (the benchmark) are presented in Column G.

Column B, the unadjusted census data, indicates what percentage of Area A residents are Caucasian (63 percent), African American (24 percent), Asian (9 percent), and Other Race (5 percent). Additional information from the census for the group of tracts that make up Area A is presented in Column C. This column shows that 407 of the Caucasian households, 459 of the African American households, 50 of the Asian households, and 27 of the Other Race households do not own vehicles.

To turn the *household* data regarding vehicle access into an estimate of the number of *individuals* without vehicles, an agency must have census information on the average number of individuals per household broken down by race (Column D). Hypothetical Area A has, on average, 2.1 people in the Caucasian households, 2.8 people in the African American households, 2.6 people in the Asian households, and 2.3 people in the Other Race households. To produce an estimate of the number of *individuals* without vehicles (Column E), we multiply for each racial group the number of households without vehicles (Column C) by the average number of individuals per household (Column D).[13] Then, by subtracting for each racial group the number of individuals without vehicles (Column E) from the total number of individuals in the area (Column A), we produce the number of individuals with vehicles (Column F). Column G provides the *adjusted* benchmark for Area A by turning the information in Column F into percentages. The result of these calculations is the percentage of individuals within each racial group in Area A who have access to vehicles.

A comparison of the *unadjusted* benchmark in Column B to the *adjusted* benchmark in Column G shows that the adjusted benchmark predicts a higher proportion of Caucasians on the road (67 percent) than does the unadjusted census data regarding residents

---

[13] Of course, all people who live in households with vehicles may not have access to those vehicles. An alternative adjustment procedure would be to multiply the total number of households in the area for each race by the average number of vehicles per household by race. This information also is available from the U.S. Census.

(63 percent). Slightly higher proportions of Asians and "Other Race" persons are predicted relative to the representation of these groups in the residential population. In contrast, the adjustment in this table reduces (from 24 percent to 19 percent) the predicted proportion of African Americans on the road in Area A. Figure 5.2 compares a hypothetical racial profile of people stopped by police in Area A to the benchmark data produced by the adjusted census information. There is little racial disparity indicated.

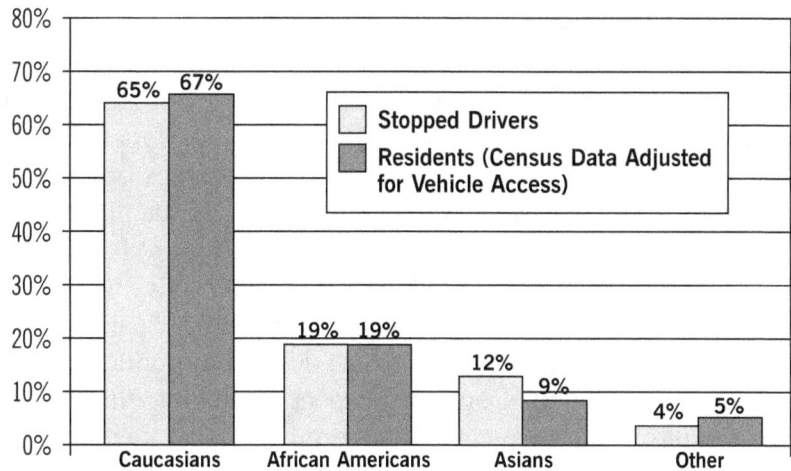

Figure 5.2. Drivers Stopped by Police in Hypothetical Area A and Area A Residents with Vehicles, by Race

The example above analyzed the data using race categories. For an agency with separate race and ethnicity variables, the results above represent half of their analyses for Hypothetical Area A. Separate additional analyses would be conducted that would examine the impact of ethnic origin, not race, on police decisions; that is the race categories would be replaced by two ethnicity categories: Hispanic and Non-Hispanic.

Calculating Measures of Disparity

We have compared in Figure 5.2 two sets of information conveyed in the form of percentages: (1) the percentage of traffic stops in the jurisdiction by race and (2) the percentage of individuals in the jurisdiction with access to vehicles by race. The researcher must turn these percentages into measures of racial/ethnic disparity. Directions on how to do this are provided in Chapter 12.

Drawing Conclusions from the Results

A report summarizing results based on census data cannot include conclusions referencing a *causal* relationship between the race/ethnicity of drivers and stopping behavior by police. It can, however, describe the disparities or lack thereof between the racial/ethnic profile of residents with access to vehicles and the racial/ethnic profile of jurisdiction-resident drivers who are stopped by police. But the cause of any disparities or even the reasons why no disparities were identified cannot be pinpointed.

A jurisdiction cannot claim, after accounting for vehicle access, that it has effectively addressed the alternative hypothesis that *racial/ethnic groups are not equally represented as drivers on jurisdiction roads*. The procedures just described produce an indirect measure, at best, of only one aspect of this hypothesis: the quantity of driving by racial/ethnic groups. The other aspect of this hypothesis—the influx of nonresidents into the jurisdiction—is not addressed.[14] Moreover, the calculations do not measure accurately the number of people without vehicles because not everyone in a vehicle-less household is without access to a vehicle, and not every person in a household with a vehicle has access to it.[15] Furthermore, even if we had produced a perfect count of individuals with vehicles, we could not assume that driving *amounts* were equal across racial/ethnic groups.

---

[14] This is a moot point, however. By excluding nonresidents from the census data, we have restricted the scope of our assessment of racially biased policing to stops of residents by police. The numerator must match the denominator.

[15] Another drawback of this method is that not all residents of a jurisdiction live in "households." These nonhousehold members include people who live in dormitories, military barracks, and other group quarters.

The performance of census benchmarking adjusted for vehicle ownership (or of any other method) must be evaluated in terms of the extent to which it accounts for the alternative hypotheses (see Chapter 2). Recall that the bias hypothesis (stopping behavior by police is caused by racial/ethnic bias) cannot be tested unless the researcher controls for all of the alternative hypotheses. Following is a summary of this benchmark's performance:

- *Racial/ethnic groups are not equally represented as residents in the jurisdiction.* This hypothesis has been addressed: census data were used to determine the actual residential representation of each racial/ethnic group.
- *Racial/ethnic groups are not equally represented as drivers on jurisdiction roads.* This hypothesis has been addressed, albeit indirectly and imperfectly.
- *Racial/ethnic groups are not equally represented as drivers on roads where stopping activity by police is high.* If analyses were conducted within subareas of the jurisdiction, the researcher has accounted for this hypothesis.
- In testing the relationship between race/ethnicity and police stops, the researcher has not accounted for the possible confounding effect of age because age information is not available for these analyses.
- *Racial/ethnic groups are not equivalent in the nature and extent of their traffic law–violating behavior.* The researcher has not in any way accounted for this possibility.

A law enforcement agency that has used this benchmarking method (adjusting census data on jurisdiction residents to account for vehicle access) should include in its report of jurisdiction results the strengths and weaknesses of the analysis as articulated above. If the report based on census benchmarking adjusted for vehicle ownership identifies disparities between the racial/ethnic profile of residents of the jurisdiction with access to vehicles and the racial/ethnic profile of jurisdiction-resident drivers stopped by police, the report should indicate that those disparities may be the result of (a) racially biased policing, (b) differences in driving quantity across residents with vehicle access, and/or (c) racial/ethnic differences in traffic law-violating behavior. The results could also represent the impact of the intervening variable, age (because we could not address this variable with this model), or could represent racial/ethnic differences in the people who live in areas where vehicle stopping activity by police is high (if analyses were not conducted within subareas.) If no disparities are found, the report should indicate that policing in the jurisdiction still could be racially biased. The constraints of measurement associated with using adjusted census data make it impossible to rule out this possibility. Indeed, as explained in Chapter 2, disparity could be masked.

This method of adjusted census benchmarking has another major drawback: it is a method for analyzing only the stops of jurisdiction residents. To match the numerator and the denominator, the researcher was instructed to include only stops of residents in the analysis. This leaves unanalyzed all of the police stops of nonresidents—stops that (1) could be considerable in number and (2) could be at particular risk of being racially biased.

ADJUSTING CENSUS DATA ON JURISDICTION RESIDENTS TO ACCOUNT FOR THE INFLUX OF NONRESIDENT DRIVERS

Let us return to the alternative hypothesis that *racial/ethnic groups are not equally represented as drivers on jurisdiction roads*. As explained in Chapter 2, the race/ethnicity of drivers on jurisdiction roads may not match the race/ethnicity of jurisdiction residents because of (1) racial/ethnic differences in driving quantity and/or (2) racial/ethnic differences in the population of people who do not live in the jurisdiction but drive in it. In adjusting for vehicle access, we have addressed indirectly the first possibility; here we focus on the second possibility. We attempt to account for these facts: (1) not all drivers on jurisdiction roads are residents of that jurisdiction, and (2) the influx of nonresidents can affect the demographic profile of drivers "available" to be stopped by police.[16]

Because of the influx of nonresidents into the jurisdiction, the demographic profile of residents produced by census data is likely to be an inaccurate estimate of drivers available to be stopped by police. For instance, if a municipal area with a substantial minority population drew a large population of Caucasians from the suburbs during the day for work, this could make the percentage of drivers on jurisdiction roads who are Caucasian higher than the percentage that would be predicted based on residential population data alone. As stated previously, nonresidents also might enter a jurisdiction to shop, go to school, seek entertainment, travel on to another jurisdiction, or for other reasons.

The influx of nonresident drivers into a jurisdiction can be accounted for in several ways. One way is by looking at the daytime population of the jurisdiction. A second method uses formulas based on those developed by Novak (forthcoming). A third approach uses formulas based on those developed by Rojek, Rosenfeld, and Decker (2002). All three methods, and the conclusions that can be drawn from them, will be explained below.

Use of Daytime Populations to Develop Racial/Ethnic Profiles of Residents and Nonresidents

Commuters traveling into or out of a jurisdiction for work can have a significant impact on the demographic profile of drivers on jurisdiction roads. These commuters have the greatest

---

[16] This second point reminds us of our objective: if we can develop a racial/ethnic profile of drivers who are at risk of being stopped by police and compare it to the racial/ethnic profile of drivers who are stopped by police, we can begin to test if racial/ethnic bias is at work.

impact on the daytime populations of jurisdictions, and information is available from the U.S. Census to estimate this impact.

Journey-to-Work Data
The journey-to-work data collected by the U.S. Census can be used to produce daytime populations broken down by race and ethnicity.[17] These data may be available from the planning department in a jurisdiction or the state data center. Jurisdictions that use one variable on their forms for measuring both race and ethnicity will need to transform the two-variable census data to produce a single race/ethnicity variable (see Appendix B). After this transformation (if it was needed), the researcher would "select in" for the analysis only those stops that occurred during daytime hours (for example, 7 A.M. to 7 P.M.). In this way the numerator (daytime stops) would match the denominator (the daytime population). Because nonjurisdiction residents are included in the denominator, they would be included in the numerator. In other words, stop data would include residents and nonresidents. Age information is available with the journey-to-work data, allowing the researcher to conduct separate analyses for age groups.

Like the adjustment for vehicle access, this adjustment produces demographic profiles of the stop population and the benchmark population. From these percentages the researcher must calculate measures of racial/ethnic disparity (see Chapter 12).

Drawing Conclusions from the Results
The limitations of these procedures are similar to those pertaining to adjustments for vehicle access. By adjusting census data

---

[17] These data are available in the Census Transportation Planning Package (CTPP), a "set of special tabulations from the Decennial Census designed for transportation planners. CTPP contains tabulations by place of residence, place of work, and for flows between home and work" (www.fhwa.dot.gov/ctpp/).

to account for the influx of nonresidents, a jurisdiction cannot claim to have addressed effectively the alternative hypothesis that *racial/ethnic groups are not equally represented as drivers on jurisdiction roads*. The procedures produce an indirect measure, at best, of only one component of that hypothesis: the influx into the jurisdiction of nonresidents. A major caveat is that only the influx of work-commuters is measured. The influx of drivers into the jurisdiction for other reasons (tourists, college students, etc.) is not assessed. Furthermore, we have not taken into account (1) not all commuters enter the jurisdiction in vehicles, and (2) the quantity of driving may not be the same for all racial/ethnic groups. Because a researcher can use this benchmark only for daytime vehicle stops, the potential for racially biased policing during the evening and nights is not analyzed. This is a significant omission.[18]

In sum, no definitive conclusions about racially biased policing in the jurisdiction can be drawn because not all of the alternative hypotheses have been addressed:

- *Racial/ethnic groups are not equally represented as residents in the jurisdiction*. We have taken this hypothesis into account.
- *Racial/ethnic groups are not equally represented as drivers on jurisdiction roads*. We have addressed this hypothesis, although indirectly and imperfectly.
- *Racial/ethnic groups are not equally represented as drivers on roads where stopping activity by police is high*. Because analyses cannot be conducted within subareas of the jurisdiction, we have not accounted for this hypothesis.
- If analyses are conducted within age groups, we have accounted for the potential intervening variable of age.
- We have not in any way accounted for the possibility that *racial/ethnic groups are not equivalent in the nature and extent of their traffic law-violating behavior*.

---

[18] An alternative method might be selected for benchmarking a jurisdiction's nighttime stops.

Use of Formulas to Develop Racial/Ethnic Profiles of Residents and Nonresidents

All of these limitations of the benchmarking method should be conveyed in the jurisdiction's report of results.

The use of daytime populations is one way to account, in part, for the influx of nonresident drivers into a jurisdiction. In this section we describe how to replicate the work of Novak (forthcoming) who developed a better way to measure this influx. First, he used information available through the stop data in the "target jurisdiction" to estimate the extent to which nonresidents from various "outside jurisdictions" were represented on target jurisdiction roads (Step 1 as shown in Table 5.2). Second, he used the census data for each of those outside jurisdictions to estimate the demographic profiles of the drivers coming from those outside jurisdictions into the target jurisdiction (Step 2 as shown in Table 5.3). Finally, he compared the racial/ethnic profile of drivers stopped by police in the target jurisdiction to the racial/ethnic profile of all drivers (residents and nonresidents) in the target jurisdiction (Step 3 as shown in Figure 5.3).

To complete these three steps, a researcher must have access to 2000 Decennial Census data (see Appendix A) and must be able to identify the jurisdiction of residence of drivers who are stopped by police from the police-citizen contact data form completed by police after a vehicle stop. Drawing on Novak's (forthcoming) model, a researcher would start by determining the proportion of stops (occurring during the reference period for the analysis) involving residents of the target jurisdiction and involving nonresidents broken down by the place where those nonresidents live. The target jurisdiction in our hypothetical example is a city—the "target city" (see Table 5.2).

Police in the target city made 95,738 stops during the reference period (Column A). Approximately 48 percent of those stops involved residents of the target city; another 22 percent involved drivers who live in the county (County X) in which the target city is located but not within the city limits of the target city; 11 percent

Table 5.2. Census Data Adjusted for Influx of Drivers: Stop Data by Residence of Drivers Stopped in Target City (Step 1)

	A	B	C
Resident Jurisdiction of Drivers Stopped by Police in Target City	Number of Stops in the Target City during the Reference Period	Percentage of Stops in the Target City	Percentage of Stops with "Miscellaneous Other" Removed
Target City (located within County X)	45,671	47.70%	50.59%
Outside City, Inside County X	20,754	21.68%	22.99%
Contiguous County A	10,429	10.89%	11.55%
Contiguous County B	8,299	8.67%	9.19%
Other Counties within MSA	5,120	5.35%	5.67%
Miscellaneous Other Counties/States	5,465	5.71%	NA
Total	95,738	100.00%	99.99%

Source: This method of analysis draws on the model introduced by Novak (forthcoming).

involved residents of contiguous County A; and 9 percent involved residents of contiguous County B (Column B). Five percent of the stops involved drivers who live in the Metropolitan Statistical Area (MSA) within which the target city is located but in counties other than X, A, or B.[19] Nearly 6 percent involved residents of counties within the state but outside the MSA or residents of other states; these residents should be excluded from the analysis because (1) this group represents a small proportion (only 6 percent in our hypothetical case) of the stops in the target city, (2) it would be too time consuming to develop demographic profiles of each place of residence of the 5,465 people in that group, and (3) the resulting profiles are likely to be unreliable anyway because of the small number of people from each of these jurisdictions. For these reasons, the percentages in Column B should be recalculated excluding these stops (see Table 5.2, Column C). The researcher now has completed the first step in Novak's model: the researcher has used data from stops by police in the target jurisdiction to estimate the extent to which nonresidents from various outside jurisdictions were represented on target jurisdiction roads.

In Step 2 the researcher uses census data to estimate the racial/ethnic profile of all drivers in the target jurisdiction (Table 5.3, Panel C). Begin with the racial/ethnic profiles of the jurisdiction of residence of the drivers stopped by police in the target city. As Table 5.2 showed, these stopped drivers could live in the target city; the part of County X outside the target city; County A; County B; and counties (other than X, A, or B) in the MSA. For each jurisdiction of residence, multiply the percentages based on census data (Table 5.3, Panel A) by the percentages based on stop data (Table 5.3, Panel B, derived from Table 5.2). This calculation

---

[19] Novak (forthcoming) used county-level census data to determine the race/ethnicity of residents of the three major counties in the relevant MSA (Counties X, A, and B). He then determined the demographics for the residents of the remaining several counties by subtracting the three-county demographic data from the demographic data for the MSA as a whole.

weights each area's demographic population characteristics by its observed proportion among stops. For example, the percentage of Caucasian drivers in the target city (36.42 percent) is produced by multiplying the percentage of target city stops of target city residents (0.5059) by the percentage of driving-age residents (age 15 and older) in the target city who are Caucasian (0.72). Similar calculations are performed for each racial/ethnic group for each geographic area included in the analysis.

The race/ethnicity categories in Panel C of Table 6.3 are then summed to provide an overall racial/ethnic profile of all drivers in the target city and thus a benchmark for the demographic profile of the drivers stopped by police.[20] The final step is to compare this profile of drivers to the deomgraphic profile of people stopped by police as shown (using hypothetical stop data) in Figure 5.3.

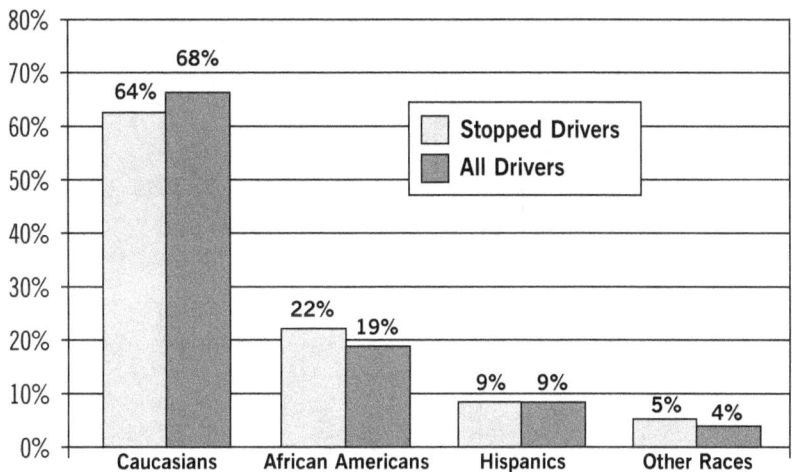

Figure 5.3. Drivers Stopped by Police in the Target City and All Drivers (Resident and Nonresident) in the Target City, by Race (Step 3)

---

[20] Note that an analogous process would be to benchmark subgroups of stops defined by driver-residence against the demographics for those areas per the census.

Table 5.3. Census Data Adjusted for Influx of Drivers: Racial/Ethnic Profile of All Drivers in the Target City (Step 2)

Resident Jurisdiction of Drivers Stopped by Police in Target City	(A) Demographics of Jurisdiction				(B) % of Stops in the Target City	(C) Demographics of Drivers in Target City			
	Caucasian	African American	Hispanic	Other		Caucasian	African American	Hispanic	Other
Target City (located within County X)	72.00%	16.00%	8.00%	4.00%	50.59%	36.42%	8.09%	4.05%	2.02%
Outside City, Inside County X	63.00%	24.00%	10.00%	3.00%	22.99%	14.48%	5.52%	2.30%	0.69%
Contiguous County A	44.00%	36.00%	12.00%	8.00%	11.55%	5.08%	4.16%	1.39%	0.92%
Contiguous County B	92.00%	3.00%	4.00%	1.00%	9.19%	8.45%	0.28%	0.37%	0.09%
Other Counties within MSA	65.00%	22.00%	9.00%	4.00%	5.67%	3.69%	1.25%	0.51%	0.23%
Total					99.99%	68.13%	19.29%	8.61%	3.96%

Source: This method of analysis draws on the model introduced by Novak (forthcoming).

The demographic profiles for each jurisdiction of residence could incorporate adjustments for vehicle access. That is, the researcher could subtract from the population of each jurisdiction broken down by race/ethnicity the estimated number of people of each racial/ethnic group who do not have access to vehicles. (See previous section in this chapter on adjusting for vehicle access.)

Additional Recommendations
In accord with recommendations explained earlier, a researcher implementing this benchmarking method should

- Select from the census data only data on people of driving age.
- Transform the two-variable census data into a single race/ethnicity variable if Hispanic origin is included in a single race/ethnicity variable on the police-citizen contact data form (see Appendix B).
- Conduct analyses within subareas of the jurisdiction. To develop the formulas within the subareas, the researcher would rely on the jurisdiction stop data to estimate, for instance, what percentage of drivers in Subarea A reside in the target jurisdiction, Jurisdiction A, Jurisdiction B, and so forth. The researcher would do the same for all subareas of the jurisdiction. (In other words, the information presented in Table 5.3 would be produced for each subarea.)
- Address the possible intervening impact of age on driving quality and thus on stopping behavior by police by determining the race/ethnicity of drivers in the target city (Table 5.3, Panel C) for two age groups: (1) legal driving age to 24 years of age and (2) age 25 and above;
- Match numerator and denominator. Because the benchmark data (the denominator) excludes all drivers who live outside of the Metropolitan Statistical Area (see Table 5.2), the numerator (the stop data) must exclude these drivers as well; and

- Calculate a measure of racial/ethnic disparity (see Chapter 12) after developing the demographic profile of the people stopped and the corresponding profile of the benchmark population.

Drawing Conclusions from the Results
The strength of this method is that it adjusts for the influx of nonresidents into the jurisdiction. Like the other methods, however, benchmarking with adjusted census data has limitations, and an agency's final report should include important caveats associated with this method.

By making the adjustments based on Novak (forthcoming), a jurisdiction cannot claim to have effectively addressed the alternative hypothesis that *racial/ethnic groups are not equally represented as drivers on jurisdiction roads*. The above procedures produce an indirect measure, at best, of the component of that hypothesis regarding the influx of nonresidents into the jurisdiction. Furthermore, these procedures are based on two dubious assumptions. First, the use of stop data to estimate the influx of drivers from various outside jurisdictions assumes that the people who are stopped by police are a representative subset (demographically) of the people from those various counties who drive on jurisdiction roads. We cannot know if this is true. Indeed, the possibility exists that racially biased policing—the phenomenon we are studying—affects who is stopped and thus the formulas. This is an important caveat related to this method.

Second, this method assumes that the demographic profile of the people traveling from the outside jurisdictions into the target jurisdiction matches the demographic profiles of all residents of the outside jurisdictions in which they live. This is a questionable assumption. For instance, the areas in the outside jurisdictions closest to the target jurisdiction could be predominantly one racial group or one ethnic group.

Once again definitive conclusions about racially biased policing in the target jurisdiction cannot be drawn because this method does not address all of the alternative hypotheses.

- We have accounted for the fact that *racial/ethnic groups are not equally represented as residents in the jurisdiction*.
- Albeit indirectly and imperfectly, we have addressed the fact that *racial/ethnic groups are not equally represented as drivers on jurisdiction roads*.
- If analyses were conducted within subareas of the jurisdiction, we have accounted for the fact that *racial/ethnic groups are not equally represented as drivers on roads where stopping activity by police is high*.
- If population estimates are broken down into two age groups, we have taken into account the potential intervening impact of age.[21]
- We have not in any way accounted for the possibility that *racial/ethnic groups are not equivalent in the nature and extent of their traffic law-violating behavior*.

Use of Formulas Accounting for Proximity of Outside Jurisdictions to Develop Racial/Ethnic Profiles of Residents and Nonresidents

The team of Rojek, Rosenfeld, and Decker (2002) at the University of Missouri, St. Louis, developed alternative methods for trying to estimate the extent to which residents of jurisdictions outside of the target jurisdiction (so-called "nonresidents") enter into the target jurisdiction. Their formulas take into consideration the proximity of outside jurisdictions to the target jurisdiction and the size of the minority populations of those jurisdictions.

Their team was selected to analyze the police-citizen contact data collected by all law enforcement agencies in the state of Missouri.[22] The estimation procedure developed by the team

---

[21] Again, if the analyst finds no disparity in the age composition of racial/ethnic groups, then analyses within age groupings are not necessary.

[22] State law required data submission, and 95 percent of the agencies submitted data for the first six months of 2000. The methods described here were used for the ninety-two municipal agencies with driving-age populations of 5,000 or greater (Rojek, Rosenfeld and Decker 2002).

was based on three assumptions about "the relationship between the residential and driving populations for any given municipality": (1) residents are more likely to drive in the target municipality than nonresidents, (2) nonresidents who live in nearby municipalities form a larger percentage of the driving population than do those who live farther away, and (3) nonresidents who reside in large municipalities form a larger proportion of the drivers than those from small municipalities (Rojek, Rosenfeld, and Decker 2002, 16). Based on these assumptions, the Missouri team's estimation procedures give more weight to residents than nonresidents of the target municipality, to the nonresidents who live in outside jurisdictions that are close to the target municipality, and to nonresidents who live in the larger municipalities.

Required Resources and Steps to Follow

To employ this method, a law enforcement agency must be able to identify the jurisdiction of residence of (1) people who have received citations and (2) people who are stopped in vehicles by police. It requires access to 2000 Decennial Census data and the ability to determine distances between the geographic center of the target jurisdiction and the geographic centers of surrounding jurisdictions using Geographic Information System (GIS) software or other methods.[23]

The first step was to measure the proximity of outside jurisdictions to the target jurisdiction. Rojek, Rosenfeld, and Decker used ArcView GIS 3.2 to determine the distances between the geographic centers of outside jurisdictions (within twenty miles of the target jurisdiction) and the geographic center of the target jurisdiction. They created inverse distance weights (1/D) so that more weight was given in their formulas to nearby municipali-

---

[23] A Geographic Information System (GIS) is a computer system that is used to assemble, store, manipulate, and/or display data on physical locations (geographic coordinates).

ties than to distant ones. This procedure addressed their assumption that nonresidents who live in nearby municipalities form a larger proportion of the driving population than those who live farther away.

The next step served both to estimate the racial/ethnic profile of nonresident drivers and take into consideration the team's assumption that nonresidents who reside in large municipalities form a larger fraction of the drivers than those from smaller municipalities. In other words, "large municipalities exert greater influence on the composite of the driving population than do smaller cities" (Decker 2002, 1). This was achieved by multiplying the inverse distance weights for each outside municipality by the numbers of Caucasian, African American, and Hispanic residents in those municipalities using census data.[24] To address their assumption that residents are more likely to drive in the municipality than nonresidents, Rojek, Rosenfeld, and Decker multiplied the numbers of Caucasian, African American, and Hispanic residents of the target municipality by two. The previously described steps resulted in weighted numbers of Caucasian, African American, and Hispanic residents for the target municipality and all other municipalities within twenty miles. They summed the populations within each racial/ethnic group and determined the percentages each group represented of the total, producing their benchmark for the target jurisdiction.

To validate its estimation procedure in three of the ninety-two target municipalities, the Missouri team used the observation method (see Chapter 9). Observers were sent to four locations within each target municipality. These target municipalities were identified by police as having "heavy traffic volume and enforcement activity." Observations were conducted across several days across different times of day. The team compared the racial/ethnic profiles based on the observation method to profiles based on

---

[24] Other racial groups comprised very small percentages of the state population.

the unadjusted census data and on the formula-based profiles (adjusted census data). For two of the three target municipalities that were used for the validation, the researchers found that the observational data were much closer to the census data adjusted using the formulas they developed than to the unadjusted census data (Rojek, Rosenfeld, and Decker 2002, 18).

For the targeted city, Clayton, the lack of fit between the demographic profile produced by the adjusted census data (based on the formula) and the profile produced by the observation data may have been attributable to the heavy influx of residents from nearby St. Louis into Clayton using the "ample public transportation linking the suburb to the city" (Rojek, Rosenfeld, and Decker 2002, 22). A great influx of residents into Clayton from outside areas, especially St. Louis, might have occurred, but these people may have entered using a form of transportation *other than* personal vehicles (for example, bus) and so they would not have been at risk of a vehicle stop by police. Indeed, researchers who use this method should acknowledge in their reports the possible variation in the use of public transportation by racial/ethnic groups.

Additional Recommendations
Researchers using this benchmarking method also should

- Consider additional adjustments for vehicle access;
- Select from the census data only data on people of driving age;
- Transform the census data from two variables into one variable if Hispanic origin is included on the law enforcement agency's data collection form as a single race/ethnicity variable (see Appendix B);
- Conduct analyses within subareas;[25]

---

[25] To develop the formulas within geographic areas, rely on the original stop data to determine, for instance, what percentage of drivers in Subarea A are from the target jurisdiction, Jurisdiction A, Jurisdiction B, and so forth. Develop these formulas for each subarea of your jurisdiction.

- Address the possible intervening impact of age by breaking down the demographic profile of residents and nonresidents into two age groups: age 15 to 24 and age 25 and above;
- Match numerator and denominator. Delete from the stop data (the numerator) the stops of people who are neither residents of the target jurisdiction nor residents of the outside jurisdictions that are encompassed in the analysis; and
- Calculate a measure of racial/ethnic disparity (see Chapter 12) after developing the profile of the people stopped and the profile of the benchmark population.

Drawing Conclusions from the Results

Again we assess the strengths and weaknesses of this method in terms of the alternative hypotheses:

- Like other methods to estimate resident/nonresident driving populations, this one addresses the hypothesis that *racial/ethnic groups are not equally represented as residents in the jurisdiction.*
- By estimating the demographic profiles of nonresidents who might enter the target jurisdiction, this method addresses, in part, the possibility that *racial/ethnic groups are not equally represented as drivers on jurisdiction roads.*
- If analyses are conducted within subareas of the jurisdiction, this method addresses the hypothesis that *racial/ethnic groups are not equally represented as drivers on jurisdiction roads where stopping activity by police is high.*
- If analyses are conducted within age groups, this method takes into account the potential impact of age on driving behavior.

- This method does not address the possibility that unequal representation of racial/ethnic groups on jurisdiction roads may be attributable, in part, to differences across racial/ethnic groups in the quantity of their driving.
- This method does not address the alternative hypothesis that *racial/ethnic groups are not equivalent in the nature and extent of their traffic law-violating behavior.*

MAKING OTHER ADJUSTMENTS TO CENSUS DATA: THE RHODE ISLAND STUDY

Researchers are looking for additional ways to adjust census data to produce more valid benchmarks. For example, Amy Farrell, Jack McDevitt, Shea Cronin, and Erica Pierce of Northeastern University have recently implemented a creative adjustment model.[26] In July 2000 the Rhode Island Traffic Stop Statistics Act was passed. The Northeastern team was contracted to analyze the data collected, in response to this legislation, by the Rhode Island State Police and all municipal police departments in the state. For the municipal police departments, Farrell's team—like Novak and the Missouri team whose work is described above—adjusted census data on jurisdiction residents to account for the influx of nonresident drivers.[27] As the authors explain (Farrell et al. 2003, 29), "we created a driving population estimate based on the idea that the demographics of a target city may be better understood by weighting the population of the target city by its surrounding cities whose drivers may drive in or through the city in question." Specifically, they developed a "driving population estimate" or DPE for each municipal department based on formulas that took into account

---

[26] See Farrell et al. (2003). The final report is available under "Reports and Publications" at www.riag.state.ri.us.

[27] The team used the observation method—described in Chapter 9—to analyze the data collected by the state police.

(1) the extent to which drivers in jurisdictions around the target city might be "pushed" from their own jurisdiction and (2) the extent to which the target city might "draw" drivers from other jurisdictions. According to Farrell et al. (2003, 30), "the DPE seeks to measure the factors that both *push* drivers out of surrounding communities and *draw* drivers into target cities from surrounding communities" (italics in original).

"Push values" were created for every municipality within thirty miles of the target jurisdiction. We refer to these as "contributing jurisdictions," and some of them were located in the neighboring states of Massachusetts and Connecticut. The "push" value of each contributing jurisdiction was based on a formula that considered: (1) the proportion of residents of a jurisdiction who own cars (based on census data), (2) the proportion of residents of a jurisdiction who drive more than ten miles to work (based on the journey-to-work data of the 2000 Census), and (3) driving time between the contributing jurisdiction and target jurisdiction measured in minutes.[28] The formula produced the number of people in each contributing jurisdiction that might be pushed into the target jurisdiction in their vehicles. The Census data for the contributing jurisdiction were then used to estimate the racial/ethnic breakdown of these drivers. Again, the formula and racial/ethnic estimates were calculated for each municipality within thirty miles of the target jurisdiction. Then the research team summed the results across all of the contributing jurisdictions of a target jurisdiction to produce estimated numbers of people within each racial/ethnic group that might be pushed into the target jurisdiction. That is, the researchers produced for each target jurisdiction a racial/ethnic profile of drivers from contributing jurisdictions by race/ethnicity that might be "pushed" onto the roads inside of the target jurisdiction.

---

[28] The team used a software program called Network Analysis to produce these drive times.

The next step was to estimate the "draw" of the target jurisdiction. (Presumably, people who are "pushed" from their own jurisdictions will be more inclined toward some neighboring jurisdictions than others.) The team identified and measured factors that would draw nonresidents into a particular target jurisdiction. It noted, for example, that people might be drawn to a neighboring target jurisdiction to go to work, eat dinner, shop, or engage in recreational activities. As the authors explain, "To determine the degree to which each city in Rhode Island 'draws' in drivers from surrounding communities, we created a measure of the relative economic and social attraction of each city" (Farrell et al. 2003, 32). Each jurisdiction was given a rank between 1 (for "high draw") and 4 (for "low draw") based on its average of the following four indicators: (1) percent of state employment, (2) percent of state retail trade, (3) percent of state food and accommodation sales, and (4) percent of state average daily road volume (p. 32). This rank was used to estimate the proportion of drivers on target city roads who were residents and the proportion of drivers who were nonresidents from the contributing jurisdictions. For instance, in "high draw" target jurisdictions, the researchers estimated that drivers were composed of 60 percent target jurisdiction residents and 40 percent contributing jurisdiction residents. In contrast, the researchers estimated that in "low draw" target jurisdictions, the drivers were composed of 90 percent target jurisdiction residents and 10 percent contributing jurisdiction residents.

The last step was to produce the race/ethnicity breakdown of the DPE for the target jurisdiction.[29] The researchers had to determine not only the DPE for each jurisdiction, but the racial/ethnic profile of that DPE. As the authors explain, "Once we deter-

---

[29] The team did not adjust the draw population for vehicle ownership; vehicle ownership data were not available by race for all cities in Rhode Island.

mined the degree of draw for each target city, we adjusted the population totals from the residential and the contributing city distributions to represent the appropriate ratio of residential to contributing city drivers in each racial category. These totals were combined resulting in the final racial demographics of the driving population estimate" (Farrell et al. 2003, 33).

We expect and hope that the Northeastern University team and other researchers working in this area will continue to develop creative ways to adjust census data to produce benchmarks. This development is particularly important for purposes of producing models suitable for the analysis of data from multiple jurisdictions (for instance, all jurisdictions within a state).

CONCLUSION

Many jurisdictions have used census benchmarking to analyze their police-citizen contact data in order to assess whether policing is racially biased. Some have merely compared jurisdiction-wide racial/ethnic profiles of residents to the racial/ethnic profiles of people stopped by police (unadjusted census benchmarking); this simplest form of census benchmarking is inexpensive and rather uncomplicated. Unfortunately, however, it is a very weak method for assessing the impact of race and ethnicity on stopping behavior by police.

This chapter has described the various ways that census benchmarking can be improved. For instance, we advocate using census data for the driving-age population instead of for all age groups, and we recommend that analyses be conducted within geographic subareas of the jurisdiction to account for the possibility that police tend to stop drivers more in some areas than in others. We direct jurisdictions to test for similarities across racial/ethnic groups in terms of their age demographics to account for the potential intervening variable of age in explaining stopping behavior by police. If age differences are detected, then analyses should be conducted within age groups.

Additionally, we have described how to adjust census data to increase the number of alternative hypotheses for which the researcher can account. Adjusted census benchmarking can incorporate two kinds of information related to driving quantity: information on vehicle access and information on the influx of nonresidents into the jurisdiction. This method addresses, in part, the alternative hypothesis that *racial/ethnic groups are not equally represented as drivers on jurisdiction roads.* While adjusted census benchmarking is superior to unadjusted census benchmarking, it does not account at all for driving quality—an important factor related to police decision making. That is, the hypothesis that *racial/ethnic groups are not equivalent in the nature and extent of their traffic law-violating behavior* is not addressed. Researchers benchmarking with adjusted census data cannot draw definitive conclusions regarding the causal link between the race/ethnicity of drivers and stopping behavior by police. In other words, the researchers (and law enforcement agencies or other stakeholders referencing their reports) cannot draw conclusions regarding the existence or lack of racially biased policing in a jurisdiction. Law enforcement agencies' reports can reference disparities or lack of disparities shown by the data, and they can reference possible explanations for the results—using the alternative hypotheses as a guide.[30]

Despite the weaknesses of adjusted census benchmarking as a diagnostic tool, some researchers (limited by resources or time) may have no option other than to use this method; this is particularly true for researchers who are charged with analyzing data

---

[30] Benchmarking with census data has some additional drawbacks. The Census Bureau has estimated that non-Hispanic African Americans were 1.84 percent undercounted in the 2000 Decennial Census. The undercounts of other minority groups, however, were not found to be statistically different from zero. As time passes, the population counts produced by the decennial census become less accurate. Although the Census Bureau prepares intercensal estimates of the population for counties and cities, these estimates are subject to considerable error (Deichert 2003).

from all or many jurisdictions within a single state.[31] The obligation of the researcher in this position is to ensure that the results are conveyed in a responsible fashion.[32] In fact, this obligation also falls to all stakeholders, including concerned residents, civil rights groups, and the media. No one interpreting results based on benchmarking with adjusted census data can legitimately draw conclusions regarding the existence or lack of racially biased policing.

That the causal connection cannot be drawn does not mean that data collection was for naught. By collecting police-citizen contact data, a law enforcement agency conveys an important message to residents: it shows that the agency is concerned about racially biased policing, is open to scrutiny, and is accountable to its constituency. Even if the results do not provide definitive conclusions regarding racial bias, they can serve as a basis for constructive police-citizen discussions regarding ways to reduce racial bias and/or perceptions of racial bias.

---

[31] Researchers analyzing statewide data (data submitted by all of the law enforcement agencies in a state or most of them) are usually limited by resource constraints to census benchmarking or comparable methods. Connecticut, Maryland, Massachusetts, Missouri, Oregon, Rhode Island, and Texas are among the states now collecting statewide data. These states are analyzing their statewide data using census benchmarking (unadjusted or adjusted), or they are comparing stop data against Department of Motor Vehicle data (see Chapter 6). Oregon, in addition to collecting statewide data to assess policing practices, is collecting information through a statewide survey, on Oregonians' perceptions of racially biased policing.

[32] The 2001 San Diego report written by Cordner, Williams, and Velasco (2002) provides a good example of responsible conclusions in a report based on census benchmarking. These researchers initiate their conclusion with the following: "Unfortunately, it cannot be determined with any confidence whether the San Diego data for 2001 indicate any systematic patterns of bias in vehicle stops or searches. As discussed above, there is evidence of disproportionate impact on Black/African American and Hispanic drivers. But there are also credible explanations for the findings that do not hinge on bias and that may even account for what initially appears to be disparate impact."

We discuss in Chapter 13 how to use vehicle stop data to achieve reform. If an agency chooses to collect data, this effort should be only one component of its comprehensive response to the issues of biased policing and the perceptions of its practice. Reforms in the realms of supervision, policy, training, community outreach to minorities, and recruitment also should be considered.[33] Additionally, police-citizen contact data need not be the only information an agency collects to assess whether policing in its jurisdiction is racially biased or perceived to be so. An agency can hold police-citizen forums to learn about citizens' concerns and perceptions,[34] scrutinize complaints by the public, or organize meetings with supervisors to assess/discuss potential problems. Multiple responses to the issues of racial/ethnic bias are possible, and multiple sources of information are available to guide agency reforms. In the context of a comprehensive agency response based on multiple sources of information, the inability to draw definitive conclusions from this benchmarking method about the nature and extent of racially biased policing becomes less important.

---

[33] See Fridell et al. (2001). This report is available at www.policeforum.org.

[34] A video and user's guide—funded by the U.S. Department of Justice, Office of Community Oriented Policing Services—can facilitate a discussion by police and citizens of racially biased policing. The video and guide can be ordered through the PERF web site, www.policeforum.org.

VI. Benchmarking with DMV Data

Some researchers have compared the racial/ethnic profile of licensed drivers who reside in a jurisdiction to the profile of the drivers stopped by police. Like adjusting census data for vehicle ownership, this method produces an indirect measure of driving quantity.[1] It accounts, in part, for the alternative hypothesis that racial/ethnic groups are not equally represented as drivers on jurisdiction roads. This method is preferable to adjusting census data for vehicle ownership, if the necessary information is available to the jurisdiction.

ASSESSING RESOURCES REQUIRED

To use this benchmarking method, a law enforcement agency must be able to obtain from the Department of Motor Vehicles (DMV) information on the race and/or ethnicity of the licensed drivers in the target jurisdiction (the jurisdiction being analyzed based on police-citizen contact forms). In some states the DMV does not have this information. In fact, the nationwide trend has been to eliminate race/ethnicity information from DMV

---

[1] Later in the chapter, we explain why this is an imperfect measure of driving quantity.

records. Even if your state's DMV collects this information, it may be incomplete. In some states it is optional for the licensed driver to specify his or her race or ethnic background.[2] Therefore, before choosing this benchmarking method, the analyst should ensure that the race/ethnicity information has been collected by the DMV, is available for at least 95 percent of the licensed drivers, and is compatible with the agency's measures of race/ethnicity, as we explain later.

The driver's license information on race and/or ethnicity from the DMV would be even more useful if it could be linked to the street address of the residence of each driver. This would allow for analyses within geographic subareas of the jurisdiction as recommended in earlier chapters.

MEASURING RACE AND ETHNICITY

The information from the DMV regarding race and/or ethnicity must be compatible with the measurement of race and/or ethnicity on the law enforcement agency's data collection form. (Of course, if the agency has not yet developed its form and has decided to use driver's license information as the benchmark, it should devise the form to match the DMV information available in the state.) An agency's form might have (1) separate race and ethnicity variables, (2) a single variable that combines race and ethnicity, or (3) only a race variable. Similarly, the driver's license information from the DMV could come in these same forms: (1) separate race and ethnicity variables, (2) a single variable combining race and ethnicity, or (3) only a race variable. If the DMV measurement of race/ethnicity matches the measurement on the agency's form, the analyst can proceed, and no transformations are required. If the DMV measurement and the

---

[2] Under such an optional system, it is likely that the missing data are not random across racial/ethnic groups. Those who choose not to identify their race or ethnic background on the DMV questionnaire may be more likely to be minorities than Caucasians.

measurement on the form do not match, refer to Appendix C for an explanation of how to make them comparable.[3]

CONDUCTING ANALYSES USING RESIDENTS ONLY

This benchmarking method compares the racial/ethnic profile of drivers stopped by police in the jurisdiction (the numerator) to the racial/ethnic profile of licensed drivers who reside in the jurisdiction (the denominator). It is preferable to account for the influx of nonresidents on jurisdiction roads, as we will explain in the next section of this chapter. If a jurisdiction does not account for the influx of out-of-jurisdiction residents, the analyst would exclude from the population of stopped drivers all of the people stopped who are not jurisdiction residents. This exclusion reflects our previously described rule of matching the numerator and the denominator (see Chapter 4).

If the data permit, the analyst should conduct comparisons within subareas of the jurisdiction. To do this, the analyst would need from the DMV the residential street addresses of the licensed drivers of the jurisdiction and the ability to link police stops geographically to the selected subareas. (See Chapter 4 for an explanation of how to select subareas.) Then, for each subarea, the analyst would compare the racial/ethnic makeup of jurisdiction residents who were stopped in the subarea (the numerator data from the police-citizen contact forms) and the racial/ethnic makeup of drivers who reside in the subarea (the denominator data from the DMV information). Only jurisdiction residents would be included in the various subarea numerators because the DMV information pertains only to jurisdiction residents. This reflects our rule that the numerator and denominator must match. To address the potential intervening impact

---

[3] Appendix B describes a similar matching process. The two-variable census data must be transformed to a one-variable format if the agency has a single-variable measure of race/ethnicity on its data collection form. Whether census data or DMV data, the principle is the same: measures of race/ethnicity must be equivalent (or transformed to be equivalent) across the stop data and the benchmark data.

of age, the analyst should determine if there is equivalence in the racial/ethnic makeup of licensed drivers in the two age groups: ages 15 to 24 and ages 25 and above (see Chapter 5). If they are not equivalent, analyses should be conducted separately within the two age groups.

Again, within each subarea, and within each age group (if necessary), the analyst would compare the racial/ethnic makeup of jurisdiction residents who were stopped in the subarea to the racial/ethnic makeup of drivers who reside in the subarea. Finally, based on these comparisons, the analyst would develop a measure of disparity (see Chapter 12).

CONDUCTING ANALYSES THAT CONSIDER THE INFLUX OF NONRESIDENTS

One reason why the race/ethnicity of drivers on jurisdiction roads may not match the race/ethnicity of jurisdiction residents is the influx of drivers who live outside the target jurisdiction. Chapter 5 described methods that utilized stop or citation information and census data to estimate the demographic profiles of both residents and nonresidents on jurisdiction roads. These techniques can be applied to this benchmarking method by substituting the driver's license demographic data for the census demographic data.

As an example, law enforcement agencies could follow the model of Rojek, Rosenfeld, and Decker (2002) that takes into consideration the proximity of outside jurisdictions (see Chapter 5), but they could substitute DMV data for census data. Alternatively, driver's license data could be substituted for census data, and the Novak (forthcoming) methods, also explained in Chapter 5, could then be implemented.

The work of Matt Zingraff, William R. Smith, Donald Tomaskovic-Devey, and others (originally reported in Zingraff et al. 2000; see also Smith et al. 2003) served as the original model for Novak (forthcoming). This team of researchers analyzed traffic stop data for the North Carolina Highway Patrol. The team faced the challenge of attempting to measure racial profiling in fifty state-trooper districts in North Carolina.[4] Zingraff and his colleagues used multiple methods in their comprehensive study. We describe here their use of driver's license data; each step is illustrated with hypothetical data: Step 1 (Table 6.1), Step 2 (Table 6.2), and Step 3 (Figure 6.1). In short, using citations issued by police in the target jurisdiction, they estimated the representation on target jurisdiction roads of both residents and nonresidents. From demographic data for people with a driver's license who lived in the various districts included in their analyses, they developed a racial/ethnic profile of the population of "drivers driving" on jurisdiction roads. We explain the methods in more detail below.

As a first step, the North Carolina team identified the resident jurisdiction of the drivers who received citations in the target jurisdiction (District 1). This step is shown with hypothetical data in Table 6.1, Column A. The team then calculated the percentage of these citations that was given to District 1 residents and to residents of the various outside jurisdictions (Column B). The citations given to residents who live outside the target jurisdiction provide a measure of the influx of residents from those districts into District 1. Finally, the team calculated the percentage of citations given to residents of each district with the "out of state" drivers removed (Column C).[5]

We turn now to Step 2. To estimate the racial/ethnic profile of the residents driving in District 1 using the methods of Zingraff et al. (2000), we use demographic data for people with a driver's license within each district. Table 6.2, Panel A, estimates the demographics of drivers for each area using DMV information obtained for all licensed drivers. Panel B reproduces the percent-

---

[4] While there are, in fact, fifty-three trooper districts in North Carolina, the researchers collapsed several of them "because of redistricting that occurred in 1998" (Zingraff et al. 2000, 11).

[5] These drivers are removed from the analysis for several reasons introduced in Chapter 5: they represent a small percentage of the stops, it would be too time consuming to develop a racial/ethnic profile of each place of residence, and the resulting profiles would likely be unreliable anyway because of the small number of people from each of the jurisdictions.

Table 6.1. Citations in the Target Jurisdiction, by Residence of Drivers, Hypothetical Data (Step 1)

Resident Jurisdiction of Drivers Receiving Citations in District 1	A Number of Citations	B Percentage of Citations in the Target Jurisdiction	C Percentage of Citations with "Out of State" Removed
District 1 (Target Jurisdiction)	45,889	52.43%	55.27%
District 2	18,422	21.05%	22.19%
District 3	7,344	8.39%	8.85%
District 4	6,245	7.14%	7.52%
District 5	5,120	5.85%	6.17%
Out of state	4,500	5.14%	NA
Total	87,520	100.00%	99.99%

ages from Table 6.1. These percentages are multiplied by the percentages for each racial/ethnic group for each district to produce the estimates in Panel C of Table 6.2. [For instance, to estimate the Caucasian "drivers driving" in District 1 who live in District 1, multiply 84 percent by 0.5527 (46.43 percent).] The bottom row of Table 6.2 indicates that the demographic profile of drivers driving in District 1 is 74 percent Caucasian, 14 percent African American, 9 percent Hispanic, and 3 percent of another race. The North Carolina team developed a 50 x 50 matrix to complete the above calculations for all fifty state-trooper districts in the state of North Carolina. That is, they performed calculations (similar to those in Tables 6.1 and 6.2 that show hypothetical data) for each of the fifty districts included in their research.

We have described the first two steps of the core model used by the North Carolina team. The team also considered the possible differential representation within racial groups of males and young people on target jurisdiction roads. Specifically, Zingraff et al. (2000) focused on the two largest race groups in North Carolina (Caucasians and African Americans), and they conducted all their analyses within groups defined by age and

Table 6.2. Racial/Ethnic Profiles of Resident and Nonresident Drivers in the Target Jurisdiction, Hypothetical Data (Step 2)

Resident Jurisdiction of Drivers Receiving Citations in District 1	(A) Racial/Ethnic Profile of People with a License					(B) Percent of Citations	(C) Racial/Ethnic Profile of Drivers in District 1			
	Caucasian	African American	Hispanic	Other			Caucasian	African American	Hispanic	Other
District 1 (Target Jurisdiction)	84.00%	8.00%	7.00%	1.00%		55.27%	46.43%	4.42%	3.87%	0.55%
District 2	60.00%	21.00%	14.00%	5.00%		22.19%	13.31%	4.66%	3.11%	1.11%
District 3	42.00%	33.00%	17.00%	8.00%		8.85%	3.72%	2.92%	1.50%	0.71%
District 4	92.00%	3.00%	4.00%	1.00%		7.52%	6.92%	0.23%	0.30%	0.08%
District 5	66.00%	21.00%	10.00%	3.00%		6.17%	4.07%	1.30%	0.62%	0.19%
Total						100.00%	74.45%	13.52%	9.40%	2.63%

gender. They compared the racial profile of drivers stopped by police to the racial profile of "drivers driving" on target jurisdiction roads for the following six groups of drivers:
- males, 16-22 years old,
- males, 23-49 years old,
- males, 50 and above,
- females, 16-22 years old,
- females, 23-49 years old, and
- females, 50 and above.

For instance, to evaluate the stops of males between the ages of 16 and 22 within a particular target jurisdiction, they compared the racial profile of males in that age group stopped by police within that district to the racial profile of male "drivers driving" in that district who are 16 to 22 years of age. Figure 6.1 (using hypothetical data) compares the racial profile of people stopped by police in the target jurisdiction (the numerator) to the racial profile of male "drivers driving" on target jurisdiction roads (the denominator). In both populations the drivers are between 16 and 22 years of age.

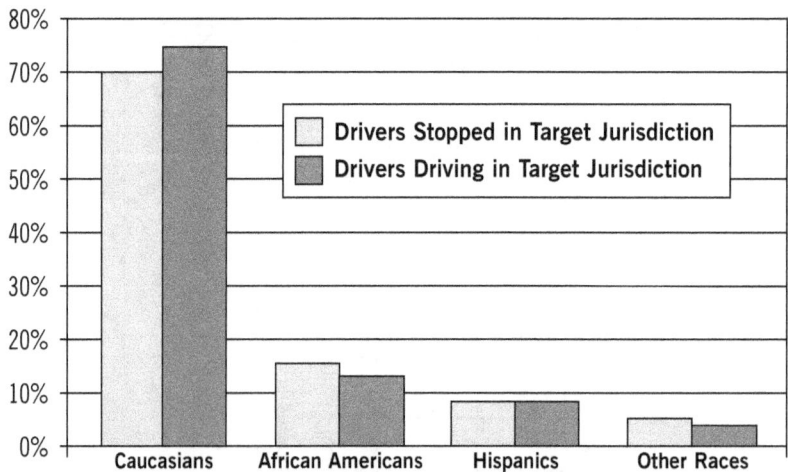

Figure 6.1. Male Drivers (Ages 16-22) Stopped by Police in the Target Jurisdiction and Driving in the Target Jurisdiction, by Race, Hypothetical Data (Step 3)

OTHER CONSIDERATIONS

In developing our estimates of "drivers driving" in the target jurisdiction, we removed those people who lived out of state (see Column C of Table 6.1). Therefore, before making our comparisons, we must remove people who live out of state from the stop data. After the demographic profiles are produced, disparity indexes can be calculated based on the instructions in Chapter 12.

DRAWING CONCLUSIONS FROM THE RESULTS

In its report summarizing the results of benchmarking with DMV data, a law enforcement agency *cannot* link stopping behavior by police in the target jurisdiction to racial bias. In other words, it cannot test the bias hypothesis because it has not addressed all of the alternative hypotheses presented in Chapter 2. Following is a summary of the performance of this benchmarking method:

- It addresses the alternative hypothesis that racial/ethnic groups are not equally represented as residents in the jurisdiction.
- By developing a benchmark comprised of only those people with a driver's license (a proxy measure of driving quantity), this method also addresses (albeit incompletely) the alternative hypothesis that racial/ethnic groups are not equally represented as drivers on jurisdiction roads. If this method is implemented in a way that accounts for the influx of drivers into the jurisdiction from outside of it—as did the North Carolina team of Zingraff et al. (2000)—the analyst has addressed the fact that not all drivers on jurisdiction roads are residents.
- If age breakdowns across racial/ethnic groups are similar, or if analyses are conducted within age groups, this method addresses the potentially confounding effect of age.
- If subareas of the jurisdiction are analyzed, this method addresses the alternative hypothesis that racial/ethnic groups may not be equally represented in areas where stopping activity by police is high.

- This method does not take into account in any way the alternative hypothesis that racial/ethnic groups may not be equivalent in the nature and extent of their traffic law–violating behavior.

CONCLUSION

Benchmarking with DMV data, like benchmarking with adjusted census data that takes into account vehicle ownership, imperfectly assesses who is driving on jurisdiction roads. The caveats associated with this method reflect three truths: not everyone with a driver's license drives, some people drive even though they do not have a driver's license, and some jurisdiction residents (particularly students and military personnel) have a driver's license from another state. Most importantly, having a driver's license is a very crude measure of driving quantity—residents of various racial/ethnic groups who have a driver's license may drive in different amounts.

Using DMV data to benchmark police-citizen contact data is superior to using census data that have been adjusted for vehicle ownership. Both benchmarking methods produce a proxy measure for driving quantity by trying to determine who is and who is not driving on jurisdiction roads. The benchmarking method that uses adjusted census data considers a person a driver if the person lives in a household with a vehicle. The method described in this chapter considers a person a driver if the person has a driver's license. Although both are imperfect, we argue that the latter is the better proxy measure of who is driving on jurisdiction roads. As noted earlier, this method will not produce conclusions regarding the existence or lack of racially biased policing in a target jurisdiction. Nonetheless, the results can be valuable as the basis for discussions between police and citizens about racially biased policing and the perceptions of its practice. We discuss how the results can be used to stimulate these discussions in Chapter 13.

Benchmarking with Data from "Blind" Enforcement Mechanisms

This chapter describes how law enforcement agencies can use "blind" enforcement mechanisms (red light cameras, radar, air patrols) to produce a benchmark against which they can compare their data on stops by patrol officers. In this method the racial/ethnic profile of technology-selected drivers is compared to the racial/ethnic profile of human-selected drivers (that is, traffic law-violating drivers stopped by police). Some agencies compare stops in which officers exercise a high degree of discretion to low-discretion stops. This benchmarking method also is explained in this chapter.

BENCHMARKING WITH DATA FROM RED LIGHT CAMERAS

Enforcement using red light cameras is blind because traffic law violators are detected and "ticketed" in a manner that does not allow for the intrusion of bias.[1] These cameras are placed at selected intersections that have a traffic light. A driver who runs the red light trips the camera, which takes a picture of the violator's license plate.

---

[1] Although individual "decisions" by the camera to "ticket" will not be biased, decisions about the geographic placement of the cameras could reflect racial or ethnic prejudice.

In this benchmarking method the analyst compares the racial/ethnic profile of the drivers "ticketed" by the camera technology to the racial/ethnic profile of the drivers stopped by police.[2] If officers are as "blind" to race/ethnicity as are the cameras, the demographic profile of the people stopped for red light violations by the officers should match the demographic profile of the people "ticketed" by the cameras in the same area. If, however, officers are targeting minorities for stops, minorities may compose a larger percentage of stops by the humans than by the technology.

Resources Required

To benchmark against red-light-camera data, a law enforcement agency must, of course, have red-light-camera technology in place. It also must be able to access Department of Motor Vehicle (DMV) data that can link the license plate photographed by the camera to the race and/or ethnicity of the owner of the vehicle.[3] An analyst should check to see that the DMV in the state maintains information on the race and/or ethnicity of registered vehicle owners. The DMV in many states does not collect this information, or it gives drivers a choice of whether or not to supply it on their license application. In addition, an agency using this benchmarking method either must have a measure of race/ethnicity on its form that matches the race/ethnicity measures of the DMV or be able to conduct a transformation to produce equivalent measures (see Chapter 6).

---

[2] The Montgomery County, Maryland, Police Department (2002) benchmarked drivers stopped by officers against (1) drivers ticketed as a result of red light cameras and (2) drivers stopped by radar.

[3] As discussed below, a drawback to this method is that the information collected regarding race/ethnicity pertains to the person to whom the vehicle is registered, which is not necessarily the driver.

General Methodology

This section explains the methodological underpinnings of "blind" and "not-blind" comparisons generally and then applies them to red-light-camera enforcement. Recall that the goal of benchmarking is to create a comparison group of people at risk of being stopped by police, assuming no bias. That is, our ideal is to develop a benchmark group that "matches" the group of drivers that officers are exposed to in their work. The alternative hypotheses outlined in Chapter 2 reflect the key factors (driving quantity, driving quality, driving location) that should match in each group.

The benchmarking methods described in Chapters 5 and 6 do not produce comparison groups that are matched across these factors. Benchmarking with unadjusted census data does not produce a close match across the key variables between the benchmark and the people at risk of being stopped by police. Therefore, the alternative hypotheses reflected by those factors cannot be ruled out. Methods that involve adjusting census data (Chapter 5) or that utilize DMV data (Chapter 6) attempt to produce a better match between the benchmark data and the people at risk of being stopped, but again they fail to address all of the factors reflected in the alternative hypotheses.

With data from red light cameras, analysts have the opportunity to maximize the match between the benchmark data and the drivers to whom police officers on patrol are exposed, but the procedures they use narrow the scope of their assessment of racially biased policing in the jurisdiction. An example will help to convey this point. To maximize the match of the two groups, an analyst might use the same intersection (for example, Intersection A) to collect both camera data and officer stop data.[4] Alternatively, in a near-ideal design, the analyst might

---

[4] A practical constraint may arise with this design. Officers may choose not to make vehicle stops for red light violations at intersections with electronic enforcement mechanisms.

compare red-light-camera data from Intersection B to officer stop data for red light violations at Intersection A. The two intersections would be very similar in terms of key variables (for example, the race/ethnicity of drivers, the drivers' behavior). The analyst would believe Intersections A and B are similar in terms of (1) the race/ethnicity of the drivers because the intersections are near each other and (2) driving behavior because both intersections have the same type of traffic—for instance, both are residential, not commercial.

Note that in both of these near-ideal examples, solid matches help the analyst to rule out the alternative hypotheses, and they produce a sound basis for assessing directly the causal relationship between the race/ethnicity of drivers and stopping behavior by police. However, the scope of the agency's assessment of racially biased policing is narrowed to one intersection (Intersection A) and to the one type of violating behavior detected by the cameras (red light violations). Using this method, an agency cannot assess the behavior of officers throughout the jurisdiction in relation to all types of vehicle stops. Rather, it can assess only what some police are doing in one particular location in response to one type of violation. In short, the agency is implementing what amounts to a "spot check" of racially biased policing.

Yet if the agency moves away from the ideal match, it decreases its ability to rule out the alternative hypotheses and thus test the bias hypothesis. We are right back to the problems with other methods because we no longer can have faith that the drivers represented in the benchmark data (those going through red-light-camera intersections) are equivalent (in terms of race/ethnicity and driving behavior) to the drivers to whom police are exposed.

The quandary is trying to identify the implementation methods that have sufficient rigor in terms of maximizing the match yet are able to provide a meaningful assessment of racially biased policing in a jurisdiction. In other words, we don't want the assessment to be too narrow in scope. Specifically, the analyst must make decisions regarding what types of stops by patrol officers should be included; these decisions concern (1) drivers' traffic law-violating behavior (for example, to include only red light violations or all moving violations) and (2) geographic location. To produce a good match, the parameters placed on the stop data (the numerator) must reflect the parameters inherent in the denominator. Below we provide guidance on how a law enforcement agency using this benchmarking method can optimize rigor and scope.

Type of Stop

In terms of which types of stops to include in the numerator, the options available for consideration include the following:

- All vehicle stops (that is, traffic stops and investigative stops),[5]
- All traffic stops (including those related to vehicle quality/maintenance) but not investigative stops,
- All traffic stops that involve moving violations (omitting stops for equipment violations),
- Only red light and stop sign violations, and
- Only red light violations.

To fully maximize the match between the stop data (the numerator) and the benchmark data (the denominator, which in this method is red-light-camera data), an agency would include only red light violations. However, to broaden the scope of its analysis, an agency could reasonably include in its numerator all red light and stop sign violations in the selected geographic areas. (The Police Executive Research Forum's Advisory Board for this project recommends including both types of violations.)

---

[5] Recall from Chapter 1 that a "traffic stop" denotes a vehicle stop because of a suspected violation of traffic laws (including codes related to quality/maintenance of vehicles). The term "investigative stop" denotes police stops of people in vehicles when there is a reasonable suspicion of criminal activity.

Note that this choice of a numerator assumes that the same people who violate red light laws violate stop sign laws at the same rate and vice versa. If an agency were to select all moving violations for its numerator, it would be making the assumption that the same people who violate red light laws violate all other moving violation restrictions at the same rate and vice versa. This assumption is much more difficult to justify. In effect, such an assumption ignores the viable alternative hypothesis that *racial/ethnic groups are not equivalent in the nature and extent of their traffic law-violating behavior*. Indeed, we strongly caution against choosing all moving violations for the numerator.

Location of Stop
The second parameter associated with the denominator that must be matched in the numerator is geographic location. In setting this parameter, analysts are asking, in essence, this question: to what geographic area(s) can we generalize the red-light-camera data? In other words, what geographic areas are equivalent in terms of who is on the road and who is violating? There is no easy formula for deciding which geographic areas might be equivalent to the red light intersections. The geographic areas defining the numerator should be chosen in the general vicinity of the red light cameras (to maximize the match in terms of the race/ethnicity of drivers), and they should resemble the red-light-camera intersections in terms of type of traffic (residential or commercial). The latter match will promote equivalence across driving behavior, as explained earlier.

Other Considerations
The numerator should include only people stopped whose vehicles are registered in-state. This is because the Department of Motor Vehicles in each state can identify only the in-state registered owners of vehicles photographed by the red light cameras, and the DMV provides race/ethnicity information only on them. Therefore, to match the numerator and the denominator, the

analyst must exclude everyone the police stopped whose vehicles are registered out of state.

Commercial vehicles also should be removed from both the numerator and denominator groups. This recommendation relates to a major caveat associated with this method: the benchmark data provided by the DMV will give the race/ethnicity of the person who has *registered* the violating vehicle. The person *driving* may not be the registered owner.

The assumption that the race/ethnicity of the driver will match the race/ethnicity of the registered owner is more viable for privately owned vehicles than for commercially owned vehicles. With privately owned vehicles, it is *reasonably* likely that the driver is (1) the registered owner and/or (2) a relative of the registered owner—someone more likely than not to be of the same race/ethnicity as the owner. For commercial vehicles, however, these assumptions are less valid. There is an increased possibility that (1) the owner of the vehicle is not the driver, and (2) the driver is not of the same race/ethnicity as the owner.

The reference periods for the numerator and denominator also should match. For example, if the agency is analyzing stops (numerator data) for a particular one-year period, it should set the same parameter on the data reflecting people ticketed by the red light cameras.

In discussions of previous methods, we highlighted the desirability of collecting information on the potential intervening variable, age. This is neither possible nor necessary for this method. Although the DMV can likely provide age information, the data will pertain to the *owner* and not necessarily the *driver*, as noted above. Although it was reasonable to assume that most nonowner drivers of privately owned vehicles will be of the same race/ethnicity as the owner, it is not reasonable to assume that the nonowner driver will be of the same age as the owner. (For instance, the driver may be the offspring of the owner.) Fortunately, however, an age assessment is not necessary for this method. Information on the potential intervening variable of age is needed when the analyst cannot produce benchmark data that are equivalent to the stop data in terms of *driving behavior*. Done correctly, this method *does* produce equivalence in driving behavior in the two groups that are compared: drivers stopped by police and drivers ticketed by the red light cameras.[6]

Variations in levels of enforcement activity also need to be addressed. With other benchmarking methods, we controlled for police activity by recommending that analyses be conducted within subareas of the jurisdiction. The counterpart recommendation for this method is to compare each red-light-camera intersection to its "matched" geographic area. These separate comparisons must be made unless two or more red-light-camera intersections and their matched geographic areas have the same driving public and the same levels of enforcement activity.

Conducting the Comparison

Law enforcement agencies benchmarking with red-light-camera data must take into account the type of stop, the location of the stop, and the other considerations noted above. Once analysts have maximized the match between the stop data and the benchmark data, they are ready to conduct the comparison. They can compare the racial/ethnic profile of the people "ticketed" by the red light cameras to the racial/ethnic profile of the people stopped by police for red light and stop sign violations in the matched geographic area (see Figure 7.1). They should conduct these analyses for each red-light-camera intersection and its matched geographic area. The final step is to calculate disparity using the instructions in Chapter 12.

---

[6] However, if stopping activity by police manifests a bias toward youths, and if the age demographics of racial/ethnic groups in the jurisdiction are not equivalent, the results of an agency's assessment of racial/ethnic bias will be impacted. For instance, if minority groups in the jurisdiction have a relatively large proportion of youths and police are biased toward stopping youths, the percentage of minority stops will be larger than would otherwise be the case.

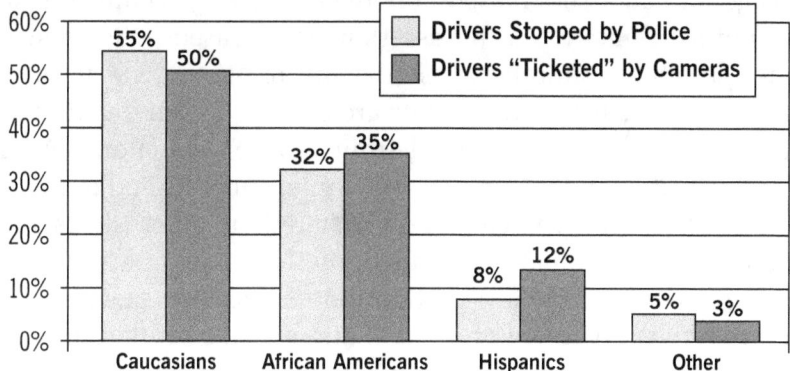

Figure 7.1. Drivers Stopped by Police for Red Light and Stop Sign Violations and Drivers "Ticketed" by Red Light Cameras, by Race/Ethnicity of Drivers (Hypothetical Data)

Drawing Conclusions from the Results

This benchmarking method has an important strength: it can create a comparison group, or benchmark, that reflects the people at risk of being stopped by police, assuming no bias. To the extent that we can create such a matched group, we have addressed the factors reflected in the alternative hypotheses and thus have correspondingly increased the confidence we can have in the results. This method, however, has several important drawbacks.

First, the measure of race/ethnicity within the benchmark group is suspect. The benchmark group is composed of the *owners* of the violating vehicles, not necessarily the *drivers.* Therefore, a law enforcement agency cannot be sure that it has accurately measured the race/ethnicity of the people "ticketed" by the red light cameras.

Second, a full assessment of biased policing in the jurisdiction is not possible with this method. If the DMV cannot provide information on ethnicity, or if the respective measures of race and/or ethnicity of the stop data and DMV data otherwise require the exclusion of ethnicity information (see Appendix C), the agency can assess biased policing only as it pertains to race and not to ethnicity. A full assessment of biased policing also is not possible for another reason: stops of drivers whose vehicles are not registered in the state are excluded from the numerator since they were excluded from the denominator.[7] As a result, jurisdiction residents (for example, students and military personnel) whose vehicles are registered in other states are excluded from the analysis. This limitation greatly narrows the scope of analysis for a jurisdiction that is close to a state line, a college/university town, or a jurisdiction with a military base.

Finally, any assessment of racially biased policing with this method is limited to certain locations for certain types of stops, and an agency's report of its findings must make this clear.[8] The results in which an agency can have confidence relate to the particular types of stops studied (red light and stop sign violations) and to the specific intersections studied. As explained earlier, the rigor of the match comes at the cost of scope. To generalize from these "spot checks" to other types of stops/violations requires an assumption without validity—namely, that the racial/ethnic profile of people who violate stop sign and red

---

[7] Although the red light cameras photograph the plates of violators whose vehicles are registered in another state, these drivers are excluded from the denominator because the data for them are not available from the DMV in the state of the target jurisdiction.

[8] Related to this caveat is the untested, but reasonable, assumption that the risk for racial bias is lowest in the context of decisions in which officers have the least amount of discretion. To the extent it exists, racial bias is presumably least likely to manifest in low-discretion stops (stops for violations that are so serious that most officers would feel a strong need to respond). Examples of low-discretion stops are stops for speeding at greater than 15 miles per hour over the speed limit, leaving the scene of an accident, and running a red light. In using red-light-camera data as a benchmark, an agency is choosing a type of traffic violation (running a red light) that is in the low-discretion category—the category in which police are least likely to manifest racial bias. Clearly, the results from this benchmarking method do not provide a full picture of policing in a jurisdiction and whether it is biased.

light laws matches the racial/ethnic profile of people who commit all moving violations. Similarly, to generalize beyond the geographic test areas to the entire jurisdiction, a law enforcement agency must assume that those areas are representative of all areas of the target jurisdiction. This is a shaky assumption as well for a number of reasons, including the likelihood that red light cameras are placed at intersections with higher than average traffic volume, violation behavior, and/or accidents.

Although sound jurisdiction-wide conclusions cannot be drawn, some geographic generalizations may be reasonable. However, generalizations beyond the red-light-camera intersection and matched areas must be accompanied in the report with a justification. The analyst needs to argue that the areas of generalization are equivalent to the camera and matched areas on the basis of driver demographics and traffic type. The report could state that "these results can be generalized only to areas within the jurisdiction that are equivalent to the test areas" and then proceed to describe those test areas. A caveat, however, is essential. The report should state that racially biased policing in the jurisdiction has not been assessed except in those areas encompassed by the agency's analyses and generalizations.

To summarize the performance of this benchmarking method, we can say that it has addressed the following alternative hypotheses to the extent it has created a matched group:

- *Racial/ethnic groups are not equally represented as residents in the jurisdiction.*
- *Racial/ethnic groups are not equally represented as drivers on jurisdiction roads.*
- *Racial/ethnic groups are not equivalent in the nature and extent of their traffic law-violating behavior.*
- *Racial/ethnic groups are not equally represented as drivers on roads where stopping activity by police is high.*

Although a good match in terms of driving quantity, driving quality, and driving location has been created between the population of drivers stopped by patrol officers and the population of drivers ticketed by the red light cameras, this method has not assessed racially biased policing in the entire target jurisdiction—only in tested areas and in areas where the results can be reasonably generalized.

BENCHMARKING WITH RADAR DATA

Radar enforcement, like red-light-camera enforcement, is "blind" to the racial/ethnic characteristics of traffic law-violating drivers, but only if it is used in certain ways.[9] The radar must be directed at all cars in a particular area, or the officer with the discretion to direct the radar at some cars and not at others must not be able to identify (because of light or distance) the racial/ethnic characteristics of the drivers. If radar is being used by a team—that is, one officer uses radar to detect speeders, and officers up ahead make the stops—the police making the actual stops (1) cannot have discretion as to which radar-identified violators to stop or (2) cannot be able to identify the violators' racial/ethnic characteristics prior to their intervention.

Conducting the Comparison

If law enforcement agencies follow the criteria for "blindness" just described, then radar stops can be used as a benchmark for assessing racially biased policing in a jurisdiction. The same procedures for benchmarking with red-light-camera data apply. Again, the nonradar police stops of vehicles included in the numerator should be as equivalent as possible to the radar stops that comprise the denominator. The equivalence or match is based on the type of stop (in other words, type of offense) and the geographic location of the stop.

---

[9] For simplicity, we use the term "radar," but this method applies to laser stops as well.

To match the numerator ("not-blind" stops by patrol officers) to the inherent parameters of the denominator ("blind" radar stops) with regard to type of offense, we recommend using only stops for speeding. To make the match with regard to geographic location of the stop, we recommend areas in the general vicinity of the radar activity. These areas are most likely to resemble the radar areas in terms of the race/ethnicity of drivers and types of traffic.

With radar benchmarks, the day of week and time of day should also be considered. Although red light cameras presumably run twenty-four hours per day, seven days per week, radar might be used only on certain days of the week and during certain times of day. Because the nature and volume of traffic vary across days of week and times of day, the numerator stops should be matched to radar stops across these temporal variables. Finally, radar stops should be excluded from the numerator. This is because, in any benchmarking method that is based on stops by police, stops that are included in the denominator should not be included in the numerator.

In short, agencies should *exclude* from the population of stops by patrol officers any stops as a result of radar, and they should *include*

- stops for speeding violations only,
- stops in geographic areas matched to the radar areas in terms of the race/ethnicity of drivers and the type of traffic, and
- stops on the days of the week and time of day that match the radar activity.

Some of the limitations of red-light-camera benchmarking because of its reliance on DMV data are not relevant to radar benchmarking. First, an agency will not be precluded from assessing the impact of ethnicity on police behavior if ethnicity information is collected for both radar stops and patrol officer stops. (As indicated in the previous section, the DMV data might not contain the ethnicity information.) Second, it will have a more credible measure of driver race/ethnicity because the race/ethnicity information will pertain to the *driver* of the vehicle and not the *owner,* as was the case with the red-light-camera data. (Note that this advantage of using the radar method allows the agency to include stops of commercial vehicles.) Finally, the agency will not have to exclude out-of-state drivers from the numerator because out-of-state drivers will be included among the radar stops.

Like benchmarking with red-light-camera data, this method incorporates driving quality into the analysis. It does this by creating the close match between drivers represented in the numerator and those represented in the denominator. Since the driving quality factor is matched, the analyst will not need to consider age as an intervening variable. The analyst will need to conduct *separate* analyses for *each* radar site and its matched geographic area for purposes of controlling for different levels of enforcement activity by police.

Drawing Conclusions from the Results

The strength of benchmarking with "blind" enforcement data (whether it be radar data or red-light-camera data) is its potential to develop a strong match between the benchmark population and the people at risk of being stopped by patrol officers. Again, to the extent that this match is maximized, the factors related to the four competing hypotheses are addressed. Like the red-light-camera method, however, this method has an important limitation: the rigor of the match comes at a cost in terms of scope (see the red-light-camera section entitled "Drawing Conclusions from the Results"). In short, conclusions can be made about specific areas and about enforcement of certain traffic laws but not about the target jurisdiction as a whole or enforcement of all traffic laws.

BENCHMARKING WITH DATA FROM AIR PATROLS

In an innovative approach to the analysis of police-citizen contact data, a team of researchers in Charleston, South Carolina, compared the racial/ethnic profile of people identified as speeders by air-patrol officers to the racial/ethnic profile of people cited for speeding by officers on ground patrol. Specifically, McConnell and Scheidegger (2001, 5-6) "compared citations issued by air-patrol officers with tickets issued by ground-patrol officers to determine if race was a determining factor in receiving a citation." This qualifies as a "blind" and "not-blind" comparison "because the race of the driver cannot be determined by the air-patrol officer." Of course, stops would not be "blind" if the ground-patrol officers receiving information on speeders from the air-patrol officers were able to discern the driver's race/ethnicity and had discretion to stop or not stop identified vehicles.[10]

McConnell and Scheidegger (2001) matched ground-patrol speeding citations (the numerator) and air-patrol speeding citations (the denominator) across day of week, time of day, and geographic area. They found that a *smaller* proportion of African Americans received ground-patrol citations than air-patrol citations. From these results they concluded that enforcement of speeding laws in the specific areas studied was not racially biased.

If a jurisdiction uses air patrols to enforce speeding laws and uses them in circumstances that are "blind" as to the race/ethnicity of drivers, this method can produce a valid benchmark against which to compare stop data. The comparison must be conducted carefully, however, in accord with the procedures described in the section on benchmarking with radar data.

---

[10] McConnell and Scheidegger (2001) support their contention that the air-patrol stops in Charleston are truly "blind." They point out that the ground-patrol officer who makes the stop is directed by police department policy to give a citation to the person identified by the air patrol. The ground-patrol officer cannot exercise any discretion in deciding whether or not to give a citation.

USING LOW-DISCRETION STOPS AS A BENCHMARK

Some agencies have compared high- and low-discretion traffic stops.[11] In effect, they are using the low-discretion stops (the denominator) as a benchmark for the high-discretion stops (the numerator). This reflects the reasonable assumption that racial/ethnic bias is more likely to manifest itself when officers have discretion in deciding whether to stop someone than when they have little choice in the matter. Circumstances where discretion is greatest and least form two ends of a continuum. Most officers will feel a strong need to respond when a driver runs a red light in a busy intersection. This is a low-discretion stop toward one end of the continuum. An officer is likely to respond to all violations of this kind, and any biases an officer might have are not likely to enter into the decision to ticket the red light violator. On the other hand, officers have great discretion in deciding whether to stop someone who is going 5 miles per hour over the speed limit (a violation at the other end of the continuum). If an officer has biases, they are more likely to influence high-discretion decisions such as this one.

For purposes of benchmarking, an agency could compare the types of traffic stops where police usually exercise little discretion (for instance, stops for red light and stop sign violations, stops for speeding 10 miles per hour over the speed limit, stops in response to a traffic accident, and checkpoint stops conducted in accordance with constitutional requirements concerning equitable treatment of all drivers) to high-discretion stops (for instance, stops on the basis of lane violations, following too closely, not wearing a seatbelt, failure to signal, failure to yield, and speeding at less than 10 miles per hour over the speed limit).[12] No category

---

[11] We do not recommend this benchmarking method for analyzing investigative stops. Instead, an agency can benchmark those stops against crime data (see Chapter 10).

[12] Law enforcement agencies will categorize stops in different ways. The analyst should confer with agency personnel to determine what types of stops they would place in the high-discretion category and what types they would place in the low-discretion category.

of stop can be listed in the numerator and in the denominator. The agency would then compare the racial/ethnic profile of the people stopped in high-discretion situations to the racial/ethnic profile of those stopped in low-discretion situations to see if the latter produces higher proportions of minority drivers.

Resources Required
To implement this method, a law enforcement agency must be able to differentiate between high-discretion and low-discretion stop data it has collected. If the agency has not yet developed its form for recording contacts between police and citizens, it will have the opportunity to include the high- and low-discretion options that make the most sense to police personnel. If the agency form is already finalized, analysts can only use the "reasons for the stop" options included on the data collection form. If the options do not break down into reasonable groups of high- and low-discretion stops, the agency should not use this benchmarking method.

Conducting the Comparison
Law enforcement agencies with the required resources outlined above can begin to conduct the comparison of data. The analyst would compare the racial/ethnic profile of drivers stopped by police for traffic offenses in high-discretion circumstances to the profile of drivers stopped by police in low-discretion circumstances. This comparison should be made within two age groups unless the age demographics of the drivers within the two groups are equivalent. The analyst also should conduct separate analyses for the jurisdiction subareas selected on the basis of the instructions provided in Chapter 4. Finally, from the racial/ethnic profiles expressed in the form of percentages, the analyst should calculate a measure of disparity (see Chapter 12).

Drawing Conclusions from the Results

Unlike benchmarking with data from "blind" enforcement mechanisms, this method does not produce a good match in traffic law-violating behavior between the people at risk of being stopped and the people who are stopped. Recall that the comparison between technological enforcement using red light cameras and enforcement by patrol officers matched stops of red light violators (the denominator) to stops of red light violators and stop sign violators (the numerator)—very similar offenses. But the use of low-discretion stops (the denominator) as a benchmark for high-discretion stops (the numerator) involves a comparison of drivers who commit very different violations. Benchmarking with data from "blind" enforcement mechanisms addresses the alternative hypothesis that *racial/ethnic groups are not equivalent in the nature and extent of their traffic law-violating behavior;* it does this by making driving behavior equivalent in the two groups. Benchmarking with data from low-discretion stops does not achieve equivalence in driving behavior.

This method, however, does address the hypotheses that *racial/ethnic groups are not equally represented as residents in the jurisdiction* and *racial/ethnic groups are not equally represented as drivers on jurisdiction roads.* If analyses were conducted within subareas, as we recommend, the method has addressed the hypothesis that *racial/ethnic groups are not equally represented as drivers on roads where stopping activity by police is high.* If analyses were conducted within age groups (or age breakdowns by race were found to be equivalent), the potentially confounding variable, age, was taken into account.

BENCHMARKING WITH "BLIND" DATA FROM A NONTECHNOLOGICAL SOURCE: PRESTOP OBSERVABILITY OF THE DRIVER'S RACE/ETHNICITY

In Chapter 4 in the section entitled "Prestop Observability of the Driver's Race/Ethnicity," we reported that some agencies on their police-citizen contact forms have officers respond to the question "Was the driver's race/ethnicity observable by police before the stop?" A response of "no" indicates the officer was "blind" as to the race/ethnicity of the driver at the time the decision to make the stop was made. As this chapter goes to press, we learn that the Public Safety and Justice division of the RAND Corporation is exploring the viability of using the information contained in this item to develop a novel, non-technological "blind" benchmarking method. Specifically, with this method the researcher compares the racial/ethnic profile of the drivers stopped in instances in which the officer could not discern race/ethnicity to the racial/ethnic profile of the drivers stopped in instances in which the officer could. As explained by Ridgeway (2003, 2), "If the relative rate of white and non-white drivers stopped differs between those instances when the officer knew (versus did not know) the driver's race in advance then there would be evidence of a race bias." The RAND researchers conducted this comparison as part of their work for the Oakland racial profiling task force. Ridgeway (2003, 2) reports on their findings:

> When looking at afternoon driving, noon to 4 pm, and considering only black and white drivers, 59% of the time the officer reported that they could not identify the race of the driver in advance. Of the stops made when the officer reported knowing the race in advance, 74% were black drivers and 26% were white drivers. When race was reported as unknown in advance, 68% were black drivers and 32% were white drivers. Statistically, advance race identification seems to be independent of the race of the driver. Whether or not the officers are able to identify race in advance, the rate at which black and white drivers are stopped does not change much.

The research team acknowledges that this analysis "requires that the officers are accurately and honestly answering the advance race identification question." Its continued work in this area is geared toward what Ridgeway (2003, 3) refers to as "relaxing this assumption." He reports that this method of testing for bias in stops is currently under peer review and that "if this method is validated, it will provide a low cost and repeatable process by which communities can monitor for bias in stops over time."

CONCLUSION

Using data obtained from red light cameras, radar, and air patrols, law enforcement agencies can compare the racial/ethnic profile of technology-selected drivers to the racial/ethnic profile of human-selected drivers (drivers stopped by patrol officers). This comparison benchmarks the data on drivers stopped by enforcement methods that are devoid of discretion (the "blind" technology) against the data on drivers stopped by methods that involve the exercise of discretion (stops by patrol officers). If officers' stopping decisions are made without racial/ethnic bias, then the racial/ethnic profile of the drivers they stop will match the racial/ethnic profile of the drivers stopped by the technology. The RAND Corporation is exploring a "blind" benchmarking method that is not technology based. In this method researchers compare groups of stops that differ in terms of the prestop observability of a driver's race/ethnicity.

When implemented in accordance with our recommendations, benchmarking with "blind" enforcement mechanisms enables a jurisdiction to conduct a strong assessment of biased policing. The results, however, are strong only for specific locations and for particular types of stops. In other words, the rigor of the methodology comes at the cost of scope. A law enforcement agency that has chosen this benchmarking method must include an essential caveat in its report of results: jurisdiction-wide conclusions about the presence or absence of racially biased policing cannot be drawn.

Benchmarking with data from low-discretion stops as a means of assessing whether racial/ethnic bias affects stopping decisions by police when they have a choice is a method with limits as well. Because these stops are for dissimilar traffic offenses, this method does not address the alternative hypothesis that *racial/ethnic groups are not equivalent in the nature and extent of their traffic law-violating behavior.* Consequently, the bias hypothesis cannot be tested.

Benchmarking with Data for Matched Officers or Matched Groups of Officers

The previous chapter described comparisons of types of stops. Stops by "blind" enforcement mechanisms were compared to stops by patrol officers, and low-discretion stops were compared to high-discretion stops. In a variation on this methodology, law enforcement agencies can compare stops by individual officers to stops by other officers, or they can compare stops by a group of officers to stops by other groups of officers.[1] These comparisons must be made across "matched" sets of officers or groups of officers to control for the factors reflected in the alternative hypotheses described in Chapter 2. For instance, an agency might compare the racial/ethnic profile of people stopped by individual patrol officers who work the same shift in the same precinct. If a particular officer stops proportionately more minority citizens than does his or her matched peers, further exploration of this officer's policing activities and decisions would be warranted. Samuel Walker has described this method of analyzing police-citizen contact data and its advantages (Walker 2001, 2002, 2003). He characterizes this method as an early warning or early intervention approach. This method has also been referred to by Walker as "internal benchmarking."

---

[1] We describe how to apply this method to the analysis of vehicle stops. As explained later in this chapter, this benchmarking method has been used to analyze arrest data as well as vehicle stop data.

ASSESSING RESOURCES REQUIRED

To implement internal benchmarking, the agency must be able to link stop data to individual officers or to groups of officers. Comparing officers to each other is preferable to comparing groups of officers. Analysis at the individual level allows the agency to identify particular officers whose stopping activity is different from his or her colleagues' stopping activity. Some agencies, however, cannot match at the individual officer level because the agency's stop data cannot be linked to individual officers. There are a variety of reasons that agencies do not collect data linked to individual officer identities.[2] Some believe, for instance, that it is easier to win officers' acceptance of the agency's data collection plan if stop data are not linked to individual officers.

THE MATCHING PROCESS

The strength of this method is directly linked to the quality of the match between the officers or groups of officers being compared. That is, the researcher wants to maximize the similarity among the officers being compared or among the groups being compared. We describe this important matching process below.

Officer-Level Matching

To assess whether Officer A, for example, is making decisions to stop vehicles based on drivers' race or ethnicity, an agency can compare Officer A's stop data to the stop data of other officers who are policing essentially the same population in essentially the same way. The goal is to compare officers similar to one another in terms of the people at risk of being stopped by them. For instance, officers on the same shift, in the same geographic area, with the same assignment would be exposed to a similar population of drivers. Because the selected officers police similar populations, all of the factors related to the alternate hypotheses (driv-

---

[2] The arguments for and against collecting data linked to individual officers are presented in Fridell et al. (2001, Chap. 8).

ing quantity, driving quality, driving location) are held constant. The racial/ethnic profile of drivers on the road, as well as the racial/ethnic profile of law violators, are roughly equivalent for these matched officers. The proportion of young drivers to which they are exposed is also similar. Therefore, law enforcement agencies using this benchmarking method do not need to account for the potential intervening variable of age.[3] Since all of the factors related to the alternative hypotheses are held constant in this comparison of individual officers, the racial/ethnic profile of the drivers they stop should be about the same unless one officer (or possibly several) is more inclined to stop drivers of particular racial/ethnic groups than are the others.[4]

Figure 8.1 illustrates benchmarking with data for matched officers. For nine of the ten matched officers, the percentage of stops of minorities is in the range of 13 percent to 21 percent. The percentage for Officer 8, however, is much higher—37 percent. This finding of disparate results does not *prove* that the officer is acting in a racially biased manner, but it should prompt a review of the policing activities of this officer.

As explained earlier, individual officers who are sufficiently matched for purposes of comparison are those who are similarly situated. The answer to the question "Which officers are policing essentially the same population in essentially the same way?" will differ for every agency. For most departments, matching individual officers by shift will make sense because the demographics of drivers and/or violators is likely to vary by time of day. However, an agency may decide not to match officers by shift if the officers in the agency rotate across all shifts during the reference period for the analysis.

---

[3] Deployment also is not an issue because we are comparing officers assigned to the same geographic areas and assigned similar responsibilities.

[4] We can identify officers who are more inclined than their matched counterparts to stop drivers based on their race/ethnicity. We cannot determine whether or not all of the officers being compared are selecting drivers to stop based on bias. We discuss this important point more thoroughly below.

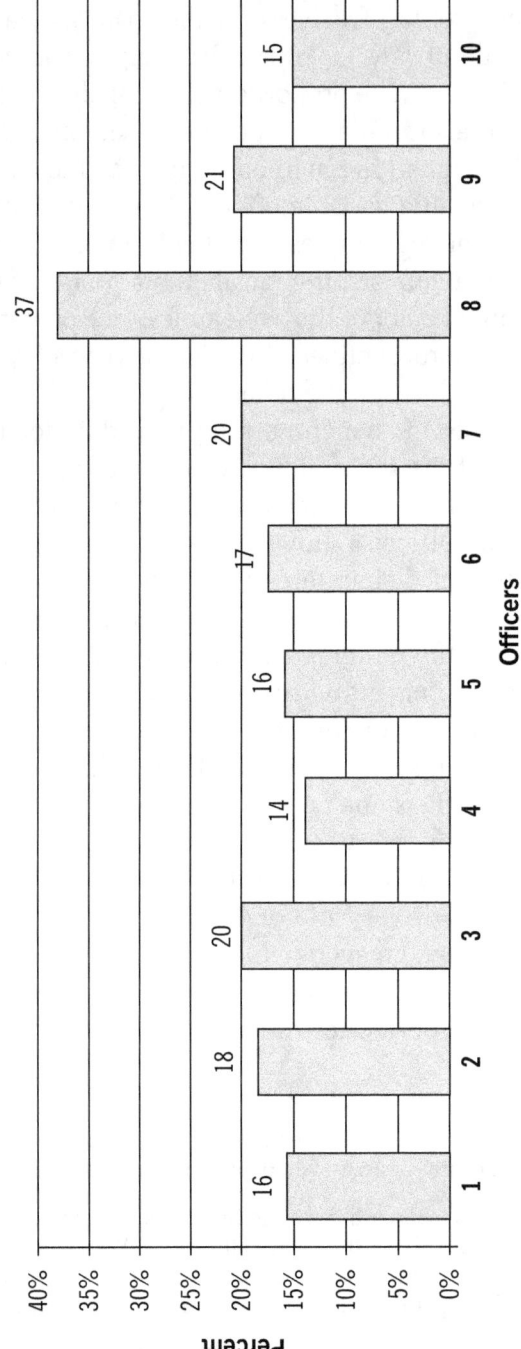

Figure 8.1. Matched Officers' Stops of Minority Drivers (Hypothetical Data)

Officers should be matched by assignment as well. It is reasonable to expect officers with different missions to stop different populations of people. For instance, officers assigned to enforce traffic laws are likely to stop a different population of drivers than would officers on general patrol; the latter stop drivers not only for traffic violations but also for investigative purposes. Therefore, traffic officers should not be matched to patrol officers, for example. In general, officers with different assignments should not be compared to each other.

We have discussed matching individual officers by shift and by assignment. Matched officers also should police the same geographic areas. By comparing officers who are assigned to the same geographic areas, an agency can be sufficiently sure that the matched officers are policing similar populations of drivers. In small agencies, however, a match across all of these variables may prove problematic. Officers assigned during the same shift to the same task and in the same area may be very few in number. To achieve comparisons within a large enough group (say, ten or more officers), small agencies may have to compare officers with the same assignment and same shift in *similar* but not the *same* geographic areas. Areas should be similar with regard to the racial/ethnic composition of the population and the nature of the traffic. Regarding the latter match, officers working in commercial areas should not be compared to officers working in primarily residential areas. If an agency is using this method to analyze investigative stops, the nature and extent of crime in the matched areas also should be equivalent.

Finally, an agency should exclude officers with a particularly low number of stops even if they fit otherwise into a selected comparison group.[5] This exclusion is necessary because analyses based on small numbers are unreliable.

---

[5] One state trooper agency eliminates officers with fewer than twenty stops. The team in St. Louis (Decker and Rojek 2002) excluded officers whose number of stops fell at least one standard deviation below the mean number of stops for the matched group.

Group-Level Matching

An agency unable to link stop data to individual officers can still implement internal benchmarking if it can identify groups of officers that are similarly situated. That is, the unit of analysis would be the group not the individual. The numerator is the aggregate racial/ethnic profile of the drivers stopped by all of the officers in the group; the denominator, or benchmark, is the racial/ethnic profile of the drivers stopped by the corresponding comparison groups. That is, the racial/ethnic profile of drivers stopped by Group A is compared to the racial/ethnic profiles of the drivers stopped by the officers in the matched Group B, matched Group C, and so forth.

To identify the matched groups, agencies should ask "Which groups of officers are policing essentially the same population in essentially the same way?" Again, the answer to this question will vary across agencies. A large agency, for example, might be able to match the group of patrol officers working the day shift in Precinct A to the patrol officers working the day shift in Precincts B and C—if Precincts A, B, and C are comparable in terms of driver demographics and the nature of the traffic. Of course, this agency could similarly compare the night-shift patrol officers in these precincts or the swing-shift officers. In the hypothetical day-shift example, three groups are compared to each other—the Precinct A group, the Precinct B group, and the Precinct C group. The greater the number of groups being compared, the greater the reliability of the results. Comparing ten groups to each other is preferable to comparing three, for example. A small agency may not be able to identify a sufficient number of groups of officers that are similarly situated. If this is the case, the agency would be precluded from using benchmarking that relies on data from matched groups of officers.

CONDUCTING THE ANALYSIS

This section provides an explanation of how to compare matched officers or matched groups of officers using work completed in St. Louis as an example.

Officer-Level Matching

As one component of their data analysis, Scott Decker and Jeffrey Rojek (2002) used officer-level matching to assess the presence or absence of racial/ethnic bias in the St. Louis, Missouri, police department. They compared traffic officers within districts to each other,[6] and they compared "district officers" (officers assigned to regular patrol) within districts to each other.[7] This produced eighteen separate analyses for the nine districts in St. Louis. For each officer they reported various types of information (including total number of traffic stops, number of traffic stops of African Americans, total number of searches, number of searches of African Americans, total arrests, number of arrests of African Americans), but their in-depth analysis focused on the stop data.[8] They translated the percentage of drivers stopped who were African American for each officer into standardized scores for purposes of comparing officers to each other.[9] As Decker and Rojek (2002, 4) explain, "The use of a standard score allows for the comparison of officers who make [a] different number of stops."

Standardized scores (or "z-scores") are calculated by subtracting from each value for each officer the mean for all officers and dividing by the standard deviation. Virtually all statistical programs provide this option. (For instance, in SPSS, an analyst would run "descriptives" on the variable representing percentage of African Americans stopped and select the option to "save

---

[6] Decker and Rojek were not able to match officers by shift because the information was not available. This was not detrimental to the analyses because officers in the agency rotated shifts. Over the course of the reference period, all of the officers would end up being exposed to the same drivers and violators.

[7] Decker and Rojek excluded six officers from the analysis because of the unique nature of their assignment.

[8] African Americans are the predominant racial minority group in the jurisdiction.

[9] As we recommend, officers with few stops were excluded. This is advisable because a small number of stops produces unreliable data.

standardized values as variables.") The standardized scores have an average of 0, and each increment of 1 represents one standard deviation. Decker and Rojek (2002, 4) point out that this score is particularly useful for interpreting the data because "each standard deviation away from the average value of 0 represents a fixed percentage of officers." An additional advantage is that the results can be displayed graphically in a manner that is easy to understand. For all standardized scores (for any variable measured for any population), 68 percent of the cases will fall within one standard deviation above or below the mean value (again, the mean value is 0). The other 32 percent of the cases have values above 1 or below -1. (Sixteen percent will be above 1, and 16 percent will be below -1.) Thus, an officer with a standardized score greater than 1 would be in the highest 16 percent of officers in terms of the rate of stopping African American drivers, an officer with a standardized score of 2 or higher would be in the highest 2.5 percent, and an officer with a standardized score less than -2 is among the lowest 2.5 percent (Decker and Rojek 2002, 5). The straightforward interpretation of these scores allows the department to identify "outliers." In any assessment of racially biased policing based on the percentage of African Americans stopped by police, the officers with high positive scores become the focus of attention.

Table 8.1 presents hypothetical data for twenty officers who have been matched across area, assignment, and shift. These officers are compared across their standardized scores based on percentage of total stops that were stops of African Americans. The rank of each officer (contained in the far right column) is based on his or her standardized score, with the rank of 1 designating the lowest standardized score (relatively low percentage of African Americans stopped) and the rank of 20 indicating the highest standardized score (relatively high percentage of African Americans stopped).

The goal of analysis at the individual level is to identify particular officers whose stopping behavior differs from that of his or her colleagues. By ordering the standardized scores from

Table 8.1. Matched Officers' Standardized Scores Based on Percentage of Drivers Stopped who are African Americans

Officer ID	Total No. of Stops	No. of Stops of African Americans	Stops of African Americans as a % of Total Stops	Standardized Score	Rank
1	30	5	16.67%	-0.94	3
2	42	8	19.05%	-0.69	6
3	56	15	26.79%	0.12	13
4	78	37	47.44%	2.28	20
5	37	12	32.43%	0.71	16
6	44	10	22.73%	-0.31	9
7	65	7	10.77%	-1.56	1
8	23	6	26.09%	0.04	11
9	55	22	40.00%	1.5	18
10	76	23	30.26%	0.48	15
11	22	5	22.73%	-0.31	10
12	45	12	26.67%	0.1	12
13	65	8	12.31%	-1.4	2
14	85	16	18.82%	-0.72	5
15	93	27	20.03%	-0.59	8
16	30	6	20.00%	-0.6	7
17	50	14	28.00%	0.24	14
18	20	8	40.00%	1.5	19
19	32	6	18.75%	-0.73	4
20	44	15	34.09%	0.88	17

lowest to highest and plotting the results, the analyst can identify these "outliers." In Figure 8.2, based on the data in Table 8.1, three outliers can be identified. Toward the right side of the figure can be seen three officers whose standardized scores are greater than 1 (Officers 9, 18, and 4 from Table 8.1 who are ranked 18, 19, and 20, respectively), including one officer (Officer 4) whose standardized score is greater than 2.[10]

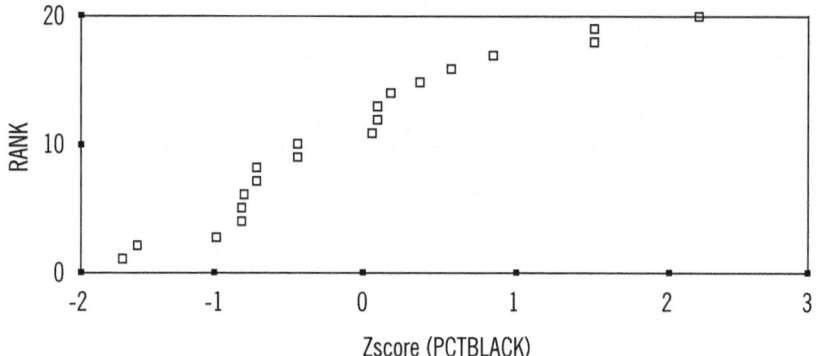

Figure 8.2. Distribution of Standardized Scores for Matched Officers

An agency might decide that a "high score" warranting a review of the officer's activities is two standard deviations above the mean. Alternatively, an agency might choose to review officers whose results are one standard deviation above the mean or maybe one standard deviation above the mean during two analysis periods (for example, two three-month periods).

---

[10] There are also "outliers" at the other end of the continuum. The officers ranked 1 and 2 in Table 8.1 stop relatively low percentages of African Americans compared to their colleagues. These outliers might warrant attention as well.

As noted earlier, Decker and Rojek focused on the percentage of African Americans stopped because African Americans are the largest racial minority group in St. Louis. Agencies with several significant minority groups can (1) analyze the percentage of drivers stopped who are minorities (combining, for instance, stops of African Americans and Hispanics), and/or (2) conduct separate analyses for each of the major racial/ethnic minority groups in the jurisdiction (for example, percentage of drivers stopped who are African American and percentage of drivers stopped who are of Middle Eastern/East Indian descent).

This benchmarking method also can be used to analyze search data (see Chapter 11).

Group-Level Matching
To compare matched groups of officers rather than individual officers, analysts should follow the same procedures reflected in Table 8.1. However, the first column would report the identification number of the group, not the officer. Columns 2 and 3 would represent the total stops made by the entire group of officers, and the total number of stops of African Americans by the group of officers. Outlier groups would be identified through the standardized scores for the groups.

DRAWING CONCLUSIONS FROM THE RESULTS

Benchmarking with data for matched officers or matched groups of officers enables analysts to identify "outliers," officers or groups of officers who stop racial/ethnic minorities at higher rates than do their matched counterparts. The degree of confidence analysts can have that policing by these officers is racially biased is entirely dependent upon the strength of the match. Perfect matches would fully account for the factors reflected in the alternative hypotheses and enable the analyst to test the bias hypothesis. But no match is perfect. For instance, in a large geographic area within which officers are being compared, the racial/ethnic profile of drivers to which particular officers are exposed may differ. Even officers with the same general assignment of "patrol" may be directed toward different activities in the course of their work. Therefore, they would not be exposed to identical populations.

In sum, *definitive conclusions about racial profiling cannot be drawn from this benchmarking method because the racial/ethnic profile of the drivers to which an officer or group of officers is exposed is not exactly the same as the racial/ethnic profile of the drivers to which the matched officers or matched group of officers are exposed.* This internal benchmarking method can pinpoint outliers, but further review is essential to assess whether the disparity is the result of bias.

There is another major caveat associated with this method— and one that must be highlighted in a law enforcement agency's report of its findings to the public. This method uses information on stopping behavior by police as both the numerator and denominator. In an officer-level match, the numerator is one officer's stop data, and the denominator is the same type of data from other similarly situated officers in the same department. Although this method of analysis can identify outliers, it cannot determine whether or not all units used in the comparison (all officers in an officer-level analysis or all groups in a group-level analysis) are practicing biased policing (Walker 2001; Engel and Calnon forthcoming).

For example, it is clear from Figure 8.1 that Officer 8 is stopping minorities at a rate disproportionate to the rate of minority stops by his or her peers. But an analyst cannot conclude that the other nine officers in the match are stopping minorities in proportions that reflect legitimate stopping criteria: they, too, might be making decisions based on racial bias. Indeed, every officer in this matched group of ten officers could be practicing biased policing. In that case Officer 8 is only the officer whose stopping decisions appear to manifest bias most strongly. Similarly, in a group-level analysis, all of the groups in the comparison could be biased. From the analysis, however, the researcher cannot determine whether the matched groups are fair or biased in their policing. The analyst is able to identify only the officers or groups that stop the highest proportion of minorities. To overcome this major obstacle (that is, the relativity of the findings), an agency could supplement internal benchmarking with other methods such as benchmarking with data from "blind" enforcement mechanisms. In using internal benchmarking in conjunction with other methods, the researcher can take advantage of the great strengths of the internal benchmarking method and counter its greatest weakness as well.

TAKING APPROPRIATE ACTION AGAINST OFFICERS OR GROUPS

The data for outliers (whether individual officers or a group of officers) should not be considered proof of racially biased policing by them. The results of high-quality-match methods, however, do raise legitimate red flags that can and should prompt further investigation by the law enforcement agency. Specifically, the results justify a comprehensive inquiry into the officer's or group's stopping activity.[11] The high rate of minority stops may have a legitimate explanation. For instance, the officer or group of officers might have a special assignment to a "hot spot" in the geographic area where minorities are present in numbers disproportionately higher than their representation in the rest of the geographic area.

Decker and Rojek recommend that senior command staff, particularly district commanders, review the data on outliers. Specifically,

> the behavior of officers who fall two or more standard deviations beyond the average for their [cohort] should be examined more closely. It should be determined if the nature of their assignment, productivity in arrests, or other factors account for the higher than average score.... In addition, officers who fall two or more standard deviations beyond the district average

---

[11] A more comprehensive review might encompass examination of other data such as complaint data, force reports, and supervisory review reports (Decker and Rojek 2002).

should have the opportunity to provide input about the reasons for such an outcome. It would be inappropriate to simply examine a standard score for an individual and conclude based solely on that score that the individual was in need of an intervention (Decker and Rojek 2002, 5-6).

Similarly, Samuel Walker (2002, 86) advocates caution when law enforcement agencies interpret the results of this benchmarking method, referred by him below as the early warning (EW) approach:

> Where the data analysis identifies potential problem officers or supervisors, the EW approach moves to the intervention stage. Intervention begins with a review of an officer's performance by supervisors. There may be extenuating circumstances that explain a particular pattern of traffic stops. The officer under review should enjoy a presumption of innocence until a full performance review is completed. The important point is that the *data represent a starting point*, the beginning of a departmental inquiry, and *are not in and of themselves conclusive*.[12] Thus, no officer is automatically presumed guilty simply because he or she has made a high number of stops of minority drivers. A flexible system involving a command review of performance can accommodate officers who may be doing professional, proactive police work.

The Ohio State Highway Patrol (Friday 2002) uses internal benchmarking to analyze arrest data. Through its review, the OSHP identifies officers who arrest minorities in proportions that are two standard deviations above the mean within their cohort. Identification as an "outlier" initiates a comprehensive evaluation of other data in order to corroborate or dispute arrest-data indications of unprofessional or biased behavior. As Figure 8.3 shows, four other sources are evaluated (warnings issued by the officer, searches conducted by the officer, in-car

---

[12] Here Walker (2002) is quoting Walker and Alpert (2000). The italics appear in the original.

video footage of the officer's actions, and previous complaints about the officer's policing practices). If these supplemental data sources indicate bias (referenced in the figure as "Unprofessional Behavior") on the part of officers, interventions are implemented (Friday 2002).

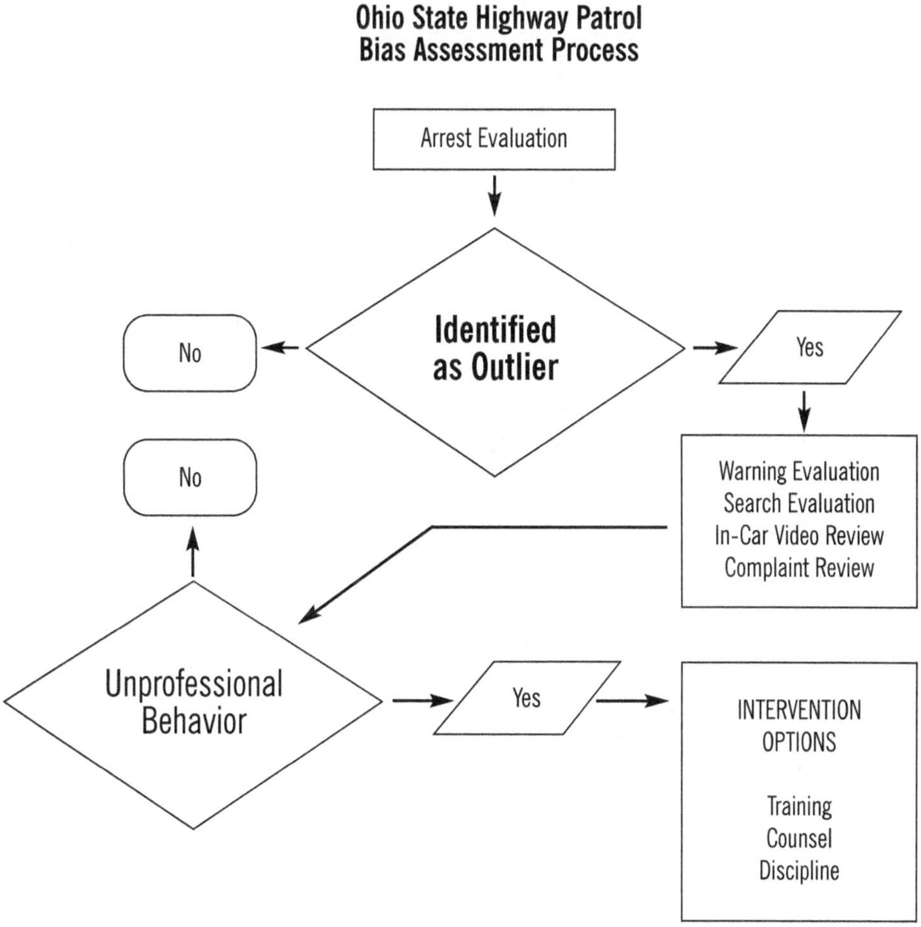

**Ohio State Highway Patrol
Bias Assessment Process**

Source: Friday (2002).

Figure 8.3. Bias Assessment Process of the Ohio State Highway Patrol

In sum, if this benchmarking method indicates disproportionate engagement of minorities by an officer or group of officers relative to matched peers' engagement of minorities, a law enforcement agency should collect additional information before it can reasonably determine whether the identified disparities are linked to bias by the officer or group. The officer or supervisor of a group may be able to explain the circumstances and factors that produced the results. The agency can also review, as did the Ohio State Highway Patrol, several other information sources to see if disparate action on the part of the officer or group is confirmed or disconfirmed. The agency should also review, as recommended by Walker (2002), the context of the officer's or group's work to determine if "extenuating circumstances" reveal legitimate reasons for the high rate of minority stops (or arrests). If disparity is confirmed and no race-neutral explanation is identified, then department interventions (training, counseling, discipline) are appropriate to correct an officer's or group's behavior.

CONCLUSION

If law enforcement agencies implement high-quality matching as described earlier, the results of this benchmarking method can identify officers or groups of officers who stop minorities for traffic violations more often than their peers. The data on these "outliers" can legitimately be used to initiate more in-depth inquiries to assess whether bias is the cause.

The stronger the match between the individual officers or groups of officers being compared, the stronger the analysis and the more confidence the researcher can have in the results. The key to the matching process is identifying officers or groups of officers who are "similarly situated" (that is, who are policing essentially the same population in essentially the same way). Because the selected officers police similar populations, all of the factors related to the alternative hypotheses (driving quantity, driving quality, and driving location) are held constant. The racial/ethnic profile of drivers and violators are roughly equivalent for these matched officers.

Although this method, implemented with strong matches, can account for all of the alternative hypotheses, there are several important caveats associated with this method. First, *the matches can never be perfect* and, as a result, we cannot be fully assured that the officers or groups of officers being compared are policing exactly the same populations. Second, this method can identify outliers within the agency but cannot determine whether or not all individuals or groups used in the comparison are practicing biased policing. Using internal benchmarking in conjunction with other methods described in this report allows the researcher to address this weakness while taking advantage of this method's strengths.

Agencies can use this method to identify and intervene with officers or groups of officers whose stopping behavior could indicate a link to racial/ethnic bias. Importantly, however, an agency should not act solely on the basis of the matched comparison results, but instead should use those results to initiate a more comprehensive inquiry. The agency should explore and rule out possible explanations other than bias for stopping behavior that is disparate from an individual's or group's peers before taking any action.

IX

Observation Benchmarking

Using the observation method, researchers compare the racial/ethnic profile of drivers observed at selected sites to the racial/ethnic profile of drivers stopped by police in the same vicinity. The observation data (the denominator) is used as a benchmark for the stop data (the numerator).[1] Law enforcement agencies that choose observation benchmarking to assess whether policing in a jurisdiction is racially biased must decide the methods, focus, location, and timing of observations. Agencies usually hire one or several researchers to help them with this assessment. Observations are conducted by individuals trained by the researchers to be the observers.

Whom should these individuals observe? In other words, what should be the population of drivers that composes the benchmark data? On this question law enforcement agencies have a choice: they can observe drivers at the selected site or traffic law-violating drivers at the selected site. This chapter will explain the factors that should influence this decision and why we recommend "violators" rather than "drivers" for the benchmark population. An alternative viewpoint is presented

---

[1] See Chapter 4 for an explanation of the concepts of "numerator" and "denominator."

in Appendix D, and a summary of the arguments for and against using violators as the benchmark is presented in Appendix E.

Observation benchmarking was the method used in the early attempts to measure racially biased policing when the issue of "racial profiling" came to national attention in the 1990s. John Lamberth applied this method to benchmark stops in New Jersey (1996a) and in Maryland (1996b).

The observation methodology has a long history in police research that extends back to the research and writings of Albert Reiss, Jr., starting in the 1960s (see, for example, Reiss 1967, 1968, 1971). More recently, the observation methodology was employed by the Project on Policing Neighborhoods (POPN) to examine police stops in Indianapolis, Indiana, and St. Petersburg, Florida (Mastrofski et al. 1998). Transportation researchers have implemented observation benchmarking to gather information about drivers (such as their seatbelt and helmet use) for the National Occupant Protection Use Survey of the National Highway Traffic Safety Administration (Glassbrenner 2002, 2003). The NHTSA observers also have collected information on the race/ethnicity, gender, and age of drivers.[2]

The observation benchmarking technique, if implemented in accordance with solid methodological standards, can be effective in addressing most or all of the factors associated with the alternative hypotheses to the bias hypothesis (see Chapter 2). These solid methodological standards pertain to the four choices referenced earlier:

- How should the observations be conducted?
- What should be observed?

---

[2] Law enforcement agencies cannot effectively use as benchmark data these national data on drivers' demographic characteristics. They should, however, contact their state or local transportation departments to determine if observation data on the race/ethnicity of drivers have been collected for their jurisdiction. This localized information might be helpful for benchmarking police stops. Transportation resources that could be useful for analyzing police-citizen contact data are discussed more fully in Chapter 10.

- What locations should be selected for observation?
- When should the observations be conducted?[3]

We discuss each of these questions below with concrete examples from relevant studies. We also explain how to train observers, conduct the observation benchmarking analysis, and draw conclusions from the results.

METHODS OF OBSERVATION

Observations can be conducted from stationary or mobile positions. With stationary methods, the researcher places observers at locations beside roadways; with mobile methods (also called "rolling" or "carousel" methods), the observers are placed in vehicles that move with traffic.

Stationary Methods

Stationary methods have been used to observe the demographic characteristics of drivers on urban and suburban roads as well as on highways. As noted earlier, John Lamberth (1996a, 1996b, 2001) has been instrumental in developing these methods. For his work in urban and suburban areas, he places observers at carefully selected intersections, and the observers record the race/ethnicity (as well as age and gender) of the drivers passing through those intersections. The demographic profile of the people passing through the intersections is compared to the demographic profile of people stopped by police in the same geographic areas.

A research team led by Geoff Alpert, conducting analysis for the Miami–Dade County Police Department, also used stationary methods of observation. It collected demographic data at or near carefully selected intersections for all drivers and for

---

[3] This list of questions corresponds closely to the "who, where, what, and when" of systematic social observation as set forth in Mastrofski et al. (1998). This valuable document about the implementation of the observation methodology to study police policy issues is available at www.ncjrs.org/pdffiles/172859.pdf.

drivers violating specified traffic codes (Alpert Group 2003). Engel, Calnon, and Dutill (2003) used stationary methods to create benchmarks for highway stops in Pennsylvania, and Lange, Blackman, and Johnson (2001) used stationary methods in New Jersey. The Miami-Dade, Pennsylvania and New Jersey teams combined human observation with radar to measure drivers' demographic characteristics and speed. The researchers placed the observers and radar technology alongside the roadways.[4]

Some have questioned whether stationary observers by the side of highways can satisfactorily assess the racial/ethnic characteristics of drivers (see, for example, Smith et al. 2003). In the study by Lange, Blackman, and Johnson (2001), one third of the data collected for analysis had to be excluded because the drivers' race/ethnicity could not be reliably determined. This was not only because of the speed of the vehicles but also because of windshield glare, bad weather, and shadows.[5]

Engel and Calnon (2003) report a different experience. These researchers tested whether observers stationed by the side of fast-moving highways would be able to discern the demographic characteristics of drivers. Their observers were able to readily capture the race and other demographic characteristics of passing motorists. Indeed, 97 percent of the observations produced agreement among observers on race using categories of "white" and "nonwhite." Importantly, observations were restricted to daylight hours and to days when weather

---

[4] In addition to this stationary method of using radar, it is technically feasible to use radar in moving vehicles. Smith et al. (2003) used in-vehicle radar to test their stopwatch method for measuring speed, not to collect benchmark data.

[5] The U.S. Department of Justice expressed concern about the research of Lange, Blackman, and Johnson and requested that they conduct additional analyses to produce a better understanding of the impact of the excluded data. Lange and his colleagues had argued that the missing data were probably neutral as to the drivers' race/ethnicity and therefore would not affect their analysis of racially biased policing.

conditions permitted sufficient visibility (Engel, Calnon, and Dutill 2003; Engel and Calnon forthcoming).

Mobile Methods

Using observation benchmarking, Smith et al. (2003) conducted a comprehensive study of stops made by the North Carolina State Highway Patrol. They rejected the stationary methods for their work because they found the observers could not discern drivers' demographic characteristics due to vehicle speeds and window glare. Instead, the research team placed a driver and three observers inside two "observer vans" that moved along selected roadway segments at the speed limit. One observer recorded the demographic characteristics of the drivers of vehicles passing the van (along with information regarding the vehicle), and the other two observers measured the speed of these vehicles using stopwatches. (The two speed measures were averaged.)

For his work in New Jersey and Maryland, Lamberth (1996a, 1996b) placed observers in cars that went up and down specified sections of the turnpikes. In New Jersey the speed of the observer car was 4 miles per hour over the speed limit; in Maryland the car went the speed limit. The car moved in the middle lane, and some observers were assigned to collect information about drivers in the lane to the left of the car, and others collected data about drivers in the lane to the right. Lamberth's team collected demographic data regarding drivers who passed the observer car (the speeders) and compared it to the demographics of drivers stopped by police in the vicinity.

To assess racial bias for the Rhode Island State Police, a team from Northeastern University's Institute on Race and Justice, led by Amy Farrell and Jack McDevitt, conducted rolling surveys on Interstate-95. Three to four people were assigned to the observation van for each shift. During each shift, the van drove the highway from one end of the state to the other multiple times. Every thirty seconds the observers coded the driver's race (as White, Black, Hispanic, Asian, or Native American) and other information (the driver's gender, the number of occupants in the vehicle, the state in which the vehicle was registered, and the license plate number) for the car next to the observation vehicle (Farrell et al. 2003).[6]

The mobile methods of observation benchmarking are particularly well suited for highway observations, although researchers for the Home Office in the United Kingdom used mobile observations in an urban area. The U.K. researchers positioned in a van a camera that was pointed toward the oncoming traffic. (This camera was positioned in such a way as to videotape drivers and pedestrians.) After the fact, driver (and pedestrian) demographics were tabulated for a random subset of the video data (see MVA and Miller 2000).

FOCUS OF OBSERVATIONS

As noted earlier, researchers using observation benchmarking need to decide whether to compare the stop data (the numerator) against demographic data for all drivers regardless of driving quality and/or for traffic law–violating drivers. The former entails collecting data on the race/ethnicity of drivers on the roadways; the latter entails collecting data on the race/ethnicity of drivers who are violating specific traffic laws. If demographic data are collected on all drivers (that is, nonviolating and violating drivers), the agency has addressed the alternative hypothesis that *racial/ethnic groups are not equally represented as drivers on jurisdiction roads.* It has not, however, addressed the alternative hypothesis that *racial/ethnic groups are not equivalent in the nature and extent of their traffic law–violating behavior.*

---

[6] The Northeastern University team decided against measuring "who is speeding" because the high speeding threshold of the state police would have required the observer van to go 80 miles per hour (McDevitt 2003). In addition to these rolling surveys, the team has conducted stationary observations within certain municipalities to benchmark their stop data.

Those who favor observing all drivers argue that everyone violates traffic laws (see Appendices D and E). This may be true, but it does not mean that everyone is equivalent in the nature and extent of their law-violating behavior. Those who violate serious traffic laws or who violate laws frequently are at greater risk of being stopped by police than are other traffic law violators. Because it is not known whether violating behavior differs across racial/ethnic groups, agencies should try to account for the possibility of this variation. It is preferable to collect demographics for drivers who are violating because this method addresses the alternative hypothesis that *racial/ethnic groups are not equivalent in the nature and extent of their traffic law–violating behavior*. The added strength of this analysis, however, comes at a cost in terms of scope, as discussed more fully below.

Of course, it would be impossible to observe, measure, and record all traffic law–violating behavior (speeding, following too closely, failing to yield, illegally changing lanes, and many other traffic transgressions). Most of the researchers who have utilized the observation method to measure violating behavior have focused on speeding violations (Lamberth 2001; Smith et al. 2003; Lange, Blackman, and Johnson 2001; Engel, Calnon, and Dutill 2003).

Measuring Speeding Behavior

As mentioned above, Lamberth, in his early studies, assessed speeding behavior by using an observer car going at a set speed (the speed limit or 4 miles per hour faster). Observers obtained a racial/ethnic profile of the drivers who passed, or were passed by, the observer car. Engel, Calnon, and Dutill (2003) used radar and observation to develop benchmarks in their study of the Pennsylvania State Police. For this study the researchers placed two observers with radar equipment at the selected observation points. In a vehicle by the side of the road or in the median, the observers used the radar to record the speed of passing vehicles, and each assessed the race of the driver.

Lange, Blackman, and Johnson (2001) also used radar to assess speed and cameras to record the race/ethnicity of the speeding drivers. An apparatus that combined radar with digital photography and a strobe light was situated at various locations at the side of the New Jersey Turnpike. The apparatus detected who was speeding,[7] measured the speed of the vehicle, flashed a strobe light to increase illumination at night and to "reduce glare and shadows within vehicles during daylight sampling," and tripped a camera that took a picture of the driver of the vehicle (Lange, Blackman, and Johnson 2001, 3).[8] The "observers" in this study were sitting at computers at another location and viewed the camera data after the fact. The observers made assessments of race, ethnicity, gender, and age. The observers could enlarge the photos to facilitate categorization and were "blind" as to the speed of the driver. Three people made the demographic assessments for each driver; at least two had to agree on categorizations of race and sex or the variables were coded as missing and the case removed from the data set.

Zingraff et al. (2000; see also Smith et al. 2003) has cautioned against the use of radar to measure speed, arguing that drivers slow down if they have their own radar detection devices that alert them to radar nearby. Engel and Calnon (2003) and Lange, Blackman, and Johnson (2001) have a different view; they argue that since *police* use of radar would *also* slow traffic, the effect is not specific to the research but rather reflects real-life conditions. In sum, researchers are split on the advisability of using radar to measure speed.

---

[7] The team "received from the State" (Lange, Blackman, and Johnson 2001, 2) information regarding the speeds at which troopers are likely to ticket. Based on this information, the team then defined speeding as 15 miles per hour or more over the posted speed limit.

[8] System operators also triggered the system manually 25 to 50 times per hour to get pictures (and thus the demographics) of a "random" subset of drivers. This produced a demographic profile of the drivers on the road, regardless of violating behavior.

The North Carolina team (Smith et al. 2003) used stopwatches rather than radar to gauge the actual speed of vehicles. The team measured the time it took for a "subject vehicle" to pass from the rear bumper to the front bumper of the "observer vehicle" moving at the speed limit. Specifically, two individuals in the observer vehicle started their stopwatches when a subject vehicle's front bumper crossed the "imaginary line" that extended from the back bumper of the observer vehicle; they stopped their watches when the vehicle's front bumper crossed the "imaginary line" that extended from the front bumper of the observer vehicle. The researchers averaged the two times and converted the average to a specific vehicle speed.[9]

When measuring speeding behavior, researchers must decide how to define speeding. Technically, a driver going even 1 mile per hour over the speed limit is speeding. Such a cut-off point, however, does not necessarily reflect speeding that puts the driver at risk of being stopped by police. Conceptually, researchers should operationalize speeding to reflect the point at which the driver is at risk of being pulled over by police. Whether that cut-off point should be 5, 10, or 15 miles per hour over the speed limit depends on the law enforcement agency's policy or practice for stopping speeding drivers. In Pennsylvania, where Engel, Calnon, and Dutill (2003) conducted their observation research, a state law holds that citations can be issued only if the driver is exceeding the speed limit by at least 6 miles per hour. In other jurisdictions informal policy rather than state law can be used by researchers to set the "min-

---

[9] These stopwatch measurements of speed were then tested at the training track used by the North Carolina State Highway Patrol. "Stopwatch recorders" timed the speed of passing cars. Those speeds were then compared to the actual speeds confirmed by radar. Zingraff et al. (2000) determined that the stopwatch method was not precise, but, importantly, it was reliably imprecise: the stopwatch measures of speed were consistently lower than the actual speeds. These tests enabled Zingraff et al. (2000) to create a "corrective equation" that they applied to all stopwatch measurements on the highway.

imum limit." A researcher could determine the most viable cut-off point by reviewing data on citations to determine practice in this regard and/or by conducting interviews or focus groups with officers. Complicating efforts to define speeding, however, is the finding of the North Carolina team that speeding thresholds may vary across roadways within a jurisdiction (Smith et al. 2003).

Speeding can be measured as a dichotomous (that is, two-part) variable or as a continuous variable. To create a dichotomous measure of speed, a researcher would select a cut-off point ("X" miles per hour over the speed limit, where "X" might be 1, 5, 15, etc.) and code data to indicate whether the driver *was* or *was not* driving at speeds above this cut-off level. Some measures of speed described earlier in the chapter (for example, those of Engel, Calnon, and Dutill 2003; Smith et al. 2003) are continuous. The stopwatch and radar methods allow the researcher to determine the actual speed of the vehicle and this number is used as the measure. As an example, cars going 53 mph and 67 mph in a 55 mph zone would, in a dichotomous coding scheme, be coded as "not speeding" and "speeding," respectively. If a researcher was using continuous measures, the two cars would be recorded as going 53 and 67 mph, respectively. Continuous measures of speed are superior to dichotomous ones because they provide more information that can aid researchers in their analysis. For instance, with speed measured as a continuous variable, the researcher's analysis can show that not all speeders are equally likely to get stopped (presumably, the greater the speed of the vehicle, the greater the likelihood of being pulled over), and the researcher can address concerns and conjectures that minority speeders are pulled over at lower speeds than are Caucasian speeders. Additionally, continuous variables can be transformed into dichotomous variables, while the converse is not true. Because of these strengths, we recommend that researchers develop, if their methods permit, a continuous measure of speeding.

Measuring Multiple Violations

In measuring only one violating behavior, such as speeding, a researcher limits the scope of the assessment of racially biased policing. The limiting parameter of the benchmark will need to be matched by a corresponding parameter limiting the numerator. That is, the researcher can use only those stops that police made on the basis of, in this case, speeding violations. This reduction in the scope of the analysis is required because one cannot assume that the same people who violate speeding laws violate other traffic laws. Therefore, it is often preferable, albeit more difficult, to measure more than one type of traffic law-violating behavior.[10]

Using the observation benchmarking method, the Miami-Dade research team (Alpert Group 2003) measured speeding (defined as 5 miles per hour over the posted speed limit), red light violations, and illegal turns.[11] At sixteen selected intersections, the team collected data on the race and gender of all drivers and of drivers violating these three types of traffic laws. The researchers assigned two people to each of three data collection tasks. One pair of observers, situated at the intersection, recorded the race and gender for all drivers passing through the intersection; during times when the traffic was too heavy to make reliable observations of race and gender, these observers focused on "the two fastest lanes of traffic"[12] (Alpert Group 2003, 9). A second pair of observers, located several blocks away from the intersection, used a radar gun to identify speeders before the traffic slowed for the intersec-

---

[10] If most of a law enforcement agency's traffic stops are for speeding, it is appropriate for the agency to focus its research on this one type of violation (Engel and Calnon 2003). Stop data for the Pennsylvania State Police, the subject of Engel, Calnon, and Dutill's research, indicated that approximately three-fourths of all stops were for speeding.

[11] Illegal turns include turning from a nonturning lane, making a u-turn at intersections where such turns are prohibited, or turning without yielding to oncoming traffic.

[12] This practice may skew the benchmark since the demographics of the drivers in the two fastest lanes may not be the same as the demographics of all drivers in all lanes.

tion. One person operated the radar gun to detect speeders, and the other observed the gender and race of the specified speeder.[13] The third pair of observers, which like the first pair was located at the intersection, recorded the race and gender of drivers who went through a red light or made illegal turns.[14]

Choosing a Denominator

We return here to the key decision facing researchers using observation benchmarking to assess whether policing in a jurisdiction is racially biased. Should the denominator (that is, the benchmark) be based on all drivers in an area (a measure of "who is driving"), or should the denominator be based on drivers violating one or more traffic laws (a measure of "who is violating")? In other words, should the racial/ethnic profile of drivers stopped by police (the numerator) be compared to the racial/ethnic profile of observed drivers or observed drivers who are violating a traffic law or laws? The answer, as we mentioned above, affects the validity and scope of the analysis. The researcher who collects "who is driving" data can benchmark all stops by police. The researcher who collects data on "who is speeding," for example, can benchmark only stops for speeding because the numerator and denominator must match.

Some researchers are collecting and analyzing data on both "who is violating" and "who is driving" to provide for a more comprehensive assessment of racially biased policing (Alpert Group 2003; Engel, Calnon, and Dutill 2003). The "who is violating" data provide for the most rigorous analysis, but this choice of a denominator reduces the scope of the study, as we

---

[13] If more than one speeding car was passing, the radar gun selected the fastest moving vehicle; the race/gender observer, too, recorded for the fastest moving vehicle.

[14] According to the Alpert Group (2003, 9-10): "Only the most obvious violations were to be recorded, thus eliminating the inclusion of debatable violations" (those that may not actually qualify as infractions of the law or be serious enough to warrant a ticket by police).

have explained. To glean the best from both methods, Engel, Calnon, and Dutill (2003) collected two sets of data. They conducted the more rigorous analysis with the "who is violating" data—an analysis that was limited in scope to stops by police for speeding. They conducted a broader, albeit less rigorous, analysis with the "who is driving" data. That is, for the latter analysis they benchmarked who is driving against who is stopped, and they included all types of stops in the analysis.

Measuring Demographics
The assessment of race/ethnicity for the benchmark data relies upon the perception of the observers—and their perception, presumably, will be in error some unknown proportion of the time. Similarly, observation is the preferred way for officers to measure race/ethnicity for purposes of filling out their data collection forms; to the extent that officers make stopping decisions based on race/ethnicity, they do so based on their perceptions of race/ethnicity, not on the basis of, for instance, information on the driver's license.[15] Since the perceptions of officers is the preferred method for identifying race/ethnicity for the numerator data, the perceptions of trained observers is equally viable as the method for obtaining the denominator data.[16]

Categories of Race/Ethnicity
With regard to the key variable of interest, the race/ethnicity of drivers, researchers need to recognize how difficult it is for both

---

[15] In fact, trainers should make it clear to officers that their perception of a driver's race/ethnicity at the time they decide to stop the driver is the information they should record on the form. Officers should not change the data they put on the form related to race if, for instance, after reviewing license information, they determine that their initial perception was incorrect.

[16] However, the vantage point of the observers is generally superior to that of the officers. As an example, observers stationed at the side of the road at an intersection (or in the median) have a better view of drivers than does the officer who, in many instances, will make a decision to stop from behind the vehicle. Therefore, researchers are not, in fact, collecting data that fully reflect what the officers on the road might see.

police and observers to make fine distinctions between racial and ethnic groups. In the context of implementing the observation method, this difficulty has ramifications for the categories of race and ethnicity used for data collection. Particularly problematic—report researchers who have used this method (for example, Alpert Group 2003; Smith et al. 2003)—is identifying *ethnicity* through observation. It also is difficult for observers—particularly stationary observers collecting data on fast-moving vehicles—to distinguish among, for instance, Middle Easterners, Hispanics, and Native Americans. The ability to discern race/ethnicity can be impacted by the time of day[17] as well as the speed of vehicles under observation.

Because of the difficulty of perceiving accurately a driver's race/ethnicity, many of the researchers implementing observation benchmarking use two or three observers. The pair or group of observers records demographic data for the same drivers, and then the researchers test and report the inter-rater reliability of the observers' findings.[18] Researchers generally require that both members of a pair of observers or two out of a group of three observers agree on the race/ethnicity of the driver.

---

[17] When selecting intersections for observation benchmarking, Lamberth (2002) considers nighttime visibility. His team chooses intersections with lighting, and sometimes it brings in additional lighting to help observers discern the demographic characteristics of drivers. Lamberth reports that missing data at night due to the inability to see driver demographics are only "slightly more" than the corresponding missing data from daylight observations (Lamberth, Lamberth, and Clayton 2003). For instance, in a particularly well-lit intersection, the Lamberth team reported that it had 2.4 percent missing data for demographics during the day and just 4.1 percent during the night (Lamberth 2003). In contrast, Rojek, Rosenfeld, and Decker (2002) report that at night their observers were unable to discern the race of drivers in 40 percent of the vehicles.

[18] In Rhode Island the team from Northeastern University's Institute on Race and Justice reports 95 percent inter-rater reliability for race/ethnicity data recorded during daytime observations. According to the team, the problems with inter-rater reliability pertained to the identification of Hispanic drivers. It reports "nearly identical" inter-rater reliability with regard to the other observation information collected (Farrell et al. 2003, 35).

Researchers have addressed the problem of discerning the demographic characteristics of drivers by broadening categories of race/ethnicity to more closely match what observers can see. For instance, Engel and Calnon (2003) originally asked observers to determine whether the drivers were Caucasian, Black, Hispanic, Asian/Pacific Islander, Native American, Middle Eastern, or Other. Both of the observers (two were assigned to watch each vehicle) had to agree on the designation. During the pilot study, however, in a significant number of instances, the observers agreed that the person was not Caucasian, but they could not agree on the specific racial/ethnic category. Because of this problem during the pilot, new instructions were given to observers in the post-pilot, formal data collection effort: if both observers could not agree on a specific racial/ethnic category for a driver they agreed was not Caucasian, the driver's race should be coded simply as "not Caucasian" (Engel and Calnon 2003).

Other researchers (Alpert Group 2003) decided to measure race only in two categories, "Black" and "Non-Black." Although conducting its research in the Miami area where there is a large population of Hispanics, Alpert's team did not ask observers to try to record ethnicity data. The team acknowledged its inability to measure Hispanic origin (and distinguish more finely among races) with any degree of acceptable accuracy. The Missouri team (Rojek, Rosenfeld, and Decker 2002) asked observers to record drivers' race/ethnicity in two categories: Whites and non-Hispanic Blacks (Rojek, Rosenfeld, and Decker 2002). The Home Office in the United Kingdom (MVA and Miller 2000) used categories of White, Black, Asian, and Other; it also gave the observer the option of coding "Non-White" when the driver was a minority, but the observer could not tell which minority group. This new option reduced the amount of missing data on the race variable.[19]

---

[19] The issues regarding the designation of categories of race/ethnicity for purposes of observation are equally relevant to decisions made by departments concerning the categories to use on their data collection forms filled out by officers.

To reduce the amount of missing data regarding race/ethnicity, agencies can use broad categories for the primary coding scheme and include a "Non-White" or "Not Caucasian" option as well. Not only should a researcher be concerned about the amount of missing data as a result of observers' inability to perceive the race/ethnicity of drivers. The researcher also must consider the possibility that the missing data are not race-neutral. As indicated earlier, it is most challenging for observers to discern between Hispanics and other races/ethnicities. If each time the observer cannot make this distinction with confidence the data are coded as missing, the resulting data could significantly under-report Hispanic drivers and/or violators. Under-reporting also could occur for other races and ethnicities that are difficult for observers to distinguish.

Another issue related to the designation of race/ethnicity categories for collecting observation data pertains to the size of the racial/ethnic groups among drivers in the jurisdiction. Initially, Lamberth (2001), in one jurisdiction, had his observers attempt to make distinctions between Caucasian, African American, Asian, Hispanic, Middle Eastern, Native American, Pacific Islander, or Other. Later, because of the small number of drivers that fit into several of these categories, he combined categories. The problem of small sample size can be exacerbated if the population of drivers chosen by law enforcement agencies for the denominator data is not all drivers but drivers violating a traffic law; this is because the number of violators within some racial/ethnic groups may be particularly small.[20]

To address the potential problem of small sample sizes, researchers should select racial/ethnic categories for the observation protocol based on (1) the method of observation (stationary or

---

[20] We are not implying that some racial/ethnic groups violate the law less than do other racial/ethnic groups (this, as we have explained, is an unknown); instead the small number could be the result of the racial/ethnic composition of the jurisdiction.

mobile) and (2) the demographic makeup of the jurisdiction population. With regard to the observation methods, the relevant overriding factor is degree of visibility. Examples are constructive in conveying this point. Observers standing in well-lit areas where traffic is slow (for example, at intersections) are likely to be able to make finer distinctions in race/ethnicity than can their counterparts at the side of highways where lighting may be inferior and cars are traveling faster. Conducting pilot tests with the observers in the relevant conditions—as Engel and Calnon (2003) did—will help the researchers determine what racial/ethnic categories are reasonable. With regard to the demographic makeup of the jurisdiction population, it is reasonable to group the smallest minority groups into the "Other Race" category. This is justified because the analyses of small numbers will not provide reliable results.

If an agency has not yet developed its data collection form and anticipates using the observation method, it might choose the racial/ethnic categories identified as reasonable for the observation protocol as the categories to include on the form. If the researchers determine that reasonable demographic categories for purposes of observation are Caucasian, African American, and Other, then the data collection form should use these categories or at least categories that can be combined into these three.[21] For example, the following (not comprehensive) list of eight categories—Hispanic Caucasian, Non-Hispanic Caucasian, African Black, Haitian Black, Other Black, Arab American, Central Asian, Eastern Asian—could be combined into three categories: Caucasian, Black, and Other. If the data

---

[21] In some jurisdictions, however, an agency might decide to include more racial/ethnic categories on its data collection form than in its observation protocol. The reason could be political: that is, an agency might be criticized by the community for not recognizing particular racial/ethnic groups on the form. Or the reason could be related to social science research: expanded categories might be useful for other benchmarking methods, such as internal benchmarking, that might be conducted using the same data. Whatever the agency's reason, the categories on the data collection form should combine easily to produce the categories used by observers.

collection form has already been developed and the demographic categories do not correspond with the categories used in the observation protocol, then adjustments may be required.[22]

Some researchers and stakeholders interested in measuring racially biased policing believe that police may stop drivers, not only on the basis of the race/ethnicity of the driver of a vehicle, but also on the basis of the race/ethnicity of the passengers, the number of passengers, or the interaction of the two. For this reason, some agencies ask officers to record on the data collection form the racial/ethnic characteristics of the passengers as well as of the driver of a vehicle. Correspondingly, some researchers—for example, Lamberth in Washtenaw County (Michigan)—have asked observers to collect demographic data for vehicle passengers. While not necessarily inadvisable, the added complication of incorporating passenger demographics into the analysis of the data may not be worth the added value of the information.

The observers may record demographic characteristics besides race and/or ethnicity. For instance, some researchers have collected information on drivers' age and gender in order to assess the impact of these variables on stopping behavior by police. Age and gender are potential intervening variables; they may independently influence driving quantity and driving quality. Lange, Blackman, and Johnson (2001), who used cameras and radar to develop benchmarks for the analysis of stops made by New Jersey troopers, had their observers record both gender and age.[23] In North Carolina, Smith et al. (2003) collected information on age and gender as well as vehicle color, vehicle type, and the state of the license plate. They extended their data collection efforts in

---

[22] See the discussion of these types of adjustments in Chapter 5 on adjusted census benchmarking.

[23] Lange, Blackman, and Johnson (2001) originally asked their teams of observers to categorize drivers as younger than 25, 25 to 45, and over 45 years of age. Because raters frequently disagreed upon classifications in the first two categories, Lange, Blackman, and Johnson subsequently changed the categories to 45 years of age and under, and over 45. This recategorization increased the reliability of the information.

this way to test whether these nondemographic factors affected decision making by police. Similarly, Engel, Calnon, and Dutill (2003) collected information on race, gender, and age of the driver; type, color, and age of the vehicle; whether or not passengers were present; and whether or not the vehicle was licensed in the state.[24] Lange, Blackman, and Johnson (2001) coded for vehicle type using the categories of truck, commercial, police, auto, motorcycle, and RV. Of these observation measures that could be added, the most important for inclusion are the variables of age and gender. An argument for including nondemographic variables is the finding by Smith et al. (2003) that age of vehicle had a small, but statistically significant, impact on stopping behavior by the North Carolina State Highway Patrol.

Thus far we have described the methods of observation (stationary and mobile). We also have examined the focus of observations (for example, whether agencies should measure "who is driving" or "who is violating" as the basis of their denominator data, what violations to measure, and how to categorize race/ethnicity). In the next section we discuss the location of observations, another area of decision making for agencies that have chosen observation benchmarking as a way to assess whether policing in their jurisdiction is racially biased.

LOCATION OF OBSERVATIONS

For both stationary and mobile methods of observation benchmarking, researchers must determine the type of locations (for example, "hot spots" versus locations representative of the target jurisdiction as a whole), the number of locations, and the geographic area. Researchers also must decide whether to select observation locations in a random or purposive manner.

---

[24] Age was coded as under 25, 25 to 65, or older than 65. Codes for type of vehicle were sedan, sports car/coupe, sport utility vehicle, minivan/wagon, pickup truck, and motorcycle. Codes for vehicle color were red, blue, green, silver/gray, black, white, and other. Codes for age of vehicle were 10 or fewer years of age and more than 10 years of age.

Site Selection Criteria

A key consideration in selecting sites is the ability of the observers to discern the race/ethnicity of drivers. Relevant factors include the speed of the vehicles, lighting at the site, and where observers stand. In some locations it is not safe for observers to stand near the traffic. Controlled intersections (intersections with a stop sign or light) have some advantages with regard to these variables when stationary methods are being used in an urban or suburban setting. Traffic is generally slower at controlled intersections than at noncontrolled intersections and nonintersections (straightaways). Intersections are also more likely than straightaways to have light sources and safe locations for observer placement.[25]

Lamberth (2002) points out that medians are desirable but not required for observations and that sites other than controlled intersections may provide sufficient visibility. Vehicle speeds and lighting may, in fact, be adequate at noncontrolled intersections or even on straightaways. In locations where there are no existing light sources, Lamberth arranges for temporary "mobile" lighting. Lange, Blackman, and Johnson (2001) also produced their own lighting for their data collection alongside the New Jersey Turnpike.[26]

As described below, Engel and Calnon (2003) and Engel, Calnon, and Dutill (2003) used stationary methods along Pennsylvania interstate and state highways. They report that

---

[25] Another advantage of intersections is that the research team can observe traffic from four directions rather than two (Lamberth 2002).

[26] Artificial lighting can have an unintended effect on the behavior of drivers. They may slow down or, if they think the lighting is a sign of a roadblock of some sort, they may even turn around to drive in the opposite direction. To preclude this latter possibility, the Lamberth team, when it uses artificial lighting, assigns observers to roadways where drivers cannot turn their vehicles around and leave the area when they see the lighting (Lamberth 2002). The tendency for drivers to slow down in response to artificial lighting does not adversely affect the efforts of researchers who are collecting benchmark data on all drivers rather than traffic law–violating drivers.

they were able to safely place observers and that the speed of the vehicles, per se, did not significantly impair observations. However, the lack of lighting (in conjunction with the speed of vehicles) precluded nighttime data collection.[27]

Law enforcement agencies conducting observation benchmarking should also remember that weather conditions can impair observers' ability to identify drivers' race/ethnicity. Engel and Calnon (2003) report that their observations alongside Pennsylvania roads were postponed several times because of blustery days. Pennsylvania's state police prohibit radar stops in bad weather because the safety of drivers detecting radar (for instance, with radar detectors) might be jeopardized if, for instance, they used their brakes suddenly. Thus, the weather kept police from conducting radar stops (the basis of Engel and Calnon's numerator data), and it kept observers from collecting the benchmark or denominator data. This represented a fortuitous matching of the numerator and the denominator.

Like stationary methods of observation benchmarking, mobile methods must be structured to ensure visibility. Observations must take place on thoroughfares with at least two lanes in each direction so that cars can pass the observer vehicle and be passed by it (Lamberth 2002). Lighting may also be a consideration during evenings and nights, but vehicle speed is less likely to be a factor since the observer vehicle is moving with the traffic.

In making site selections, the researcher should also consider volume of activity. That is, the researcher should strive to select sites that have sufficient numbers of both police stops (numerator data) and cars and/or violators passing by the sites to be observed (denominator data) to produce reliable results. There are no easy formulas for determining whether the volume of activity at potential sites is sufficient. A researcher might use

---

[27] Alpert's team also had to forgo nighttime observations due to lack of visibility (Alpert Group 2003).

department data on police stops and/or local transportation department information regarding road usage to identify sites with the greatest volume of stops or traffic.

Random and Purposive Site Selection

In random selection of sites for observation benchmarking, the researcher identifies the locations in a jurisdiction that meet certain criteria and then randomly selects from among those locations. In purposive selection, the researcher will rely completely on specific criteria to select the sites and will not use random selection during this process. Both methods of site selection—random and purposive—produce "spot checks" of racially biased policing. Instead of assessing bias across the entire jurisdiction, the researcher assesses bias in certain specified locations only. The advantage of random selection is that it allows the researcher to generalize. In other words, the results from the selected sites can be applied to other locations in the city that meet the criteria for inclusion in the pool from which the sites were selected. Sometimes, however, a researcher is unable to use random selection for choosing sites because an insufficient number of sites meets the criteria. In short, the pool from which to select the sites in this manner may be too small.

We turn now to the set of criteria that could be used by researchers for random selection (also called random sampling). For instance, to facilitate the ability of the observers to see the vehicles and drivers within them, the researcher might decide that only intersections (not nonintersection portions of roads) will be selected. The researcher also might decide that all of the observation intersections must have a sufficient volume of activity and set a particular cut-off point for inclusion based on an available measure of volume such as traffic stops by police.

After the researcher develops a group of eligible intersections based on the minimum criteria, she or he might begin selecting randomly from among them or incorporate additional selection criteria. For instance, to achieve geographic diversity, the researcher might divide the jurisdiction into sections and select sites from within each of them. The researcher might decide to select from among geographic areas stratified or grouped by other variables such as racial makeup (high minority, low minority, evenly mixed) or traffic type (commercial, residential, mixed).

With purposive site selection, the researcher purposively (not randomly) selects particular sites that meet particular objectives, such as visibility on the part of observers, sufficient volume of activity, geographic diversity, heterogeneity across racial makeup, heterogeneity across traffic type, and so forth. Some additional criteria are introduced in the examples of site selection methods provided below.

How Social Scientists Have Selected Sites

Lamberth (2001) initiated the site selection process in Washtenaw County, Michigan, by analyzing citation data provided by the department. After identifying areas with sufficient numbers of stops to produce reliable data, his team traveled to the county to view the areas that produced sufficient numbers of police stops. It chose eleven intersections as observation sites that maximized geographic coverage of the jurisdiction and facilitated observers' ability to see vehicle occupants. The team selected intersections because the traffic is slowed, and intersections are more likely than straightaways to be well lit; both of these factors enhance the ability of observers to discern the race/ethnicity of drivers. In addition to geographic coverage and visibility, intersections were chosen based on the extent to which the traffic at the intersection was representative of traffic in the area. For example, an intersection with traffic characteristic of the traffic within a five-block radius was preferable to an intersection with traffic characteristic of the traffic within only a two-block radius. In jurisdictions where many more locations are viable than are needed, Lamberth selects randomly from among them.

The Miami-Dade team (Alpert Group 2003) also chose to observe at intersections and used a multistep process for selecting its sites. First, it compiled a list of intersections on the basis of accident volume and ability to discern driver race/ethnicity.[28] Second, it presented this list of intersections to commanders within districts and asked them to identify the racial composition of the area surrounding each intersection.[29] This process produced a list of intersections within three types of neighborhoods: predominantly Caucasian, predominantly African American, and neighborhoods with a mixture of different races.[30]

Site selection might be accomplished by a less sophisticated method than that used by Alpert's Miami-Dade team. A law enforcement agency might use census data to group divisions, beats, or neighborhoods within its jurisdiction into the following categories: (1) high levels of racial/ethnic minorities, (2) low levels of racial/ethnic minorities, and (3) fairly equal levels of

---

[28] Data on accidents at intersections were supplied by the police department. To identify intersections that provided driver visibility, the team relied upon a previously conducted observation study. The same intersections were chosen that had been selected by a team of researchers measuring seatbelt use with the observation method.

[29] The team wanted to ensure diversity of sites in terms of racial makeup. Research has shown that some police behaviors and/or strategies vary by neighborhood. (See, for instance, Meehan and Ponder 2002.) Therefore, when law enforcement agencies attempt to assess whether policing in their jurisdiction is racially biased, they should study varying racial environments. Although the Alpert Group (2003) originally used commanders' perceptions to classify intersections, it later developed a more sophisticated approach. Specifically, it used four measures to classify intersections by racial composition: the perception of the police, the race of residents for the census block around the intersection, the race of residents for the census tract around the intersection, and the racial makeup of drivers observed driving through the intersection.

[30] The Alpert Group (2003) also added an intersection to its list based on community input. At a community meeting the team explained the observation benchmarking methodology, and resident participants expressed disappointment that no observations would be conducted within a particular "important" Black neighborhood. In response, the researchers added an intersection from this area to their list of sites.

Caucasians and racial/ethnic minorities. The researcher would then further divide the areas by type of traffic, such as high-density commercial or low-density residential. (This scheme reflects area stratification based on racial makeup and traffic type. It will work only in jurisdictions with numerous intersections.) Finally, the researcher would randomly select intersections from within each of the resulting subgroups.

For their mobile survey along North Carolina roadways under the jurisdiction of the state's highway patrol, Smith et al. (2003) selected fourteen stretches of roadway, each between ten and fifteen miles long: three sites on Interstate 95, four on Interstate 85, two on Interstate 40, and another five on U.S. or N.C. highways.[31] All were four-lane highways because two-lane highways would not permit a sufficient number of vehicles to pass the observer vehicle, and six- or eight-lane highways were too distracting to the observers and complicated in terms of data collection. These stretches along four-lane highways were purposively selected by researchers on the basis of the following criteria:

- They had to have a sufficient number of traffic stops by police (as measured by citations given along the stretches during the months preceding the observation).
- They had to have "appreciable numbers of African Americans driving on the segment" (Smith et al. 2003, 260).
- They could not be too busy because this would jeopardize the safety of the observers.[32]

---

[31] The number of stretches was based on budgetary considerations; that is, the team picked as many as the budget would allow.

[32] Also for safety reasons, the observers did not work during rush hours. An additional criteria was convenience: the roadway had to be sufficiently close to Raleigh, the home base of the research team.

In their project designed to measure whether the Pennsylvania State Police were racially biased, Engel, Calnon, and Dutill (2003) developed a sophisticated method for selecting roadway observation sites. By virtue of their task, they did not select intersections within urban areas but rather sections of highways (under the jurisdiction of the state police) within urban, suburban, and rural areas. Site selection was based on (1) general extent of roadway usage, (2) roadway usage by minorities, and (3) the degree to which the race/ethnicity of drivers on the roadways was expected to reflect the race/ethnicity of the residential population in the surrounding area. To begin, Engel, Calnon, and Dutill gauged general roadway usage in this manner. For each of the sixty-seven counties in Pennsylvania, they used census data to obtain the total residential population. With information from the Pennsylvania Department of Transportation, they then obtained for each county the number of interstate miles and the total miles of roadway. As a proxy measure of roadway usage by minorities, they gathered census information for each county on the percentage of residents who were African American and the percentage who were Hispanic.

The third selection factor (the degree to which drivers on the roadways were expected to reflect the surrounding residential population) need not be used by researchers replicating the Pennsylvania team's model. This factor is not directly related to the research objective of determining whether racially biased policing exists. Rather, it was used to help the Pennsylvania researchers evaluate the extent to which census benchmarking and observation benchmarking produce similar racial/ethnic profiles. In certain geographic areas, the racial/ethnic profile of residents produced by census data may resemble the racial/ethnic profile of drivers produced by observation data. In jurisdictions where the two profiles match, future analyses within those areas can rely on census benchmarking.

To measure whether roadway usage by drivers in various counties was likely to reflect residential populations, the research team developed two dichotomous variables: "the presence of tourist attractions, colleges and universities or historical sites" and "the presence of seasonal attractions (e.g., amusement parks, water parks, ski resorts, etc.)" (Engel, Calnon, and Dutill 2003, 5-6). The team reasoned that counties with tourist attractions, colleges, and so forth would have more non-resident drivers on the roads than counties without these attractions and facilities.

With factor analysis the team identified a single construct that it then used to rank the counties as high, medium, medium-low, and low. The single construct or "underlying dimension could be thought of as something that measures (roadway usage), larger volumes of travel by minorities, or travel patterns that may not match residential populations" (Engel and Calnon forthcoming). The team selected counties from within each group. Proportionately more counties were selected as it moved from the low to the high groupings.

Having selected twenty counties based on these procedures, the team selected specific stretches of roads within the selected counties for purposes of observation. To do this, Engel, Calnon, and Dutill (2003) asked station commanders (lieutenants) of the Pennsylvania State Police to identify potential observation sites based on four criteria. First, the site had to have a relatively high volume of traffic. Second, the site had to be representative of the travel patterns in the county. Third, the site had to be in an area where troopers issue a significant number of citations. Fourth, the site had to be suitable for safe and effective observation; in other words, the team chose locations where the observers could safely and effectively use radar, as well as observe the race/ethnicity of drivers.

TIMING OF OBSERVATIONS

Observation benchmarking requires researchers to make decisions not only about the method, focus, and location of observations but also about their timing (the days of the week, the times of the day, and the length of the reference period). Decisions related to timing are important because the racial/ethnic composition of drivers on the roadways may vary considerably across days of week, times of day, or even seasons of the year.[33] Choices related to the timing of observations (the denominator data) will affect time-related choices with regard to the stop (numerator) data.

Days of the Week
In selecting days of the week for scheduling observations, researchers strive for "representativeness" in the nature and extent of traffic behavior. Observations could cover all days of the week or, to be more efficient, researchers could develop "categories of days." For example, a researcher might make the reasonable assumption that traffic on Mondays, Tuesdays, Wednesdays, and Thursdays is essentially similar in the area being studied but traffic on Fridays, Saturdays, and Sundays are each unique. (Although Fridays in an urban area would include commuting traffic that is similar to that on other weekdays, Friday evening traffic might be characterized by an influx of suburban residents to entertainment establishments. Saturday traffic might differ because of greater than normal travel to commercial shopping areas or daytime entertainment establishments, and Sunday traffic might be uniquely affected by the population that travels to religious gatherings or events.) Because of these traffic patterns, researchers in most jurisdictions could categorize days as (1) Mondays through Thursdays, (2) Fridays, (3) Saturdays, and (4) Sundays, unless there were particular characteristics of the jurisdiction that required more or fewer categories. The Home Office in the United Kingdom (MVA and Miller 2000) used different categories for selecting observation times: (1) Monday through Thursday, and Friday morning ("typical weekdays"), (2) Friday mid-day through

---

[33] Gaines (2002) conducted observations in Riverside, California, and found larger proportions of minority drivers at night and during the early mornings. Farmer (2001) reported differences in driver demographics on the New Jersey Turnpike across time of day and days of week, and Smith et al. (2003) found racial differences in driving populations across time of day.

"early" Saturday morning, (3) Saturday afternoon through "early" Sunday morning.[34] This categorization is another viable option for jurisdictions.

After identifying categories of days or days/times (as in the scheme of the Home Office), researchers must schedule the times of day for observations.

Times of Day

The times of day for collecting observation data should also reflect the goal of representativeness. For example, researchers would not conduct observations from 6 P.M. to midnight if they wanted to benchmark stops made during all times of the day. Without observation times that provide for representativeness, the observations will produce skewed data regarding the demographics of drivers or violators.

Hypothetical Variation in Driving Population by Time of Day
Many, if not most, intersections have a different type of driving population at various times of day. During the middle of the day, most drivers at one hypothetical intersection might be Caucasian females. During the morning and evening hours—when stopping activity by police is greatest at this intersection—the population of male and minority drivers might be larger than at mid-day. If most of the observations are conducted during the day, then the researcher will produce a benchmark that mischaracterizes the drivers to which the police are most frequently exposed when they are in the area. (This variation within an intersection may also cut across days of the week.)

Random or Purposive Selection of Times of Day
Like the selection of sites, the selection of observation times can be purposive or random. Again, random selection enhances

---

[34] Except for the "early" hours, Sunday was not included in the analysis. That is, the Sunday stops by police were not analyzed, and observations were not conducted.

generalizeability. To schedule observations, researchers can randomly select blocks of time (for example, four-hour blocks) for each intersection or for a group of intersections.[35] Alternatively, researchers can stratify blocks of time by days of the week and shift (for example, day, evening, night). Researchers might decide not to select (whether randomly or purposively) the same number of blocks (let us say five blocks of time) from each grouping of days and shifts. Instead, the researchers might tailor the number of time blocks from each grouping to the volume of traffic activity as measured by traffic flow or traffic stops.[36] Thus, if researchers have information indicating that traffic volume in the jurisdiction as a whole is twice as high on weekdays during the evening shift than at other day/time categories, they could select twice as many time blocks for observations during weekday evenings.

If observation time blocks have been selected that provide for representativeness across days and times and the observations taken during those days and times are proportionate to activity volume, researchers can conduct analyses for all days and all times combined. However, if representativeness and proportionality are not achieved, researchers should conduct separate analyses for different days or categories of days and/or for the various times of day (for example, day shift, evening shift, night shift). For each analysis of this type, the researchers must match the numerator to the denominator. For instance, Saturday observations must be matched with Saturday stops or evening observations with evening stops. Even a researcher who has produced representativeness and proportionality might choose to conduct separate analyses within time categories. With separate analyses, a law enforcement agency may be able to determine whether

---

[35] If researchers choose a time block (say, 4 p.m. to 8 p.m.) for the entire group of intersections, they may not have a sufficiently large number of observers to collect data at all of the sites at the same time.

[36] For traffic flow data, researchers can contact the local transportation department. The police department can provide information on traffic stops.

disparity in stops across racial/ethnic groups, if it exists, is stronger during certain shifts and/or during certain days of the week. This specific information can be used for purposes of interventions to alleviate problems.

How Social Scientists Have Selected Observation Times

Observation methodologists have selected observation times in different ways. Lamberth schedules multiple observation periods at each selected site or stretch of roadway "during randomly selected times of the week and hours of the day" (Lamberth 2001, 4). The length of time and the location of the site are governed by the number of cars that need to be observed. The Lamberth team members seek to observe 1,000 to 3,000 motorists at each site.[37]

Because of the lack of visibility at night, the Miami-Dade team (Alpert Group 2003) observed its sixteen sites only during the daytime and evenings. To prevent observer fatigue, it selected four-hour blocks within eight-hour shifts: 9 A.M. to 1 P.M. for the day shift that ran 6 A.M. to 2 P.M., and 4 P.M. to 8 P.M. for the evening shift that ran from 2 P.M. to 10 P.M.[38] The team randomly selected days of the week, excluding Sundays because of the low number of observations for the benchmark data and the low number of police stops for the numerator data.[39] Each site was observed for a total of eight hours, producing 128 hours of observation data during a six-month period.

---

[37] This range produces a sufficient number of observations for reliable analysis, but the number of motorists is not so high that all inference tests will show significance merely by virtue of the large sample. Preliminary observations at selected sites produce estimates of how much observing time will be required to see the fixed number of motorists.

[38] The researchers determined that observations running the full eight-hour shift would increase the fatigue of the observers, thus affecting the validity of the data. Rush hours were avoided because the traffic proved too unwieldy for observers to identify the race/ethnicity of the drivers.

[39] Agencies observing speeding vehicles may want to exclude rush hours. The traffic density then may produce insufficient numbers in terms of both speeding vehicles and police stops for speeding (Engel and Calnon 2003).

From mid-May through the end of June, the North Carolina team observed fourteen sites for six hours a day (9:30 A.M. to 11:30 A.M., 1 P.M. to 3 P.M., and 6 P.M. to 8 P.M.) across four weekdays during a single week for each site.[40] Thus, the total was twenty-four hours of observation for each site. It did not observe at night, at noon, or during the morning and evening rush time—periods when troopers were more likely to be attending to accidents than disseminating speeding tickets. (Recall that speeding violations were what the team was measuring with observation.)

Within each of the selected twenty counties in Pennsylvania, Engel and her team conducted approximately 75 hours of observation, for a total of 1,500 hours of observation. (The number of sites within each county varied.) They scheduled their observations to provide variation across days of the week, times of day, and months of the year "to allow for day, time, and seasonal variation in traffic patterns" (Engel, Calnon, and Dutill 2003, 8).

During a three-month period, Lange, Blackman, and Johnson (2001) collected forty-eight hours of data at each of their fourteen observation locations along the New Jersey Turnpike. The researchers do not provide detail regarding their selections of times; they state that "images were taken at each location on a weekend and weekday. No sampling occurred on holidays or Mother's Day" (Lange, Blackman, and Johnson 2001, 6).

Reference Period

In some jurisdictions the nature and extent of traffic vary during different times of the year. (For example, a southwestern city experiences an influx of northern tourists during the winter months, and a university town with a popular football team has more traffic during the fall.) This seasonal variation will affect

---

[40] They used these observation data to benchmark police stops and citations that occurred during May through July.

the population of drivers on the roadways and thus the racial/ethnic profile of drivers will vary by season. On the other hand, other jurisdictions may have no seasonal variation in their traffic.[41]

Researchers can handle suspected seasonal variation in several ways. One option, the one chosen by Farrell et al. (2003), is to conduct the analyses using a full year of data; that is, the researcher would conduct observations at various points throughout a twelve-month period.[42] A twelve-month reference period, however, may not be economically feasible or politically viable. Residents may not expect to wait a year for the results of the analysis. Researchers who choose a reference period of less than one year (for example, six months) must include in the report a caveat that the results do not necessarily apply to the parts of the year for which data were not analyzed. As noted earlier, the researcher will need to adjust the stop data to match the time period encompassed by the observation data. That is, if observation data are collected during the period of January through April, the researcher will select for numerator data only stops made by police during that same period, or a reasonably comparable one.[43]

---

[41] For instance, in Washtenaw County there was "little difference in the reported race of the transient population between Fall and Spring (data collection)," according to Lamberth (2001, 5).

[42] Such a long reference period for the analysis of stops has an advantage: officers are likely to get used to the ongoing data collection effort over time and behave more naturally.

[43] Similar to the consequences of seasonal variation is the possible negative impact on representativeness of special events, such as a major festival or basketball conference championship. Researchers may choose to analyze those events separately; that is, they may collect observation data for the event and analyze the stops during that event using the corresponding observation data. If, on the other hand, no observations were conducted during the special event, researchers may reasonably choose to remove from the stop data, the stops that occurred in the location, and during the time, of the special event. In the same vein, researchers should be attuned to major changes in driving behavior that may be caused by, for instance, the opening of a new plant.

TRAINING OBSERVERS

Researchers conducting observation benchmarking for law enforcement agencies need to answer the questions we have posed thus far: How should the observations be conducted? What should be observed? What locations should be selected for observation? When should the observations be conducted? They also must train the individuals who will be making the observations in order to ensure that they collect data that are as accurate as possible (enhancing validity) and do so in a manner similar to each other (enhancing reliability).

Lange, Blackman, and Johnson (2001) selected observers based on their ability to accurately classify the race/ethnicity of selected drivers. They showed applicants videotaped records of drivers whose race/ethnicity was known by the researchers. (These drivers had self-identified their race and/or ethnicity.) Applicants were assessed on the extent to which their racial/ethnic classifications of the videotaped drivers matched the self-classifications by the pictured drivers. The observers who were selected were then trained to perform accurate classifications—again through the use of existing videotaped images of drivers. "Through group discussion of images with known self-identification, we made the process of racial and ethnic classification as systematic and uniform as possible for the visual cues to be used," explained Lange, Blackman, and Johnson (2001, 2).

The Lamberth (2001) team begins training observers by explaining the observation benchmarking study and the critical role of the observers in it. The observers' tasks are then described. The team also organizes "hands-on practice in the field" (Lamberth 2001, 3). Under supervision, the observers conduct pilot observations and record their findings on data sheets. They receive feedback on their work. Additional training is required if observers are using radar or otherwise measuring violating behavior. Observers for the Miami-Dade and Pennsylvania teams were instructed by certified trainers in the use of radar. The Pennsylvania observers received four hours of classroom instruction on the use of radar, four hours of hands-on radar practice, four hours of classroom instruction on the observation methodology, and four hours of observation training in the field.

If more than one observer collects data for the same drivers, the reliability of the data is increased. Engel, Calnon, and Dutill (2003) used two observers. Both observers had to agree on the categorization of each driver's race/ethnicity, or the information was coded as "missing." Lange, Blackman, and Johnson (2001) had three observers recording each driver's demographic characteristics. Two of the three had to agree on at least the driver's race and sex or the case was removed from the data set.[44]

CONDUCTING THE ANALYSIS

To begin to conduct the analysis, the researcher should identify the police stops (the numerator data) that correspond with the observation (or denominator) data at each site. The numerator and denominator data are matched in several respects. As in other benchmarking methods, matching reduces the scope of the analysis but increases the researcher's ability to draw conclusions regarding racially biased policing. A potential drawback of the matching process is that it may reduce the numbers of stops in the numerator and/or the number of observations in the denominator to the point that some analyses become unreliable. Therefore, the researcher must balance the need for matching against this potential drawback to various subanalyses.[45]

The stop data are matched to the observation data with regard to the violations observed. That is, if the researcher is observing who is speeding and who is violating red light ordi-

---

[44] Lamberth (2002) argues that unanimity of two observers is superior to the agreement of two out of three observers.

[45] As Jack McDevitt (2003) of the Northeastern University team points out, a researcher could aggregate some of the data originally disaggregated through matching if patterns among the disaggregated data are similar.

nances, the strongest analysis will involve only those police stops that were for speeding and/or red light violations. (Of course, if the researcher is collecting observation data for all drivers, not violators, this matching of the numerator and the denominator with regard to the type of stop is not relevant.)

The researcher should also match stop data and observation data geographically. To do this, the researcher conceives of a radius around each observation site and uses for the analysis of that site only the police stops that occurred within the radius. There is no fixed, standard size that is appropriate in all jurisdictions. The researcher should select a radius around the site that she or he believes contains the same type of traffic—in terms of density, nature (residential or commercial), and driver demographics—as that going directly by the site under observation. Lamberth (2002, 1) sets his perimeters at "two blocks or more" around the benchmark sites.

The stop data and observation data also should match with regard to time of day and reference period. If only daytime observations are conducted to ensure sufficient visibility of driver demographics, only daytime stops by police should be included in the analysis. Similarly, if observations are conducted in the spring, the analysis should only include stops conducted in the spring.

Let us consider the example of hypothetical City A. At fifteen sites (intersections) observers collected demographic data for all drivers violating speeding, red light, and/or stop sign laws. The observation data were collected during randomly selected time blocks between 7 A.M. and 7 P.M. on all days of the week for the period January through June. Around each site the researcher identified a perimeter within which the traffic resembled the traffic going through the intersection. Then, within each of these fifteen geographic areas, the researcher selected the police stops that occurred from January to June for speeding, red light, and/or stop sign violations between the hours of 7 A.M. and 7 P.M. For each of the fifteen sites, the researcher compared the demographic profile of the people stopped to the profile of the people observed. A Likelihood Ratio for each site was developed to indicate the relative likelihood of one group being stopped compared with another (see Chapter 12).

Instead of analyzing data site by site, researchers can analyze the data by neighborhood type. The Alpert Group (2003), as noted earlier, classified intersections in Miami-Dade County with regard to whether they were in neighborhoods that were predominantly Caucasian, predominantly African American, or a mixture of races. The observation data and stop data for the intersections within each category were aggregated for purposes of analyses. (Note that this scheme does not necessarily control for variations in police deployment.[46])

We conclude this section by describing the analysis conducted by the North Carolina team (Smith et al. 2003). We explain the team's unit of analysis (roadway areas/stretches), how it matched stop data and observation data, and how it analyzed this data and presented its findings.

The North Carolina team (Smith et al. 2003, 390) compared the extent to which African Americans (the largest minority group in the state) were stopped by police to the representation of African Americans among speeders (as determined by observation). Separate analyses were conducted for each of the fourteen sites. The numerators (stops for speeding) matched the denominator geographically and with regard to time of year. The stop data were for "highway areas" ("a stretch of highway within an area of a county," roughly a fourth of a county in size), and observations were for fifteen-mile stretches within those highway areas. Stops covered the period May through July. Recall that the observations for each site were conducted during a one-week period during the period encompassing mid-May through the end of June.

---

[46] Recall that controlling for police deployment is desirable to address the alternative hypothesis that *racial/ethnic groups are not equally represented as drivers on roads where stopping activity by police is high*. However, the Miami-Dade team was precluded from controlling for deployment because the police department changed deployment patterns within geographic areas on a daily basis.

The North Carolina team used two "denominators" developed from its observation data; specifically, it measured the proportion of African Americans who were speeding for two different speed thresholds: "percent over median threshold speed" (MTS) and "percent over decile threshold speed" (DTS). The MTS denotes the speed (above the posted speed limit) at or under which one-half of the drivers are issued citations. The DTS denotes the speed (above the posted speed limit) at or under which 10 percent of the drivers are issued citations.

Table 9.1, containing hypothetical data, will help us explain how the North Carolina team conducted its analysis. Along Segment D, as an example, the posted speed limit is 65 miles per hour. The Median Threshold Speed (the "high estimate of the speed that will result in a stop") for this segment is 80; the First Decile Threshold Speed ("the low estimate of the speed that will result in a stop") is 77. Thirteen percent of the people stopped at greater than the MTS, and 18 percent of the people stopped at greater than the DTS, were African American. Sixteen percent of the people stopped for speeding by the police were African American. The North Carolina team that developed this method would interpret these hypothetical results as indicating no bias. According to this method, if bias is absent, the percent of people stopped for speeding by the police that are African American should be "somewhere between" 13 and 18 percent—which it is in this example for Segment D. Their reticence to make definitive claims regarding how the data can be interpreted is based on their general concern as social scientists that not all relevant variables have been included in the analysis and on specific concerns related to measurement error, as well.[47] The researchers are careful not to generalize their results to geographic areas beyond those that they analyzed.

---

[47] The researchers note they can accurately measure speed within plus or minus 2 miles per hour and yet the interval between the MTS and DTS for all segments was just 1 to 3 miles per hour. These facts imply that the use of the MTS and DTS proportions of African Americans as endpoints on a range relies on the ability to measure speed more precisely.

Table 9.1. North Carolina Team's Method of Analysis, Hypothetical Data

Highway Segment	Miles per Hour		% of Drivers Over MTS Who Are African American	Miles per Hour First Decile Threshold Speed (DTS)	% of Drivers Over DTS Who Are African American	% of Drivers Stopped for Speeding Who Are African American
	Posted Speed Limit	Median Threshold Speed (MTS)				
A	55	70	15	67	14	21
B	55	70	25	69	18	24
C	65	80	18	77	15	19
D	65	80	13	77	18	16
E	65	82	16	79	12	16
F	70	82	14	79	17	21
G	70	85	22	80	16	22

Source: Based on Smith et al. (2003).

DRAWING CONCLUSIONS FROM THE RESULTS

The observation method, conducted in accordance with standard social science methods, can provide meaningful information for a jurisdiction exploring the existence of racially biased policing. The assessment, however, is limited because the researcher is only able to conduct "spot checks" of racially biased policing. Returning to the example of City A, we explain that the researcher will have a strong assessment of racially biased policing but only in the geographic areas, during the time periods, and for the violations under study. With observation benchmarking, like other benchmarking methods, the stronger the "match" between the numerator and denominator data, the greater the confidence the researcher can have in the results. As conveyed earlier, however, this increased confidence comes at a cost in terms of the scope of the assessment.

The observation benchmarking method addresses the alternative hypotheses (explained in Chapter 2) that *racial/ethnic groups are not equally represented as residents in the jurisdiction* and that *racial/ethnic groups are not equally represented as drivers on jurisdiction roads*. If analyses are conducted separately for specific geographic locations, the method addresses the hypothesis that *racial/ethnic groups are not equally represented as drivers on roads where stopping activity by police is high*. If observations are made of drivers rather than violators, the method does not address the alternative hypothesis that *racial/ethnic groups are not equivalent in the nature and extent of their traffic law-violating behavior*. If, however, the observations are made of drivers violating particular traffic laws, the method addresses this final hypothesis.

CONCLUSION

Using the observation method, researchers compare the racial/ethnic profile of drivers observed at selected sites and times to the racial/ethnic profile of drivers stopped by police in the same vicinity at the same times. Researchers using observations to develop a benchmark for stop data must make decisions regarding the following issues: whether to use mobile or stationary methods of observation, whether to observe the race/ethnicity of persons who are driving or the race/ethnicity of drivers who are violating traffic laws, what racial/ethnic categories to use, what other demographic information to collect regarding drivers and vehicles, where to conduct the observations, and when to conduct the observations.

Once the observation data (that is, the denominator data) have been collected, researchers must match this data to the stop data (the numerator data) with regard to geographic location, time of day, the reference period, and the type of violating behavior (if observations are made of "who is violating"). Implemented in accordance with the recommendations in this chapter, the observation method is very strong with regard to its ability to account for the factors associated with the alternative hypotheses. This strength allows the researchers to determine if disparities exist across racial/ethnic groups with regard to drivers stopped by police and, importantly, to determine with a fair degree of confidence whether disparity is explained by the bias hypothesis. The assessment, however, is limited to a "spot check" of racially biased policing.

Other Benchmarking Methods

Law enforcement agencies can assess whether policing in their jurisdiction is racially biased by implementing one of the benchmarking methods described in detail in Chapters 5 through 9. Specifically, they can compare their data on stopping activity by police to adjusted census data (Chapter 5); Department of Motor Vehicle data (Chapter 6); data from blind enforcement mechanisms such as red light cameras, radar, and air patrols (Chapter 7); stop data on peer officers or units (Chapter 8); and observation data (Chapter 9). The benchmarking methods described in this chapter are covered in less depth because they have not been fully explored by researchers or have more limited application than the methods described in earlier chapters. This chapter examines

- Crime data benchmarking,
- Crash (auto accident) data benchmarking,
- Transportation data benchmarking,
- Survey data benchmarking,
- Geographic information system (GIS) resources, and
- Other analytical tools.

CRIME DATA BENCHMARKING

As noted in Chapter 4, traffic stops and investigative stops, in theory, should be analyzed separately. The factors that put a person at legitimate risk of being stopped by police for a traffic violation are different from the factors that put a person at legitimate risk of being stopped by police for purposes of investigating a crime. In practice, however, separating traffic and investigative stops into two clear groups is difficult if not impossible. This is because of "pretext stops": stops made on the basis of a traffic violation but motivated by the officer's desire to investigate a possible crime. Because of this problem of pretext stops, all vehicle stops—traffic stops and investigative stops—should be analyzed together.

On the stops that officers identify as investigative stops, a jurisdiction might choose to conduct additional separate analyses. If the jurisdiction chooses to do this additional analysis on the investigative subset of stops, crime data can be legitimately used as a benchmark. This section examines in more depth why crime data (the denominator data) should be used only to benchmark investigative stops (the numerator data) and not traffic stops or even all vehicle stops.[1] For the jurisdictions that choose to use crime data to benchmark investigative stops, we also discuss the types of measures of crime that are and are not appropriate. Crime data were used in a comprehensive analysis of "stops and frisks" conducted by members of the New York City Police Department (NYPD); this section concludes with a description of this model study of pedestrian detentions (Spitzer 1999).

Using Crime Data:
The Right Choice for the Numerator Data
A benchmark based solely on crime data can be used to benchmark investigative stops, but not traffic stops or all vehicle stops. As noted earlier, using crime data to benchmark *traffic* stops requires one to make a tenuous assumption—namely, that the same people who commit traffic violations are the ones who com-

---

[1] See Chapter 4 for an explanation of numerator and denominator data.

mit crimes and vice versa. A few researchers, however, have pointed to pretext stops as justification for using crime data as a benchmark for traffic stops. It is true that many traffic stops are really investigative stops: on the pretext of a traffic violation, an officer stops a driver to investigate a crime. But the latter justification for using crime data as a benchmark for traffic stops, as we will explain, fails because of its inability to help researchers interpret police-citizen contact data accurately.

To explain this point we will use a hypothetical jurisdiction that first benchmarks its data on vehicle stops (which include both traffic and investigative stops) against census data; it finds that minorities are over-represented among people stopped relative to their representation in the resident population. Next the jurisdiction benchmarks its vehicle stop data against crime data; it finds that minorities are not over-represented among people stopped relative to their representation among criminal law suspects or violators. In fact, minorities are under-represented when this benchmark is used.

What valid conclusions about the existence of racially biased policing in this jurisdiction can be drawn from these findings? None. This hypothetical jurisdiction might *incorrectly* reason this way:

- Many traffic stops are pretext stops to investigate possible criminal activity.
- Minorities are disproportionately represented among crime suspects and therefore we would expect more traffic stops of minorities.
- In fact, the results indicate more traffic stops of minorities than nonminorities occurred, lending support to the contention that racially biased policing does not exist in the jurisdiction.

This explanation for the findings is not sound. It is true that traffic stops are frequently pretext stops (see, for instance, Cordner, Williams, and Velasco 2002), and measures of crime frequently indicate that minorities are disproportionately represented among crime suspects. But the findings of the hypothetical jurisdiction are as consistent with the existence of racially biased policing as the lack thereof. The police could be conducting the pretext stops based on an expectation that minorities are more likely to be criminal. That is, the police could pull over more minorities for pretext stops (which, by definition, are justified on their face by a traffic violation, not by reasonable suspicion that criminal activity is afoot) because they think that minorities commit more crime. If they are using this stereotype as the basis for their decisions, they are engaging in racially biased policing. (One definition of racial profiling is stopping minorities more than nonminorities because of a belief that they are more likely to commit a crime.)

Because researchers cannot assume that traffic violators are criminals or vice versa and because the pretext stop argument does not help researchers assess the existence of racially biased policing, crime data are not useful for benchmarking traffic stops. Crime data are useful for benchmarking investigative stops (not traffic stops or all vehicle stops) and, as explained below as Gary Cordner and his team in San Diego tried to estimate their occurrence among all vehicle stops (Cordner, Williams, and Velasco 2002).

Investigative Stops Compared to Census and Crime Data

Cordner and his team produced a hybrid benchmark based on census data and crime data in an innovative attempt to estimate the extent to which vehicle stops were pretext stops.[2] As we have explained, some proportion of traffic stops made by police are motivated by the observed traffic violation, and some proportion are made by police on the basis of a traffic violation but are motivated by the officer's desire to investigate possible criminal activity (pretext stops). Cordner and his team asked thirty-three offi-

---

[2] The crime data were victims' and witnesses' descriptions of the race/ethnicity of criminal suspects.

cers to estimate the percentage of their traffic stops that were motivated by a desire to investigate a crime, not by traffic violations per se; the average was approximately 25 percent. The team argued that crime data were relevant for benchmarking investigative stops and, since an estimated 25 percent of the traffic stops they were examining were investigative stops, 25 percent of the benchmark should similarly reflect crime data.

Table 10.1 shows the team's hybrid benchmark based on census data (75 percent of the benchmark) and crime data (25 percent of the benchmark). The first row presents the traffic stops motivated by traffic violations and applies census data to those stops to predict for each racial group the number of stops that police would make absent bias for every 75 traffic stops made: 11.2 stops of Asian/Pacific Islanders, 5.4 stops of Black/African Americans, 16.8 stops of Hispanics, and 41.6 stops of Whites. The second row presents the traffic stops that are pretext stops—stops based on suspicions of criminal activity. For these estimates, the team used data on criminals' demographics as described by victims and witnesses. With these data the team estimated that of every group of 25 stops, the police, absent bias, would stop 4.4 Asian/Pacific Islanders, 6.0 Black/African Americans, 6.9 Hispanics, and 7.8 Whites. The third row provides the sum of the first two rows for each racial group. Here we see the estimated breakdown of stops by racial group for every 100 stops. The final row shows the profile of the group of drivers actually stopped by the San Diego Police Department during 2001. Comparing those data to the hybrid benchmark indicates that Hispanics are slightly over-represented among stops compared to the benchmark, but that the other groups are proportionately represented.

The team was cautious in its interpretation of the results of its hybrid benchmarking experiment. It acknowledged the "crude estimate" of pretext stops, the less than ideal information it used to develop a profile of criminal suspects, and the "lack of precedent for this type of approach" (Cordner, Williams, and Velasco 2002, 3). Nonetheless, this alternative analysis has two

Table 10.1. Vehicle Stops by San Diego Police Officers in 2001: Comparing Actual Stops to a Benchmark Made Up of Crime and Census Data

Type of Stop	Type of Benchmark Data Used	Number of Drivers Stopped by Racial/Ethnic Group			
		Asian/Pacific Islander	Black/African American	Hispanic	White
Vehicle stops motivated by traffic violations[a]	Census Data	11.2	5.4	16.8	41.6
Vehicle stops motivated by a desire to investigate crime[b]	Crime Data	4.4	6	6.9	7.8
Estimated vehicle stops[c]	Census and Crime Data	15.6	11.4	23.7	49.4
Actual vehicle stops		11.7	10.4	27.7	50.2

Source: Cordner, Williams, and Velasco (2002, Table 27).

Note: For every 100 vehicle stops, the San Diego Police Department estimated that 75 were for traffic violations and 25 were pretext stops (that is, the pretext for the stop was a traffic violation but the real reason for the stop was crime-related).

[a] Proportionate to the racial/ethnic composition of the residential population, the 75 traffic stops would include this number of stops of each racial/ethnic group.

[b] Proportionate to the racial/ethnic composition of described criminal suspects, the 25 stops motivated by the officer's desire to investigate a possible crime would include this number of stops of each racial/ethnic group.

[c] One would expect this racial/ethnic composition of 100 vehicle stops based on findings in the first two rows.

benefits noted by the team. "First, it attempts to incorporate the reality of pretext stops—that officers make a lot of stops for non-traffic reasons, not 2 to 3 percent as the vehicle stop forms indicate. Second, it demonstrates the potential consequence of building a more realistic benchmark into the analysis, rather than settling for using the driving age population" (Cordner, Williams, and Velasco 2002, 3).

Viable Measures of Crime

Researchers conducting crime data benchmarking must decide carefully what measures of crime to use. To assess whether racial profiling in their jurisdiction exists, the researchers will compare the racial/ethnic profile of drivers stopped by police in an investigation of possible criminal activity (the numerator or investigative stop data) to the racial/ethnic profile of people who appear in recorded data on crime in the jurisdiction (the denominator or crime data). Therefore, the first criterion for viable measures of crime is that they be linked to the race/ethnicity of the suspect or perpetrator. The second criterion is that the measures reflect as closely as possible actual crime as opposed to crime responded to by police.

These types of crime data are difficult for researchers to obtain. Indeed, arrest data are imperfect measures of crime. Although arrest data from the Uniform Crime Report (UCR) contain race/ethnicity information, the demographic profile of people arrested in a particular jurisdiction reflects two factors: (1) who commits crime and (2) whom the police identify and target for arrest. Regarding the latter, the decisions made by police regarding whom to target for arrest could be affected by racial bias. Thus, if a jurisdiction is arresting more minority criminals than Caucasian criminals due to police bias, the benchmark data used here to assess racially biased policing (arrest data) will itself reflect that racial bias. If a law enforcement agency is racially biased in both its arrests and investigative stops of vehicles and if it uses arrest data as a benchmark for investigative stops, its bias will not be revealed in the results. And like arrest data, data on jurisdiction residents who are on probation or parole are flawed measures of crime. The same problem with the data arises. The people on probation or parole could reflect biased practices by police and others in the criminal justice system.

What, then, are viable measures of crime that researchers can use in crime data benchmarking? Measures of crime used by social science researchers include (1) data on arrests involving minimal police discretion and (2) information from victims and witnesses regarding the race/ethnicity of perpetrators. Regarding the former, Thomas (2002) and Spitzer (1999) have compared investigative stop data to arrest data (a problematic measure as we have seen), but, importantly, many have not used this arrest data for all crime categories. Rather, they have carefully selected subsets of arrest data to help them avoid the problem of police bias skewing the results. Cordner and his teams (Cordner, Williams, and Zuniga 2001; Cordner, Williams, and Velasco 2002) used the second of these measures of crime. Specifically, they developed a racial/ethnic profile of criminals in San Diego based on crime reports in which victims and witnesses provided descriptions of the race/ethnicity of the perpetrators. The San Diego team selected this measure of crime because of its strength with regard to the criterion stated earlier: the measure is minimally affected by police discretion. The team acknowledges that its attempt to identify who committed a crime is limited to only criminal acts where the victim and perpetrator came face to face.

In her analysis of data from the Denver Police Department, Thomas (2002) identified three measures of crime activity that were (1) linked to race/ethnicity data of the alleged perpetrator and (2) minimally affected by police discretion. Thomas referred to these as "nondiscretionary measures" of crime. One measure was data on crime reported to the police that included victims' descriptions of the race/ethnicity of the alleged perpetrator. Another was police records of citizens' complaints of vice and narcotics activity; the complaints included race/ethnicity data on the suspects. The third measure was arrest data but only for "arrests made by officers where they had little or no discretion in the decision to arrest" (Thomas 2002, 12). For the most part, the arrests were for crimes so serious that officers would be disinclined to release the person without sanction. Thomas had the police department identify "nondiscretionary arrests." They included arrests for arson, aggravated assault, auto theft, burglary, false imprisonment, forgery, hit and run, possession of a dangerous weapon, robbery, sexual assault, manslaughter, murder, and other serious crimes. Using viable measures of crime such as those used by Thomas (2002), a researcher can compare the racial/ethnic profile of drivers stopped by police to investigate crime (so-called investigative stops) to the racial/ethnic profile of suspected criminals within subareas of the jurisdiction.[3]

Investigative Stops of Pedestrians
Crime data can be used to benchmark investigative stops of pedestrians as well as drivers. While there has been little research or even commentary on the analysis and interpretation of pedestrian stop data, a key exception is the work conducted in New York City for the Attorney General of New York (Spitzer 1999).[4]

Following the shooting in February 1999 of Amadou Diallo by NYPD officers, the Attorney General of New York, Eliot Spitzer, conducted a full-scale review of the NYPD's "stop and frisk" practices. As part of this review, Spitzer commissioned researchers at Columbia University, led by Jeffrey Fagan, to

---

[3] The importance of conducting analyses within subareas of a jurisdiction is explained in Chapter 4 in the section entitled "Geographic Location of Stop." A researcher implementing this method, should also refer to the section in Chapter 7 entitled "Using Low-Discretion Stops as a Benchmark." We explain some of the pitfalls of benchmarking stops against a subset of incidents defined according to their level of police discretion. See, specifically, the section in Chapter 7 entitled "Drawing Conclusions from the Results."

[4] Another exception is the study conducted by Boniface (2000) in Great Britain using observation methodology.

assess whether stop and frisk activity conducted by the NYPD was racially/ethnically neutral. Fagan's team conducted several different analyses of the data that were collected by officers for each detention they undertook. The team analyzed stop rates for racial groups. It also analyzed the rates at which stops led to arrests.

Calculating Stop Rates for Racial Groups
The research team calculated the rates at which police stopped each racial group in its study (the groups being White, Black, Hispanic, and Other) using residential census data as the denominator in the rate calculation. The researchers developed these rates, not to draw conclusions regarding whether police actions were racially biased, but to better understand the nature and extent of stop and frisk activity across racial groups and within various contexts. The researchers found that "minorities, and in particular Blacks" were more likely than Whites to be subject to detention by police. The researchers were appropriately cautious in their interpretation of these data. "Without considering other factors, including crime data," these data alone do "not demonstrate that there is a problem with how the police conduct their operations." The data, however, "demonstrate, with statistical reliability, that the perception in the minority community that the police 'stop' more minorities than non-minorities, and are effecting more 'stops' in minority neighborhoods than in White ones in general, has an objective basis in fact" (Spitzer 1999, Chap. 5, 7).[5]

---

[5] The team used Poisson random effects regression analyses to examine the stop rates of the various racial/ethnic groups. Its unit of analysis was precincts, and its equation allowed the team to control for race-specific crime rates and the racial/ethnic composition of the population within those precincts. Even after controlling for crime by Blacks and Hispanics in precincts and for Black and Hispanic residential representation, the team found that Blacks and Hispanics were significantly more likely than Whites to be stopped by police (Spitzer 1999). For a fuller discussion of multivariate analyses, see Chapter 12.

The team examined the stop rates of each racial group across geographic subareas of New York City, across commands/units of the NYPD (for example, regular patrol, street crime unit, narcotics task force), and across groups of precincts categorized by their racial/ethnic composition. Each precinct was defined in terms of its percentage of Black residents (under 10 percent, 10 to 40 percent, over 50 percent) and Hispanic residents, and then it was grouped with like neighborhoods for the analysis. Fagan's team compared rates across these groups of precincts to explore whether police behavior might vary by neighborhood context.[6] These analyses allowed the researchers to determine, for instance, that the rate at which African Americans were stopped (relevant to their representation in the residential population) was greatest in the "strongly-White neighborhoods" (Spitzer 1999, Chap. 5, 7).[7]

Calculating Rates at which Stops Lead to Arrests
As another aspect of its comprehensive analysis, Fagan's team calculated the rates at which stops lead to arrests. This can be considered a stop effectiveness measure. Detentions sometimes lead to probable cause for arrest (for example, if contraband is found during the frisk), and sometimes they do not. A stop and frisk can be considered "successful" if an arrest is made; the officer had reasonable suspicion that criminal activity was afoot, and he or she was right.[8] Fagan's team assessed whether

---

[6] Meehan and Ponder (2002) have found that police behavior does vary by neighborhood context. They examined racially biased policing by looking not just at vehicle stops by police but also at mobile data terminal (MDT) queries conducted by police concerning vehicles and/or drivers, including criminal history. These authors report that African Americans' likelihood of being the subject of MDT queries or stopped by police increased "dramatically" in predominantly Caucasian areas. See also Cordner, Williams, and Velasco (2002).

[7] The Alpert Group (2003), conducting analyses for the Miami-Dade Police Department, also analyzed data within neighborhood groups defined by racial composition.

[8] As the researchers point out, stops that do not result in an arrest are not necessarily illegal or improper.

the stop decisions by police were equally effective across racial/ethnic groups. Presumably, if police were using the same threshold of evidence in deciding whom to stop across all races/ethnicities, then the effectiveness of the stops would be similar across all racial/ethnic groups. The team found that "for every 'stop' that resulted in an arrest, 9.0 stops were made" (Spitzer 1999, Chap. 5, 9). This means that police made nine stops of individuals for every "success." The 9.0 figure is the overall rate at which stops lead to arrests for all command/unit types and all racial groups (see Table 10.2, last row, column 3). If police have a lower threshold of evidence for investigating one group than another—for instance, if they are more inclined to stop minorities than Caucasians—the effectiveness measure would indicate more minorities stopped per each "successful" stop of a minority. Indeed, this is what Table 10.2 shows. More Blacks were stopped for every stop that resulted in an arrest compared to Hispanics, Whites, and members of other races. Specifically, "police 'stopped' 9.5 Blacks for every 'stop' that yielded an arrest, and 8.8 Hispanics, but only 7.9 Whites per one arrest" (Spitzer 1999, Chap. 5, 9).

Column 3 labeled "Ratio of Stops to Arrests" provides a stop effectiveness measure for each police command/unit. For instance, the narcotics task force made many more stops for each arrest (26.7) than did the other units. At the other end of the continuum, the highway and traffic enforcement unit made an arrest for every 6.3 stops. The research team (Spitzer 1999) points out that variations in effectiveness of stops would reasonably vary across commands/units with different missions.

The commands/units can also be compared with regard to the ratio of stops to arrest by race of the person stopped. Nonspecialized officers (labeled "precinct command" in the table) conducted the overwhelming majority of stops in New York (129,538 of the 174,919 stops, or 74.1 percent). Stops by these officers showed the least divergence in rates across racial/ethnic groups: 8.6 stops of Blacks for every arrest of a Black individual (column 4) and corresponding figures of 8.3,

Table 10.2. Ratio of Stops to Arrests, by NYPD Command/Unit, January 1998 through March 1999

Type of Command/Unit	(1) Total Stops	(2) Total Arrests	(3) Ratio of Stops to Arrests	Ratio of Stops to Arrest by Race of Person Stopped			
				(4) Black	(5) Hispanic	(6) White	(7) Other
Precinct Command	129,538	15,452	8.4	8.6	8.3	7.7	8.9
Street Crime Unit	19,091	1,279	14.9	16.3	14.5	9.6	15.9
Public Housing	8,158	1,134	7.2	7.4	7.3	4.6	8.3
Boro Patrol - Task Force	6,028	675	8.9	10.9	7.5	9.0	7.8
Boro Patrol - Citywide	3,782	261	14.5	15.5	16.6	8.9	9.7
Transit	3,738	331	11.3	12.3	10.0	11.5	7.8
Other	2,008	140	14.3	16.8	12.7	11.0	13.8
Narcotics - Task Force	1,816	68	26.7	21.5	37.9	23.5	48.0
Narcotics - Citywide	576	40	14.4	12.7	25.6	10.9	2.0
Highway and Traffic	184	29	6.3	14.2	5.0	3.2	12.0
Total	174,919	19,409	9.0	9.5	8.8	7.9	9.0

Source: Spitzer (1999, Table I.B1, Ch. 5, p. 12).

7.7, and 8.9 for Hispanics, Whites, and Others, respectively (columns 5-7). The researchers conducted similar analyses comparing all precincts with each other.

The core of the model of analysis used by the Fagan team—assessing the effectiveness of a police action based on a measure of success—has other applications. In fact, this assessment method is a version of the "outcome test" described in Chapter 11 in the context of search "hit rates" (the rate at which searches turn up contraband). This method of assessment could also be used to evaluate the outcome of traffic stops (for example, citation, warning, no disposition). In the search hit-rate context, the success of a search is measured by whether contraband was found. In the "stop and frisk" context, the success of the detention is measured by whether an arrest was made. In the traffic stop context, success might be a citation or warning (versus "no disposition").

The strength of this method (and the confidence researchers can have in the results) is inversely related to the amount of police discretion associated with the "outcome" used in the test. Arguably, police have no discretion in deciding the disposition of a search: they either do or do not find something illegal on the person. At the other end of the continuum, police often have a great deal of discretion in deciding the outcome of a traffic stop. They can give a citation, they can give a warning, or they can decide "no disposition." In between these two extremes is the amount of discretion an officer has to arrest someone if the officer finds contraband during a search. We assume that the more serious the law violation (and carrying contraband is more serious than many traffic violations), the less discretion the officer has. Again, the strength of the outcome test is inversely related to the level of discretion associated with the outcome. The following example illustrates this important negative correlation.

The success measure for a detention (an arrest), unlike the "hit" in a search, is ultimately in the hands of the officer. Generally, the officer can choose not to make an arrest even if he or she does detect criminal activity as a result of the detention. The decision to arrest or to not arrest may not be race-neutral for all officers. The use of discretion in the arrest decision can affect the "results" of this application of the outcome test and produce misleading conclusions. Consider hypothetical results showing 9.5 stops for every arrest of an African American and 9.5 stops for every arrest of a Caucasian. Assume for the sake of the illustration that the officers whose stops produced these results always made an arrest when they found contraband; that is, assume that there was no discretion exercised in their arrest decisions. What would happen to these figures if the officers, their discretion restored, started to let many of the Caucasians off without an arrest when contraband was found but continued to arrest all African Americans on whom contraband was found? This would increase the number of stops made for every arrest of a Caucasian; stops of Caucasians would then appear less effective than in the previous scenario in which we envisioned no discretion. This bias favoring Caucasians might produce results showing 12.0 stops for every arrest of a Caucasian—greater than the figure for African Americans (9.5). In such a situation, researchers might erroneously conclude that there is bias against Caucasians, not African Americans, because they show more Caucasians than African Americans stopped for every "success" (arrest). In fact, in our illustration, the reverse is actually true.

In a converse example, picture a law enforcement agency that favors African Americans by not arresting them if the frisk turns up contraband—behavior, if you will, manifesting bias against Caucasians. The bias in favor of African Americans will produce results indicating less effective stops of African Americans than of Caucasians. Those results might easily be misinterpreted to indicate bias against African Americans when, in fact, African Americans are the ones being treated leniently.

In sum, the version of the outcome model used by Fagan mirrors that used to evaluate searches using "hit rates" and can be applied to traffic stop dispositions as well.[9] However, to the extent that there is police discretion associated with the outcome being used to measure success, the confidence researchers can have in results pertaining to the existence of racial bias is reduced. Although rates such as those found by Fagan—showing differential effectiveness of detentions across race—are red flags for racially biased policing, definitive conclusions about the existence or absence of racial bias cannot be drawn. Indeed, the Fagan team was appropriately cautious when interpreting its findings. In Chapter 11 we will explain how the outcome test applied to searches provides results in which researchers can have more confidence.

Summary
Crime data can be used to benchmark vehicular and pedestrian investigative stops. Crime data are not an appropriate benchmark for traffic stops or even for all vehicle stops (most of which are usually traffic stops). We described the creative hybrid benchmark that Cordner, Williams, and Velasco (2002) used in San Diego. They presented their model with appropriate cautions. We explained it here, not to promote their model necessarily but to stimulate other researchers in their thinking about pretext stops and the challenge they pose to benchmarking.

Crime measures need to have race/ethnicity information linked to the data, and they need to reflect, as much as possible, actual crime and not the criminal justice system's response to it. The study conducted by Fagan and his team in New York City (Spitzer 1999) is a viable model for analyzing investigative stops (vehicular or pedestrian), but the relatively high degree of

---

[9] In this model, citation and warning dispositions might be compared to "no disposition" stops. The rates would indicate the number of stops that occur for every stop that results in either a citation or warning. If, however, "no disposition" stops are quite rare, the reliabilty of the data for this analysis may be questionable.

police discretion involved in stop and frisk decisions makes it difficult to draw conclusions about the existence or absence of racially biased policing from ratios of stops to arrests.

CRASH DATA BENCHMARKING

In crash data benchmarking researchers can compare the racial/ethnic profile of drivers stopped by police (the numerator) to the racial/ethnic profile of drivers involved in crashes (the denominator).[10] Most researchers have used crash data to estimate "who is driving" rather than "who is driving poorly."[11] In the two major studies described below, the North Carolina team (Smith et al. 2003) developed its benchmark using data on all people involved in crashes; the Miami-Dade team (Alpert Group 2003) used data only on the drivers adjudged not to be at fault in the crashes.

Types and Sources of Crash Data

Law enforcement agencies that have chosen crash data benchmarking to try to assess whether policing in their jurisdiction is racially biased must decide whether to use data on fatal crashes, nonfatal crashes, or a combination of the two types of data. This section will explain the types and sources of crash data and their weaknesses in terms of social science research.

Data on Fatal Crashes

Information on people *killed* in vehicle crashes nationwide is available from the Fatal Accident Reporting System (FARS) of the National Highway Traffic Safety Administration (NHTSA) of the U.S. Department of Transportation. These data have several advantages: they are computerized, they are available free of

---

[10] Researchers variously describe the denominator data as crash data or vehicle accident data.

[11] See Chapter 9 for an explanation concerning researchers' choice of population for analysis.

charge from the federal government, they include the race/ethnicity of the people killed in the crashes, and they represent a clearly defined subset of accidents (all of those involving a fatality).[12] Arguably, however, of the various subsets of people involved in crashes (everyone involved, the not-at-fault drivers, those killed in crashes), those *killed* in crashes are least likely to reflect a representative subset of either drivers or poor drivers. This is because factors that increase or decrease the likelihood of a fatality in a crash are not evenly distributed across racial/ethnic groups. For instance, some studies indicate that seatbelt use is lower among minorities than among Caucasians (Braver 2003; Colon 1992), and other studies indicate that failure to wear a seatbelt increases the likelihood of a fatality in a crash (Cummings, Wells, and Rivara 2003; National Center for Statistics and Analysis 2002; Cummings 2002). Moreover, vehicles that include the best safety features are relatively expensive, and racial/ethnic minorities are disproportionately represented among lower-income groups that might not be able to afford these vehicles. In short, the racial/ethnic profile of people killed in crashes may not match closely the racial/ethnic profile of people who drive or drive poorly.[13] And a close match is needed to draw sound conclusions from this benchmarking method about whether policing in a jurisdiction is racially biased.

Data on Fatal and Nonfatal Crashes

A law enforcement agency interested in implementing crash data benchmarking is likely to have its own data set on fatal and

---

[12] More information about FARS can be found at www-nrd.nhtsa.dot.gov/departments/nrd-01/summaries/FARS_98.html.

[13] Zingraff et al. (2000) raise further questions about the viability of using fatality data to create benchmarks. The North Carolina team of researchers found no correlation between frequency of fatalities and a measure of driving quantity within districts.

nonfatal crashes.[14] However, like the FARS information, these data may have problems that may make them less than viable for use in benchmarking. First of all, and critically important, not all police departments have in their reports the race/ethnicity data for the drivers involved in the accidents.[15] Second, these data may be incomplete because of the unsystematic reporting of crashes by jurisdiction residents. Under-reporting of vehicle crashes may occur more for one racial/ethnic group than another, or under-reporting may correlate with a nonracial/nonethnic factor, such as socioeconomic status, that is, in turn, correlated with race/ethnicity. Cordner, Williams, and Zuniga (2001), in their analysis of the data collected by the San Diego Police Department, decided against using crash data because they suspected that Hispanics in San Diego—an unknown proportion of which are illegal immigrants—would be disproportionately represented among the people who do not report vehicle accidents for fear that they would be identified as being in the country illegally. Third, data on fatal and nonfatal crashes may be influenced not just by the unsystematic reporting of crashes by drivers but by less-than-systematic filing of crash reports by officers called to or coming upon the scene of the accident. That is, officers within the same agency may make different decisions regarding when it is and is not appropriate to file an accident report. While it is acceptable for the accident reports within an agency to reflect a subset of the accidents that come to the attention of the police, the subset must be a systematic one (for instance, all accidents involving damage greater than $500 or involving an injury).

---

[14] A researcher or civil rights group without direct access to police data may be able to obtain data on fatal and nonfatal crashes from a state-level agency that receives crash reports from local law enforcement departments. Contact the Office of the Highway Safety Representative in your state to identify possible sources of this information. See footnote 25 in this chapter for more information.

[15] Even if a department does collect race/ethnicity information, these data will not be available for the at-fault drivers of hit-and-run accidents.

An unsystematic subset could be skewed with regard to the racial/ethnic characteristics of drivers. For example, officers working in high-crime areas where they are kept very busy may be less likely to take reports on minor accidents than are officers working in areas where there are fewer problems requiring their attention arise. If these two types of areas also vary by racial/ethnic composition, the accident reports for the jurisdiction will not be representative of people involved in accidents.

In the jurisdiction being studied to assess racially biased policing, more than one law enforcement agency may respond to vehicle crashes. For example, within an incorporated area in a county, both the sheriff and a municipal law enforcement agency may respond to crashes. In that case the researcher would access the crash data from both the sheriff's office and from the municipal agency for the geographic area under study. Researchers analyzing state patrol data will likely find that local agencies respond to crashes in the same areas patrolled by the state patrol; collecting the crash data from all relevant agencies may be unwieldy. In North Carolina (see Smith et al. 2003), it was more than unwieldy. It was impossible because many of the local jurisdictions in North Carolina did not collect information on the race/ethnicity of drivers involved in accidents.

Working with crash data will be particularly challenging for researchers if the data are not computerized. The Alpert Group (2003), analyzing the Miami-Dade County Police Department data, had to extract information on crashes from the original hard-copy accident reports on file at the police department. Another problem that can arise with these data relates to sample size. Although there may be numerous crashes within a jurisdiction as a whole, within particular subareas (even particular intersections) the number of crashes available for analysis may be too few to provide reliable assessments. This was an issue for the North Carolina team. It chose to aggregate three years of accidents for the various subareas being studied "to get a sufficient number of accidents to justify statistical comparisons." Importantly, the team affirmed "stability in the demographic composition of drivers [involved in accidents] over a three-year period" (Smith et al. 2003, 81).

Recommended Criteria for Crash Data
The choice of crash data can be problematic for researchers for the reasons we have described. If a jurisdiction decides to use crash data as a benchmark, it should make sure that
   (1) Race and/or ethnicity information on the drivers involved in the crashes is available.
   (2) The researchers have reasonable confidence that racial/ethnic groups in the jurisdiction report crashes at similar rates.
   (3) The researchers have reasonable confidence that the filing of accident reports by officers is systematic (that is, filed for all crashes reported to police or filed for some clearly defined subset of crashes).
   (4) The crashes in the data set can be linked to their geographic locations within the jurisdiction. Researchers then can conduct subarea analyses (see Chapter 4).

Studies Using Crash Data
Innovative researchers have been exploring the use of crash data to benchmark police-citizen contact data. Indeed, two groups of researchers have conducted tests of whether crash data can be used to measure who is driving or even who is driving poorly. Because this research is still in its early stages, we are not yet in a position to evaluate the effectiveness of crash data as a benchmark nor to provide detailed "how to" information for implementing this method. We describe how crash data have been used by the North Carolina team of researchers (Smith et al. 2003) and the Miami-Dade team in Florida (Alpert Group 2003). We hope that this information will stimulate further study of whether and how crash data can be used to benchmark police–citizen contact data.

Both the North Carolina and Miami-Dade teams used multiple benchmarking methods in their work (that is, they developed benchmarks in addition to those based on crash data), and both used other measures of driving to assess the crash data. The projects differ from each other in terms of the benchmark population. The North Carolina group developed a profile of "who is driving" using the race/ethnicity of all parties to crashes, whereas the Miami-Dade team developed a profile of "who is driving" using the race/ethnicity of only the not-at-fault drivers.

The North Carolina Study

Smith et al. (2003), in their analysis of data for the North Carolina State Highway Patrol (NCSHP), developed profiles of who is driving in various geographic areas of the state using crash data. They developed the profiles using the race/ethnicity of all of the drivers involved in the fatal and nonfatal crashes for which the members of the state highway patrol submitted reports. For their subarea unit of analysis, they chose highway patrol districts. That is, for each district, they compared the profile of drivers involved in crashes to the profile of drivers given citations and/or warnings by the highway patrol. (It is important to note here that the North Carolina team benchmarked the crash data against citation/warning data, not stop data, because the team did not have confidence in the validity of the stop data collected by the highway patrol during the team's study.)

William Smith and his colleagues did not analyze a subgroup of drivers involved in accidents—such as those identified as the at-fault drivers or not-at-fault drivers.[16] They note that the determination of who is at fault and not-at-fault is made by law enforcement, and these decisions could be racially biased. Indeed, the North Carolina team advocates using crash measures that are not affected by law enforcement discretion

---

[16] It is not possible to identify all of the not-at-fault drivers in crashes in North Carolina. In North Carolina a determination of who is at fault in a crash is not made by law enforcement unless (1) there is bodily injury and (2) at least one of the involved drivers is uninsured. Therefore, a valid profile of the population of not-at-fault drivers could not be produced (Zingraff 2003b).

(Zingraff 2003b). Another advantage, according to the team, of using the race/ethnicity of all drivers involved in crashes is that it increases the number of people who were part of the profile, providing more reliable data.

To assess whether the crash data produced a valid benchmark, the North Carolina team compared the crash data to data developed by the American Automobile Association (AAA) on vehicular miles driven per district. The correlation between the NCSHP data on crashes and the AAA data on vehicular miles was 0.585. The team described this correlation as "moderately strong" and said it validated the use of crash data as a measure of who is driving: "We conclude from this preliminary analysis of the NCSHP accident data that there is a plausible foundation for using such data as a basis for further comparisons. For example, we could use the accident data to compare the percent of accidents with African American drivers to the percent of those cited who are African American" (Smith et al. 2003, 386).

The Miami-Dade Study
As detailed in the Chapter 9 section entitled "Choice of a Numerator," researchers implementing observation benchmarking must decide whether to compare the racial/ethnic profile of drivers stopped in a jurisdiction to the racial/ethnic profile of *all drivers* in the vicinity or to *violating drivers*. We recommended the population of violators but presented the alternative view in Appendix D. Similarly, there is no consensus answer to the question of whether the profile of drivers involved in crashes reflects "who is driving" or "who is driving dangerously." And the answer might vary depending on whether the profile was based on information on all drivers involved in crashes, the at-fault drivers, or the not-at-fault drivers. For its analyses in unincorporated Miami-Dade County, Florida, the team led by Geoff Alpert made a decision, based on the traffic safety research literature, to use information on the not-at-fault drivers to develop a profile of who is driving. The key underlying assumption of this literature reviewed by the Alpert team is that not-at-fault

drivers in two-vehicle crashes are a representative subset of the driving population. This assumption is at the core of what traffic safety researchers call the "quasi-induced exposure method" (see, for instance, Lyles, Stamatiadis, and Lighthizer 1991; Stamatiadis and Deacon 1997). These researchers believe the racial/ethnic profile of the not-at-fault drivers reflects the racial/ethnic profile of the driving population as a whole. To understand why, consider the at-fault drivers in crashes. Clearly, they have not selected the crash victim based on the victim's demographic characteristics; they hit whatever vehicle was in their way. Therefore, according to these traffic safety researchers, the not-at-fault parties in crashes are demographically representative of the driving population.

As Alpert, Smith, and Dunham (2003) report, the assumption that the not-at-fault drivers reflect a representative subset of drivers on the road has not been fully affirmed by empirical research. There has been "limited empirical testing" (Alpert, Smith, and Dunham 2003, 12) of the assumption. Lyles, Stamatiadis, and Lighthizer (1991), Stamatiadis and Deacon (1997), and DeYoung, Peck, and Helander (1997) have conducted some tests, but more research is required. According to Alpert, Smith, and Dunham (2003, 15-16), "If this method can be further validated as a reliable estimation of the racial composition of drivers, then not-at-fault crash data can serve as an alternative and potentially superior benchmark against which to compare police traffic stop data." At eleven intersections, the Alpert team compared the racial profile of people traversing through the intersection, based on observation data, to the racial profile of the not-at-fault drivers involved in crashes at that intersection. A correspondence between the two profiles would provide support for the assumption of the quasi-induced exposure method that not-at-fault drivers are a representative subset of drivers on the road.

The Alpert team assessed the correspondence between the crash data and observation data at several levels of aggregation (or "levels of analysis"), a practice recommended in earlier chapters because findings vary across levels. The assumption that not-at-fault drivers are a representative subset of drivers on the road is strongest at the lowest levels of aggregation (Stamatiadis and Deacon 1997, 39). What this means is that a researcher should not develop a single profile of not-at-fault drivers for the jurisdiction as a whole across all days of the week and across all times of day. Instead, profiles should be developed within various subsets of place and time categories and used to benchmark stops for the same place and time.[17]

In a hypothetical jurisdiction, City A, consider the possibility that high-crash-prone areas/intersections are not evenly dispersed. The intersections in City A where most crashes occur are in the areas of the city where minority residents predominate. Because these crash-prone areas are near minority residential areas, minorities are disproportionately represented as drivers (both at-fault and not-at-fault drivers) in crashes. If the crash data were aggregated to the whole-city level and if the profile of not-at-fault drivers was used to benchmark all stops in the city, the benchmark would overestimate the representation of minority drivers. That benchmark would reflect, not who is on the roads, but rather who is driving in areas where crashes are most likely to occur.

In Chapter 4 we noted that aggregated jurisdiction-level statistics could produce misleading results and recommended subarea analyses; our examples in that chapter related to the impact of deployment on the numerator data. In the case of crashes, the aggregation of data could affect the denominator as well as the numerator, but the same remedy applies: analyses

---

[17] Smith et al. (2003) also argue for "small [geographic] units of analysis" for analyses involving crash data. They note that the racial/ethnic profile of drivers varies by type of road (for example, rural versus urban). They also note that the level of accidents varies by type of road. If, for instance, minorities are heavily represented on the types of roads that incur the most accidents, the minority proportion of "who is driving" will be inflated if all data on all roads are aggregated.

of subareas of the jurisdiction. The greater incidence of crashes in Area A compared to Area B in a hypothetical jurisdiction will not skew the results if researchers conduct separate analyses (that is, if they compare the demographics of not-at-fault drivers in Area A to the drivers stopped in Area A and the demographics of not-at-fault drivers in Area B to the drivers stopped in Area B). This is because the profile of the not-at-fault drivers is more likely to mirror the actual profile of drivers if the comparison is conducted within small units (subareas) rather than large geographic units (the whole jurisdiction).

The Alpert team compared the profile of drivers produced by crash data to the profile of drivers produced by its observation data. It made this comparison at three levels of aggregation. At the lowest level of aggregation, the team compared the crash and observation profiles at each of eleven individual intersections. For each intersection, it compared the profile of drivers produced by the crash data to the profile of drivers produced by the observation data. At the highest level of aggregation, the team combined all the data from the individual intersections to produce one comparison: it compared the profile of drivers produced by summing all the crash data from the intersections to the profile of drivers produced by summing all of the observation data from the intersections.

At the middle level of aggregation, the team aggregated data from the eleven intersections into three groups defined by the racial composition of the area in which the intersections were located: "predominantly non-Black, substantially Black, or racially-mixed areas" (see Chapter 9). The Alpert team found correspondence between the profiles produced by crash data and the profiles produced by observation data at the middle and highest levels of aggregation but not at the lowest level. These mixed results provide neither a confirmation nor disconfirmation of the quasi-induced exposure method. Indeed, the correspondence found by the team could be the product of accumulated error (that is, a "lucky" set of results). That this could happen is indicated in Table 10.3.

Table 10.3. False Indication of Correspondence between Measures of Who is Driving at the Jurisdiction Level, Hypothetical Data

Race/Ethnicity	Area A			
	# Observed Driving	Percent Observed Driving	# NAF[a]	Percent of NAF
Caucasians	800	80%	60	60%
Minorities	200	20%	40	40%
Total	1,000	100%	100	100%
Race/Ethnicity	Area B			
	# Observed Driving	Percent Drivers Observed Driving	# NAF	Percent of NAF
Caucasians	200	20%	40	40%
Minorities	800	80%	60	60%
Total	1,000	100%	100	100%
Race/Ethnicity	Total Jurisdiction[b]			
	# Observed Driving	Percent Observed Driving	# NAF	Percent of NAF[c]
Caucasians	1000	50%	100	50%
Minorities	1000	50%	100	50%
Total	2,000	100%	200	100%

[a] Not-at-fault drivers in crashes.

[b] A plus Area B.

[c] False indication of correspondence.

The table shows that data producing a lack of correspondence between the racial/ethnic profiles that are generated using the observation method and using the quasi-induced exposure method at the lowest levels of aggregation can, in fact, produce a misleading correspondence when the data are aggregated. In Area A there is poor correspondence between the profile of who is driving based on observations (20 percent of the drivers are minorities) and the profile of who is driving based on the not-at-fault drivers involved in crashes (40 percent of the drivers are minorities). In Area B the observation method estimates 80 percent of the drivers are minorities, and the quasi-induced exposure method estimates only 60 percent are minorities. The lack of correspondence in the two areas indicates poor performance for the quasi-induced exposure method, yet when the results are aggregated—combining the findings from Area A and Area B—a correspondence is produced. At the "Total Jurisdiction" level, both measures indicate that 50 percent of the drivers on the roads are minorities.

Without knowing the subarea results, one might presume from the aggregated data that the researchers have found empirical support for the quasi-induced method. But "two wrongs do not make a right." The convergence of profiles at the jurisdiction level of analysis (the "right" if you will) is merely the lucky mathematical product of two wrongs. Our manipulation of the racial makeup of the two areas allows us to produce this "lucky" result. Recall that the Alpert team, in creating its middle level of aggregation, removes the impact of area makeup by conducting analyses within groups defined by racial/ethnic composition.

The Alpert team's best tests of the quasi-induced method come with the analyses at the lower and middle levels of aggregation—the individual intersection analysis and the analysis of intersections grouped by type of neighborhoods as defined by racial makeup. For these analyses, however, the Alpert team reports mixed results: a lack of correspondence when looking at individual intersections but a good correspondence when looking at intersections grouped by type of neighborhood. The researchers note that their results could be impacted by the small sample sizes: too few crashes and too few intersections. The team calls for further research to test the viability of the quasi-induced exposure method for producing benchmarks for police–citizen contact data.

A finding that the demographics of not-at-fault drivers in crashes match the demographics of drivers on the road could be a great boon to benchmarking efforts. As Alpert, Smith, and Dunham (2003, 26) report:

> If our findings in Miami-Dade County can be replicated, then these data will serve as a less costly and more comprehensive estimate of the driving population than traffic observation methods currently provide. Moreover, they will not be susceptible to the daytime bias inherent in observational data (which is usually gathered only during the day) and unlike observation data, can be aggregated or disaggregated in a variety of ways to help facilitate comparisons of traffic stops.

Summary

Crash data may have potential for developing benchmarks for analyzing police–citizen contact data. Theoretically, at least, they might be used to measure either who is driving or who is driving poorly (the latter arguably producing a "who is violating" benchmark). The two teams that have examined crash data have developed "who is driving" benchmarks using racial/ethnic data of either all drivers involved in crashes (Smith et al. 2003) or the not-at-fault drivers (Alpert, Smith, and Dunham 2003).[18] Each of these teams compared the crash data to other measures of driving. The North Carolina team reports a "moderately strong corre-

---

[18] The Alpert team is currently assessing the correspondence between the profile of *at-fault* drivers and its observation data on violators (Alpert 2003b). That is, it is testing to see if demographic information regarding the at-fault drivers can produce a valid profile of "who is violating." Another potential source of valuable benchmarking information might be the data collected by automobile insurance agencies regarding who is involved in accidents.

lation" between miles driven and level of accidents within districts within North Carolina. The Alpert team found mixed results when it compared the racial/ethnic profile of drivers produced from information on not-at-fault drivers with the racial/ethnic profile of drivers produced from observation data. These two teams have laid the groundwork for further exploration of the validity of using crash data to develop benchmarks.

TRANSPORTATION DATA BENCHMARKING

State and local transportation data can help researchers compare the racial/ethnic profile of drivers stopped by police to the racial/ethnic profile of drivers driving on jurisdiction roads (or violating traffic laws on jurisdiction roads). In making this comparison, researchers will find useful transportation data that include information about drivers' driving behavior and race/ethnicity. We describe in this section various sources of transportation data and the relative usefulness of the data in assessing whether policing in a jurisdiction is racially biased. As we explain, national data provide researchers with valuable information about accidents, safety-related behaviors, and other transportation issues but are ill-suited for estimating jurisdiction-level transportation behavior.

In our discussion of crash data benchmarking, we mentioned the Fatal Accident Reporting System (FARS) data collected by the U.S. Department of Transportation. This information on crashes nationwide that lead to fatalities includes the race/ethnicity of the people killed. Transportation data meeting the necessary requirements (information on drivers' behavior and race/ethnicity) include, in addition to the FARS data mentioned earlier, data produced through observation and through travel surveys or diaries.[19]

---

[19] Eck, Liu, and Bostaph (2003), as part of their analyses of the Cincinnati vehicle stop data, used information from the Cincinnati City Traffic Engineering Department to determine traffic volume in various areas at various times of day and then used the observation method to ascribe demographic information to that volume.

Observation Data

Observation data have been used for many years by transportation planners. Of value to researchers attempting to measure racially biased policing in a particular jurisdiction are observation data collected at the *local* and *state levels* by stationary and mobile methods. At the *national* level, observation data are collected for the National Occupant Protection Use Survey (NOPUS) under the direction of the National Highway Traffic Safety Administration (NHTSA). The original purpose of NOPUS, initiated in 1994, was to provide an assessment of national seatbelt use (Glassbrenner 2002); currently data are collected on drivers to assess the extent of motorcycle helmet and child restraint use as well. Demographic data—including race but not ethnicity—are collected for the drivers observed. While valuable data for measuring the demographics of drivers and safety behaviors, the national data are not useful to individual jurisdictions analyzing their police–citizen contact data because it is not viable to assume that the demographic profile of drivers produced by a national study will mirror the demographic profile of drivers in a particular jurisdiction.[20]

Travel Surveys and Diaries

Transportation planners also gather travel behavior information through surveys of randomly selected households. Respondents to the survey may be asked to complete a travel diary. These diaries help transportation planners construct traffic forecasting models for various areas (Smith 2003). The National Household Transportation Survey (NHTS), referenced in Chapter 2 and again in Chapter 5, is conducted by the U.S. Department of Transportation approximately every five years. This phone survey of representative households collects comprehensive data

---

[20] Observation data also are available from cameras located on selected roadways to collect various types of information regarding road usage. Cameras inside tunnels and above highways in Atlanta and Los Angeles, for example, provide real-time information on congestion and other conditions.

regarding transportation-related resources and behaviors. For instance, information is collected regarding the number of vehicles in the household, annual miles driven, incidence of public transportation use in the past two months, usual distance to work, and usual travel time to work. In addition to responding to the phone survey items, respondents maintain a travel diary in which they log all daily trips for a designated period and, for each of those trips, report its purpose, time, origin, destination, method of transportation, travel time, and distance. Respondents to the NHTS report their race and ethnicity and other demographic characteristics.[21] Measures that can be produced from these data are many and include average minutes of driving (per day, week, year); average driving miles (per day, week, year); and number of "person trips" per year by mode (car, foot). This information would allow a researcher to develop a racial/ethnic profile of drivers on jurisdiction roads and compare it to a racial/ethnic profile of drivers stopped by police in the same jurisdiction.[22] (As explained in earlier chapters, it is preferable for the researcher to develop profiles of drivers within subareas of the jurisdiction.) Unfortunately, most jurisdictions cannot use data from the National Household Transportation Survey to benchmark their vehicle stop data. NHTS is a national survey producing national, not local, data. As we noted in our description of the observation data collected at the national level (NOPUS), it is not viable to assume that the demographic profile of drivers produced by a national study will mirror the demographic profile of drivers in a particular jurisdiction. Moreover, there are generally not enough NHTS respondents within individual jurisdictions to produce a reliable profile. These data, however, can be produced at the local level; a jurisdiction can "purchase" a sufficient sam-

---

[21] Additional information regarding the NHTS can be found at http://npts.oml.gov.

[22] A department will likely need the services of a transportation researcher familiar with manipulating NHTS data (for example, someone at a local university who has used these data).

ple to produce valid jurisdiction-level results. That is, a jurisdiction (for instance, city, county, state) can request an NHTS "add on" that directs the U.S. Department of Transportation to sample more residents in the jurisdiction than it would have for purposes of the national survey. Sufficient numbers of residents are then surveyed to produce a reliable assessment of the transportation behaviors of residents within those jurisdictions.[23]

Some local jurisdictions and states conduct their own travel behavior surveys independent of the NHTS. The data produced by these surveys—if race/ethnicity data are included—can be used by a researcher to develop a benchmark for "who is driving." An example of a local survey is the Household Activity and Travel Behavior Survey conducted in Eugene, Oregon, in 1994 (Smith 2003).[24]

Summary

A researcher exploring resources that might be useful for analyzing police–citizen contact data should get in touch with transportation officials at the state and local levels to identify any viable data sources. Large jurisdictions often have transportation planning offices. At the state level, a starting point for inquiry could be the Office of the Highway Safety Representative (HSR), an entity that exists in every state to receive federal funds.[25] Like the other benchmarking methods

---

[23] The Texas Criminal Justice Reform Coalition (tasked with analyzing vehicle stop data submitted by Texas law enforcement agencies) is planning to use NHTS data to develop benchmarks in the jurisdictions that have purchased "add-ons" (Moswoswe 2003).

[24] Like the survey in Eugene, local surveys may be conducted infrequently. Researchers should not use data that are more than two years old unless they can reasonably argue that transportation behavior has not changed since the survey was conducted. This will be a difficult argument to make in many jurisdictions.

[25] To find out about the HSR in a particular state, the researcher would look under "state information" on the web site of the Governor's Highway Safety Association at www.naghsr.org.

described in this report, transportation data benchmarking involves effort by researchers to develop profiles of people who are driving (or violating) on jurisdiction roads. To measure racially biased policing, a resourceful researcher may find existing transportation data that can be compared to data collected by police, or the researcher may be able to spearhead an effort to collect new data that are beneficial to, and funded by, multiple agencies (for example, the local transportation planning department and the local police agency).

SURVEY DATA BENCHMARKING

Some researchers have used survey data to try and assess whether policing in a particular jurisdiction is racially biased. With data from survey respondents regarding whether or not they were stopped by police, their race/ethnicity, and their driving behavior, researchers can assess whether decisions by police are impacted by driver demographics. Continued experimentation and exploration by innovative researchers are required before the validity of this benchmarking method, and of the other methods discussed in this chapter, can be fully affirmed.[26]

Overview of the Survey Method

Researchers who have implemented survey data benchmarking to measure racially biased policing have conducted surveys (written surveys, telephone interviews, or face-to-face interviews) of scientifically selected residents of the jurisdiction. The respondents are asked about (1) incidents over a specified time period in which they were stopped in their vehicles by police and (2) the quantity, quality, and location of their driving.

---

[26] Survey data also have been used to measure perceptions of racially biased policing among the general citizenry of a jurisdiction or among persons stopped by police (see, for example, Gallup Organization 1999; Campbell DeLong Resources, Inc. 1999). Another use of survey data was noted in Chapter 4; a task force in one jurisdiction proposed using survey data to cross-check information included on the contact data form filled out by police.

In effect, these surveys collect both numerator and denominator data. The information on stops can be used instead of police-collected data to measure the nature and extent of vehicle stopping behavior. The information on driving quantity, quality, and location provides the researcher with information on the various factors, referenced throughout this report, that can affect a driver's risk of being stopped by police.

Strengths of the Survey Method
A major advantage of this method is that the researcher produces numerator data on the people the police *don't stop* as well as about those they *do stop*. The survey goes to a scientifically selected sample of residents, some of whom have been stopped by police during the designated reference period and some of whom have not. All of the other benchmarking methods discussed in this report rely upon the contact data collected by police to produce the numerator; that data can produce information only on people who were stopped. With survey data from respondents regarding whether or not they were stopped by police,[27] researchers can determine if there is disparity in the level of stops of various racial/ethnic groups. A survey is valuable because it can link that disparity to causes by collecting from respondents information pertaining to the alternative hypotheses (that is, information regarding driving quantity, quality, and location). Information can also be collected on age to allow for an assessment of the impact of that potential intervening variable. The data on stops and the factors related to the alternative hypotheses are collected from a single population. In other words, researchers obtain stop and driving information from the same group of people. This is an important strength of survey data benchmarking. Other methods do not have this

---

[27] The survey could be structured to produce not only a dichotomous variable (whether or not a person was stopped during a designated time period) but also a continuous variable (the number of times a person was stopped during a designated time period).

benefit. With the observation method, for example, the information on stops comes from police-collected data on vehicle stops; the information on who is driving or who is violating comes from the population of people who pass by the selected observation location in their vehicles. It is possible that not one individual who is represented in the stop data (the numerator) is also represented in the observation data (the denominator); researchers just assume—albeit not unreasonably—that the folks going through the intersection represent the same *types of folks* who could be stopped by police, assuming no bias. In contrast, with the survey data the numerator and denominator populations are identical. Information on stops by police and on behaviors related to the risk of being stopped (driving quantity, quality, and location) comes from a single representative sample of individuals. With this database, researchers can use multivariate analyses to test the impact of race/ethnicity on police decisions to stop, controlling for risk-related behaviors. There are other benefits associated with survey data benchmarking:

- It makes unnecessary the collection of data by police because the survey collects data on stops. This relieves the department of the tasks of creating a new form for recording contacts between citizens and police and training officers in how to use the new form. Indeed, it removes from individual officers the task of filling a form out following each stop.
- It makes moot the concerns that some officers (1) do not fill out forms for each stop for which they are required to complete a form or (2) report invalid information on the form.
- It makes possible the collection of more comprehensive information regarding each stop. Researchers can reasonably ask more questions of a survey respondent (who must answer the questions only once) than they can ask of an officer who might need to fill out the contact data form many times per day.

Based on the strengths of the survey method, some jurisdictions might conclude that it is the perfect way to measure racially biased policing. Indeed, it would be but for all the caveats associated with the survey method generally and with the method as applied to the measurement of racial bias.

Weaknesses of the Survey Method
Regardless of the subject matter, the survey method suffers from several drawbacks pertaining to the fallibility of the respondents. For instance, the respondents may not accurately report the information that is solicited because their memories fail. They may forget some stops by police or provide faulty reports of driving quantity or quality based on their less-than-perfect memories. The faulty memories may lead to "telescoping," a term to describe the reporting of an incident as occurring during the reference period when, in fact, it occurred before the start of the reference period. Some answers may not be fully accurate—not because of the faulty memories of the respondents—but because the respondents want to "look good" or "say the right thing." This "social desirability effect" could be particularly applicable to the questions in a survey to measure racially biased policing (Smith et al. 2003; Engel and Calnon forthcoming). Some respondents may under-report stops by police because they are embarrassed about them or want others to think that their driving quality is better than it truly is. As we will discuss in the context of the North Carolina survey, if faulty memories (including telescoping) and the social desirability effect do not manifest equally across racial/ethnic groups, the survey method will produce distorted assessments of racially biased policing.

Another drawback to this method is that some valuable information provided by police on the contact data form cannot be replicated in a survey. For instance, the survey respondent may not know the actual reason for the stop, particularly if the stop does not result in a citation, or the respondent may not know the legal basis for a search. Although some may criticize the stop information generated by police on the contact data form for being limited to the police perspective, others can fault the survey method for providing only the perspective of citizens.

Citizens' lack of information may extend to the identity of the agency conducting the stop. Consider this example. City X uses the survey method to assess racially biased policing. It asks the respondents to report, among other things, how many times they have been stopped by City X police during the past six months. Many of the respondents report stops occurring during the reference period that were conducted by law enforcement agencies other than the police department of City X (for example, the local sheriff's department, the state police). Respondents may not be sensitive to the distinctions between law enforcement agencies, or perhaps they cannot remember at this later date which agency made the stop. This will result in an inflated measure of stops for the police of City X.

Another potential drawback of the survey method is the difficulty of taking deployment variations into consideration. Legitimate variations in police deployment can affect who is stopped; to remedy this, we have recommended that researchers conduct analyses within multiple geographic subareas. Subarea analyses, however, can pose particular difficulties in the context of the survey method. Conducting such analyses requires (1) a complicated process by which each respondent's reported stops are linked to geographic locations or (2) the analysis of subarea data with subareas defined by the residence of the respondent. The latter method incorrectly assumes that the respondent drives only in his/her residential area, and it could result in sample sizes too small for reliable analyses.

In the next section we describe the survey component of the comprehensive research conducted by Smith et al. (2003) in North Carolina. This team not only developed a model for using survey methodology that could be customized for other jurisdictions, but it also conducted an assessment of the validity of survey data for purposes of measuring racially biased policing.

The North Carolina Survey

The North Carolina team (Smith et al. 2003; Tomaskovic-Dewey, Wright, and Czaja 2003) conducted telephone interviews of a stratified random sample of licensed North Carolina drivers.[28] Respondents were asked about the number and type of vehicle stops they experienced in the past year; their perceptions of the treatment they received from police; the quantity, quality, and location of their driving; and their personal demographic information (race, age, gender, home ownership status, and urban/rural residency). Respondents also reported whether or not they were new drivers and the model and year of the vehicles they typically drove.[29] Regarding the vehicle stops, respondents reported the overall number of times they were stopped in the previous year, as well as the number of stops by their local police and by the North Carolina State Highway Patrol. They provided information about driving quantity for various periods of time and the extent to which they drove on the interstate (a measure of location). Questions related to driving quality addressed speeding, lane changing, passing, adhering to stop signs, and other driving behaviors; this information was used to develop a scale of risky driving behavior. The survey also assessed "ticket avoidance mechanisms," such as use of radar detectors, cruise control, and/or CB radios.

To assess the validity of the survey method for measuring racially biased policing, the North Carolina team sought to determine whether and to what extent African Americans and Caucasians under-reported police stops. In its report, the team mentioned many of the caveats associated with the survey method. The team took particular note of the possibility that surveys asking drivers if they have been stopped by police may

---

[28] It surveyed only African Americans, the predominant racial minority in the state, and Caucasians. The stratification was based on race to ensure sufficient numbers of African Americans.

[29] To review the North Carolina survey, go to the web site of the Police Executive Research Forum, www.policeforum.org.

be highly vulnerable to the "social desirability effect" mentioned earlier. Previous literature on this effect points to possible variations in its manifestation across demographic groups. Researchers on the North Carolina team referenced literature showing stronger social desirability effects on survey responses among African Americans (Smith et al. 2003; Tomaskovic-Dewey, Wright, and Czaja 2003). For this reason, the researchers note, African Americans might have under-reported in the survey vehicle stops by law enforcement.[30]

To determine whether there was under-reporting of police stops by African Americans and/or Caucasians, the North Carolina research team conducted the interview described above with an additional special sample of North Carolina drivers. The respondents selected for this study were licensed drivers in the state who had received a speeding citation in the six months prior to the survey. In this "reverse record check" study, because all of the respondents were known to have been stopped by police, the researchers knew that a report of "no stops" during the one-year reference period represented under-reporting.

The researchers found that both groups under-report their speeding stops, and African Americans do so at a slightly higher rate than Caucasians (Smith et al. 2003). Under-reporting by African Americans on a survey used to assess racially biased policing could negatively affect the findings: unless the data from respondents were "adjusted" to correct for the greater under-reporting by African Americans than by Caucasians, the survey results would underestimate racially biased policing.

Using the finding from its "reverse record check" study, the North Carolina team did adjust its data. In fact, the team developed two different adjustments or "weights" to apply to its data analysis: "record check weights" and "DMV weights." The

---

[30] The authors also suggest a reason why African Americans might over-report police stops. "The current politicization of the 'Driving While Black' phenomena would encourage African Americans to recall and report driving stops" (Tomaskovic-Dewey, Wright, and Czaja 2003, 9).

former was developed to account for the difference in under-reporting of stops on the survey. The team applied this weight to the information regarding stops provided by the subjects in the stratified random sample. Smith et al. (2003, 345) report:

> From the main survey of drivers we have data on 1,477 white drivers and 1,368 African American drivers. Of the 1,477 white drivers, 18.1 percent report being pulled over by police in the last year. African Americans report being pulled over about 45 percent more often—26.3 percent of the African American respondents report being pulled over by the police in the last year. The reverse record check of results suggests that both of these are likely to be under-estimates.... We saw that whites reported only 74.8 percent of actual stops and African Americans reported even less—at 66.9 percent. We can calculate, based on reported stops, the likely actual incident of stops within race. For whites, the number is 356 (267 self-reported stops divided by .748) and for African Americans, our estimated number of stops is 538 (360 self-reported stops divided by .669).

The second weight was not linked to the reverse record check study. The team weighted the survey data to the distribution of licensed drivers in North Carolina (the "DMV weights"). That is, it weighted its survey data to produce a sample that reflected licensed drivers with regard to age and gender within race categories.

To assess racially biased policing, the team conducted both bivariate and multivariate analyses of their data. Based on their bivariate analyses using the DMV weights, the researchers report that driving quantity and driving quality cannot explain away the higher rate at which African Americans were stopped by the North Carolina State Highway Patrol. In North Carolina "African American drivers drive 32,681 miles before being stopped. Whites in North Carolina report driving more than twice as far, 68,944 miles per stop" (Smith et al. 2003, 191). The traffic law-violating behavior did not appear to explain the difference since African Americans reported slightly less risky behavior (and more safety-promoting behavior) than did Caucasians.[31]

In their multivariate analyses to try to identify factors that influence law enforcement decisions, other researchers have used databases that do not include the key variables of driving quantity, quality, and location. In contrast, the North Carolina team through its survey produced a single database that included information on stops; driver demographics; and driving quantity, quality, and location.[32] It conducted various multivariate analyses including a set of logistic regressions with "stop or no stop in the last year" as the dependent variable and respondent race, driving quantity, and driving quality represented among the independent variables. That is, the researchers assessed the impact of these factors on whether or not a person was stopped in the past year. All models were estimated using both the DMV weights and the record check weights, and separate analyses were conducted for dependent variables reflecting stops by any law enforcement agency, stops by local law enforcement, and stops by the highway patrol. Below, for the sake of brevity and simplicity, we convey the results of analysis using DMV weights to identify the factors that influence stops by any law enforcement agency.

Without controlling for other demographic characteristics (for example, age and gender) and without controlling for driving behavior, the North Carolina team estimated disparity in the extent to which Caucasians and African Americans were stopped by any police agency. The odds of an African American being stopped at least once in North Carolina in the prior year were reported as 1.63 times higher than for Caucasians. Then controlling for other demographics and self-reported driving

---

[31] Smith et al. (2003) acknowledge the possibility that these two racial groups are not equivalent in the extent to which they fully acknowledge risky behaviors.

[32] Recall that the measurement of driving location was limited to a question pertaining to use of interstates.

behaviors, the North Carolina team again assessed the relative odds of Caucasians and African Americans being stopped. The team reports that drivers in North Carolina are more likely to be stopped if they drive more, engage in risky behaviors, drive older vehicles, and/or are young. Self-reported speeding was not significantly associated with being stopped.

The results from the study indicate, however, that the quantity and quality of driving do not entirely predict who will be stopped by police in North Carolina. According to Smith's team (2003), even after these and other factors are accounted for, the racial disparity in stops persists: the odds of an African American being stopped by any police agency are still higher—1.71 times higher—than they are for Caucasians. Summarizing their findings (and referencing results produced with both the DMV and record check weights), the researchers report that "the degree of unexplained racial disparity, as measured as the relative odds ratio of African American to Caucasian police stops is somewhere between 1.71 [DMV weights] and 2.15 [record check weights]. This is a substantial level of unexplained racial disparity and so [indicates] potential racial bias in police stops" (Smith et al. 2003, 201).

The researchers conducted various other analyses, including analyses that looked separately at stops by local police in North Carolina and stops by the North Carolina State Highway Patrol. Unexplained racial disparity remained in both models after all other variables were controlled for, but the disparity was much greater for local police than for the highway patrol. The researchers' multiple models produced interesting nuanced results. For example, the researchers write that "the estimated racial disparity in stops by the NCSHP is much smaller [than the racial disparity in stops by local police], but still statistically significant after controls for driver characteristics and reported driving behavior. The NCSHP does not stop African American males at higher rates that African American females net of driving behavior." The researchers note that race is linked to other attributes of the stop decision by the highway patrol: "Older whites and whites driving late-model cars are less likely to be stopped than are other whites. African Americans who report more risky behaviors are more likely to be stopped. This suggests that the NCSHP troopers are reacting not simply to the race of the driver, but to the combination of race and other status attributes for whites and race and driving behavior for African Americans" (Smith et al. 2003, 209–210).

This summary of results indicates the type of information related to racially biased policing that can be produced with a survey of jurisdiction residents that gathers information on police stops; driving quantity, quality, and location; and driver demographics. The North Carolina team conducted a test of one weakness of the survey method applied to the issue of racially biased policing—the differential manifestation across racial groups of the social desirability effect. Smith et al. (2003) found that both Caucasians and African Americans under-report their vehicle stops by police, but under-reporting by African Americans is greater than by Caucasians. By measuring the impact of the social desirability effect across these two racial groups, they were able to adjust their data based on those findings. Absent jurisdiction-specific weighting information, the weights used by the North Carolina team arguably might be useful for similar research conducted in other jurisdictions. However, the North Carolina team notes that, ideally, jurisdictions using the survey method should replicate their social desirability assessment and produce appropriate weights for that jurisdiction's data (Tomaskovic-Devey, Wright, and Czaja 2003). The North Carolina team calls upon other researchers to conduct "reverse record check" surveys so that "multiple data sources for constructing weights" might be available (Tomaskovic-Devey, Wright, and Czaja 2003, 19).

Other Studies Using Survey Data

The North Carolina survey gathered the "full package" of information required to assess the existence of racially biased policing: information on survey respondents' demographic characteristics, law enforcement stops, and driving quantity, quality, and location. Other surveys have collected some but not all of these categories of information. We describe these briefly. In this section we also describe efforts to measure the perception of racially biased policing.

Farmer (2001) describes a survey to measure the racial/ethnic composition of drivers on the New Jersey toll road. The National Personal Transportation Survey (NPTS) conducted by the U.S. Department of Transportation gathers information on the transportation behaviors of U.S. residents that can be used to understand driving quantity, quality, and location for various demographic groups.

The Bureau of Justice Statistics (BJS) of the U.S. Department of Justice used survey methodology to collect information from a scientifically selected sample of U.S. residents regarding their contacts with police. In the Police Public Contact Survey, a supplement to the National Crime Victimization Survey, residents 16 years of age or older are asked about the number and nature of their contacts with police during the previous year. Information is collected on various aspects of these contacts including, but not limited to, whether the stop was a vehicle or pedestrian stop, whether the respondent perceived the stop to be legitimate, whether a search was conducted, whether the search was perceived to be legitimate, the outcome of the stop (for example, arrest, citation), and whether force was used or threatened.[33] This valuable nationwide information includes not only citizens' contacts with police but also citizens' perceptions of those interactions. As an example of their findings, BJS researchers report that in 1999 African American males were stopped in their vehicles an average of 2.7 times, and young white males were stopped an average of 1.7 times (Schmitt, Langan, and Durose 2002). In the BJS survey, unlike the North Carolina survey, little information is collected that would allow

---

[33] The Police Public Contact Survey is available at www.ojp.usdoj.gov/bjs/pub/pdf/ppcs99.pdf.

a researcher to pinpoint with any scientific confidence the causes of the disparity.

Questions from the BJS survey, however, could be replicated by a jurisdiction and asked to a sample of residents. Their answers could then be compared to the national data. Though it would not be cost-effective to replicate the entire, quite lengthy survey, key questions might include the following:

- Did the respondent have face-to-face contact with police in the past twelve months?
- What was the respondent's perception of the reason for the face-to-face interaction with police?
- Was the respondent questioned, ticketed, arrested, and/or searched during the encounter?
- What was the respondent's perception of the legitimacy of any search?
- Was physical force used or threatened?

As indicated above, the Police Public Contact Survey includes items that solicit the perceptions of the respondent regarding the stop. While our focus has been on measuring whether police actually engage in racially biased behavior, it is important for a jurisdiction to understand whether its residents *perceive* policing to be racially biased (Fridell et al. 2001; Lundman and Kaufman 2003). The survey method can be used to measure these perceptions. Researchers could develop a survey, and police could ask drivers they stop to complete it and return it to the agency.[34] The survey would ask drivers to report their perceptions regarding the stop. Or a jurisdiction could ask questions of a broad representative sample of residents about their perceptions of racially biased policing; a special survey on the topic of racially biased policing

---

[34] To promote the likelihood that officers will disseminate these surveys following every stop, the jurisdiction could broadly publicize the survey so that residents would expect the survey following a stop and officers would be deterred from noncompliance.

could be designed or specific questions on this topic could be added to a regular agency survey of its residents.

The state of Oregon asked questions pertaining to perceived police bias (not just racial bias) on its Oregon Annual Social Indicators Survey. One question from the 2001 survey reads: "How often, if at all, do you believe Oregon police officers allow race, ethnicity, or national origin to unfairly influence their decision to stop someone—never, rarely, sometimes, often, or always?"[35] In one of its national surveys on this topic, the Gallup Organization has asked respondents to gauge the frequency with which "police officers (stop) motorists of certain racial or ethnic groups because the officers believe that these groups are more likely than others to commit certain types of crimes" (The Gallup Organization 1999). The North Carolina team (Smith et al. 2003) included questions in its survey of drivers that were related to police bias. For instance, the survey asked, "Do you think the following kinds of drivers are more likely to be pulled over by police than other drivers?" The "kinds of drivers" included young drivers, male drivers, African American drivers, Latino drivers, and "people driving run-down cars."

Summary

Survey methods can be used to explore racially biased policing by gathering information on residents' race/ethnicity; vehicle stops; driving quantity, quality, and location; and/or perceptions of police behavior. The North Carolina team used a survey to collect information in all of these categories; other researchers have collected information in one or more categories. There is a wealth of accumulated information on how to conduct scientifically sound surveys. We do not even attempt to summarize that information here. Researchers conducting survey data benchmarking should be familiar with this methodology and/or utilize the services of a social scientist who is familiar with it.

---

[35] The Oregon Annual Social Indicators Survey for 2001 is available on the web site of the Police Executive Research Forum, www.policeforum.org.

USING GEOGRAPHIC INFORMATION SYSTEMS (GIS) RESOURCES

A Geographic Information System is a computer system that is used to assemble, store, manipulate, and/or display data on physical locations (geographic coordinates). Although these spatial data, by themselves, cannot provide evidence that racially biased policing is or is not occurring in a jurisdiction, they can be used to select subsets of stops for analyses and to produce maps for inclusion in a jurisdiction's report on its findings.

Using GIS to Select Subsets of Stops for Analyses

As explained in Chapter 4 and repeated in succeeding chapters, researchers should identify subsets of stops—defined by their geographic location—for purposes of conducting analyses of geographic subareas. If the subsets for the denominator data are, for example, observations at Intersection X, researchers would analyze only the stops made by police in or around Intersection X (the numerator data). If GIS resources link stops to their geographic location, then this information can be used to select subsets of stops by geographic area.[36]

---

[36] As Lawson (2003, 1) explains, researchers "must determine the appropriate geography for their analysis. For example, a point in space can be located using the latitude/longitude coordinates available using GPS (Global Positioning Systems). A street address can be located using an index of street addresses available from software providers or other commercial vendors. If the location is described as a street, between the closest cross streets, a street address range segment is the appropriate geography. Areas or polygons must be drawn to meet the boundaries of a district, beat, service area, or analysis subarea. After these features are created, the data associated with the incident can then be linked to a specific location or area. Additional issues pertain to the source and quality of the data collected to produce geographic location information. An agency planning to geocode stop data would, of course, need to request on their data collection form the location of the stop. Although street addresses are a fairly routine geocoding processing technique, many traffic stops will not correspond to a particular street address. The officer will need to designate a street and the two closest cross streets or an area. If the descriptions of the locations are too vague, there is little an analyst can do to clarify this data."

Using GIS to Produce Descriptive Information on the Jurisdiction

GIS data can also be used to produce maps for inclusion in a jurisdiction's report that convey descriptive information regarding the jurisdiction and its subareas, the stop data collected, and findings of disparity or lack thereof. Maps can be produced that describe various aspects of the jurisdiction and the subareas selected for separate analyses even if GIS data are not incorporated into the stop data. That is, these maps can be produced to convey other department information that is GIS encoded or to convey data collected by other entities (for example, the U.S. Census Bureau) that can be summarized within geographic areas. As examples, maps of the jurisdiction might show the subareas selected for analysis and, within those subareas, convey information regarding the density of traffic accidents (for example, accidents per 1,000 residents), calls for service, reported crimes, or other measures of problems and/or police activity.

In her report for the Denver Police Department, Thomas (2002) used spatial information to describe various aspects of subareas of the jurisdiction. As one measure of police activity, for instance, Thomas mapped citizen-initiated calls for service that resulted in the dispatch of police to handle the call. Specifically, she mapped absolute numbers of calls within various subareas (precincts) of the jurisdiction. Rates, such as dispatched calls for service per capita, instead of numbers can be used to convey variation across subareas as well. A spatial display of arrests also can convey police activity by geographic location. Thomas (2002, 38) mapped the location of problem-solving projects to show "areas of high concern by community and police."[37] The Alpert Group (2003) used maps in its work for the Miami-Dade County Police Department to convey arrests per 10,000 people and race-specific arrests per 10,000 people for various geographic areas.[38]

---

[37] Thomas (2002) also included maps for vice/narcotics complaints, firearms offenses, and the race/ethnicity of identified suspects for specified crimes.

[38] Eck, Lui, and Bostaph (2003) also made extensive use of maps in their report regarding Cincinnati vehicle stops.

Census data might also be used to provide descriptive information regarding a jurisdiction and the geographic subareas. This information might be valuable even if the researcher is not conducting census benchmarking. For instance, the Institute on Race and Poverty, which is associated with the University of Minnesota Law School, includes in its reports maps that convey within census tracts the driving-age population by race. Specifically, within each census tract the Institute presents a pie chart showing the residential population by racial/ethnic group. Alternatively, by color coding subareas or census tracts, a researcher might convey the density of racial/ethnic minorities or the density of a particular racial/ethnic group.

If an agency has linked its stop data to GIS information, this spatial data can also be used to produce maps that describe police stopping activity within a jurisdiction (the numerator data). For instance, Engel, Calnon, and Dutill (2003) used maps to show the density of traffic stops in the various municipalities of Pennsylvania counties. The corresponding map for a single municipality might, for instance, indicate with color variations the density of police stops (for example, stops per 10,000 driving-age residents) within the various subareas. Depending on what data are being collected, volumes of stops might be conveyed separately for traffic stops, vehicle investigative stops, and pedestrian stops.

Maps might also show for each subarea the percentage of stops for each racial/ethnic group. Then one map for each racial/ethnic group might convey the percentage of stops within each subarea of people of that racial/ethnic group. This information could be presented separately for traffic stops, vehicle investigative stops, and pedestrian stops.[39]

Maps also can be used to convey information about analysis methods. Next to their maps showing density of vehicle stops, Engel, Calnon, and Dutill (2003) provide maps showing where they conducted their observations. These maps were presented

---

[39] Similar information might be conveyed for volume of searches and race/ethnicity of persons searched. Analyses of searches are covered in Chapter 11.

to demonstrate that observations were undertaken in the areas with the most police stops.

Maps can show whether and in what areas stops of certain groups are disproportionate to their representation in the benchmark population. A researcher conducting adjusted census benchmarking might use maps to show the extent to which the "allocation" of stops across demographic groups within subareas of the jurisdiction corresponds to the demographic profile of driving-age residents in those same subareas. While there are various ways to convey this information, a straightforward approach is to produce a "disparity index" for each subarea for each major racial/ethnic group. Chapter 12 explains how to calculate disparity indexes. A value of 1.0 indicates no disparity in the stops relative to the benchmark of the particular group for which the index was produced. For example, a subarea disparity index of 1.0 would be produced for African Americans if 19 percent of stops were of African Americans, and African Americans made up 19 percent of the benchmark population (for example, residential population, people with a driver's license, drivers on the road, violators). A value greater than 1.0 indicates over-representation of a group among those stopped relative to the benchmark, and a value less than 1.0 indicates under-representation. The researcher could use various colors to shade the subareas indicating whether and to what extent the index is above and below 1.0.[40] This is what Engel, Calnon, and Dutill (2003) did in their analysis of the stops of the Pennsylvania State Police. Three separate maps of Pennsylvania—one for Black drivers, one for Hispanic drivers, and one for all Nonwhite[41] drivers—showed counties color coded to

---

[40] The Institute of Race and Poverty made extensive use of maps in their analyses conducted for sixty-five jurisdictions in Minnesota. To convey disparity they portrayed for each racial/ethnic group for each census tract both the absolute difference and relative difference between stops and expected stops. Their reports are available at www.crimeandjustice.org/pages/publications/ recialprofilingstudy.htm.

[41] The "Nonwhite" category in their study combines all minority racial/ethnic groups.

indicate whether racial/ethnic groups were over-represented, under-represented, or proportionately represented among people stopped relative to their representation in the population of residents 16 years of age or older. (Disparity indices, described above, were used to convey levels of disparity.)

Maps showing levels of disparity do not prove or disprove racially biased policing. The maps produced by Engel, Calnon, and Dutill (2003) did display disparity in stops relative to the driving-age population, but, as they note, the disparity might be the result of racial bias or any one or more of the factors reflected in the alternative hypotheses to the bias hypothesis. Maps like these represent what might be called the "spatial analysis version" of unadjusted census benchmarking and should be accompanied in a report by all the caveats associated with that method.

Researchers assessing whether the volume of police stops around a jurisdiction is justified by measures of police activity and/or crime/traffic problems can use maps to portray their findings (see, for instance, Eck, Lui, and Bostaph 2003).[42] Presumably, most traffic stops by police will be in areas where traffic problems are greatest, and most investigative stops by police will be in areas where crime problems are greatest. Of course, factors other than traffic and crime can justify police presence/activity in an area (for example, citizens' requests for an increased presence by police). However, these comparisons (between traffic stops and traffic problems; investigative stops and crime problems) enable researchers to take a first step toward exploring whether racial/ethnic bias is influencing police activity levels. An agency might identify, for instance, an area where the volume of police investigative stops is not justified by independent measures of criminal activity. This information could prompt researchers to look further at these questions: Could the demographics of the area (high proportions of racial/ethnic minorities) and stereotypes/biases regarding crim-

---

[42] Mapping can supplement but is not required for these types of analysis.

inal activity associated with those demographics be responsible for this high volume of police activity? Or do legitimate factors explain stopping activity by police?

To assess whether volumes of stops or searches appear to be justified in the various areas of the jurisdiction, the researcher might use GIS resources to convey the level of correspondence between

- volume of police traffic stops and reported auto accidents,
- volume of police traffic stops and hit/run accidents,
- volume of investigative stops (vehicle and/or pedestrian) and measures of criminal activity (for example, reported crime),
- volume of all police stops (traffic and investigative) and calls for service to which police were dispatched, or
- volume of searches and measures of criminal activity.[43]

Summary

Spatial information associated with police stop data can help researchers select stops for analysis based on the geographic location of the stop. Indeed, GIS information is useful for implementing all benchmarking methods. Spatial information associated with stop data and/or with other information (such as information related to police activity or crime/traffic problems) can describe the jurisdiction and identify disparities in police stops. Alone, however, spatial information cannot provide information regarding whether policing in a jurisdiction is racially biased.

---

[43] A comparison of levels of criminal activity to levels of traffic stops or even to levels of all vehicle stops (which, in most jurisdictions, are primarily traffic stops) rests upon the weak assumption of a strong correspondence between traffic problems and crime problems. For these reasons, it would be misleading to compare, for example, the volume of traffic stops within areas to the volume of criminal activity. This would be the spatial analysis equivalent of benchmarking traffic stops against crime data, a practice we do not recommend. (See the section in this chapter entitled "Crime Data Benchmarking.")

OTHER ANALYTICAL TOOLS

Other tools have been used to assess the existence of racially biased policing. For example, in-car videos have been used in Volusia County, Florida, to document stop information, and a "reverse sting" operation in Illinois by a Hispanic private investigator was conducted to determine if police would target him for a stop (see Harris 2002). Meehan and Ponder (2002) of Oakland University in Michigan used information on "queries" conducted by police using their Mobile Data Terminals (MDTs) to study police actions other than vehicle and pedestrian stops in their assessment of policing and possible racial bias. In this section we briefly explain these studies.

Data from In-Car Cameras

Using tapes from in-car video cameras, the *Sentinel Tribune* gathered information on vehicle stops by deputies in the Volusia County Sheriff's Office (Harris 2002). Sheriff Robert Vogel, an advocate of drug courier profiles, had become the target of numerous complaints by minorities who claimed that the race/ethnicity of drivers was used as part of those profiles.[44] Since no comprehensive data were collected on the stops made by the deputies, the newspaper used Florida's public records laws to obtain the in-car videotapes. Newspaper personnel then used the tapes to produce a racial/ethnic profile of the drivers who were stopped by the deputies and to assess whether minority drivers were specifically targeted by them. Of the almost 1,100 drivers stopped, more than 70 percent were either African American or Hispanic. The *Sentinal* reported that this percentage was much larger than the corresponding proportions of African Americans and Hispanics among driving-age residents

---

[44] A drug courier profile lists presumed characteristics of someone who is transporting drugs. It is used to guide law enforcement personnel in their decisions regarding whom to investigate for suspected drug crimes. Profiles might list characteristics pertaining to a driver, passengers, vehicle, vehicle location, and so forth.

of Florida.[45] The newspaper staff also reported that minority drivers were stopped for longer periods of time than were Caucasians, and minorities were more likely to be searched.

A Reverse Sting

A "reverse sting" was used to assess whether the Illinois State Police targeted racial/ethnic minorities for vehicle stops (Harris 2002). Following numerous complaints by African Americans and Hispanics in Illinois of racial profiling by the state police, a Hispanic private investigator was hired by a lawsuit plaintiff's lawyer to assess the existence of racial profiling. The investigator, Peso Chavez, drove in areas where complaints of racial profiling were high. He followed all traffic laws as confirmed by the paralegal who was hired to follow him and document his driving behavior. After following Chavez for twenty miles a deputy pulled Chavez over for allegedly changing lanes without signaling. (The paralegal disputes this claim by the deputy.) The deputy brought a drug-sniffing dog to the scene to walk around the car and told Chavez that the dog had been "alerted" to drugs (although none were present in the car). The deputy and a backup officer put Chavez into the back seat of the patrol car and conducted a thorough search of his vehicle. This incident became evidence in the lawsuit against the state police; the plaintiffs, however, did not win their case.[46]

---

[45] The *Sentinel* used a nontraditional tool for collecting numerator data, but, inadvisably, benchmarked its numerator data against state-level census information. That is, the team compounded the weaknesses of using unadjusted census benchmarking by using state-level versus local-level data. It is important to note, however, that the conclusions drawn by Sentinel reporters were based on more than just the comparison of the profiles of stopped drivers and the Florida driving-age population.

[46] *Chavez v. Ill. State Police*, Nos. 99-3691 and 00.1462, slip opinion (7th Circuit, 2001).

Police Queries of Vehicles and Drivers

Law enforcement agencies that have attempted to determine whether racially biased policing exists in their jurisdiction have focused on vehicle stops. Jurisdictions that require police officers to fill out forms for all traffic or vehicle stops usually do not require forms for the many other activities in which police engage.[47] Defined broadly, racially biased policing is the inappropriate use of race to make law enforcement decisions (Fridell et al. 2001, 5). Clearly, these decisions could be decisions other than those associated with vehicle stops. Therefore, assessments of racially biased policing should extend beyond the vehicle stop context.

Meehan and Ponder (2002) have done just that. Their goal was to answer two questions: "(1) Do police officers proactively surveil African American drivers at a rate that is significantly higher than their proportion of the actual population of drivers on the road? and (2) Does police behavior vary by place?" (Meehan and Ponder 2002, 413). With regard to the latter question, Meehan and Ponder wanted to determine if the impact of race/ethnicity on query decisions varied within different contexts as defined by the racial/ethnic composition of the drivers in the geographic area.

To answer these questions, Meehan and Ponder looked at the vehicle-related and driver-related queries conducted by officers using Mobile Data Terminals (MDTs). An officer can enter a license plate number into his or her MDT and pull up information from national, state, and/or local databases regarding the year, make, and model of the vehicle; the name and address of the vehicle's registered owner; and whether the vehicle is stolen. The officer can then conduct an electronic query to find out if the registered owner has, for instance, a criminal record, any outstanding warrants, or a history of traffic law violations.

---

[47] The general emphasis upon vehicle stops is not unreasonable. More than 50 percent of police-citizen contacts are in the context of a motor vehicle stop (Langan et al. 2001).

The probation/parole status of the registered owner can also be determined. All of this information can be retrieved without stopping the vehicle and without specific grounds for suspicion. It can occur without the officer's supervisor's knowledge. Meehan and Ponder (2002) developed a database composed of these electronic queries.

Meehan and Ponder conducted their research in 2000 in a predominantly Caucasian (98 percent), blue collar, suburban police department that served 75,000 residents and employed 100 sworn officers. The city under study shares a border with a city that is comprised primarily of African American residents (75 percent). The researchers developed a racial/ethnic profile of drivers who were the subject of a particular subset of queries. That is, the team did not analyze all queries made by officers but focused on queries that reflected officer surveillance unassociated with reactive police work.[48] This subset of queries, the researchers argued, reflected "pure" surveillance activities (Meehan and Ponder 2002, 411). Using observation methodology, Meehan and Ponder produced a benchmark reflecting "who is driving." With the query and observation data they were able to compare "the rates at which African American and white drivers were the objects of officers' proactive MDT query behavior" to "the racial composition of drivers on the roadway" (Meehan and Ponder 2002, 413). They made these comparisons within geographic subareas that varied in terms of the racial composition of drivers and residents. (The closer the subareas were to the predominantly African American contiguous city, the higher the percentages of African American drivers and residents.)

Combining data for all subareas, the researchers report that 27 percent of the queries involved African American drivers;

---

[48] Specifically, the team eliminated queries that were associated with police responses to calls for service (including responses to vehicle accidents) and queries associated with making arrests. The team also excluded the queries that resulted in vehicle stops, arguing that those queries may have been precipitated by observed traffic violations.

and only 13 percent of the driving population was African American. Therefore, Meehan and Ponder (2002, 415) conclude that "African American drivers are twice as likely as are white drivers to be queried (2.1 versus 0.8)." Looking at the results within the eight subareas, the researchers report that African Americans are only slightly more likely than Caucasians to be queried in three areas with the highest proportions of African American drivers and residents. The African Americans' chances of being the subject of queries "increased dramatically" (417) in the areas comprised of predominantly Caucasian drivers (92 to 94 percent). According to the research team, "profiling, as measured by the proactive surveillance of African American drivers," significantly increases as African Americans travel farther from African American communities and into neighborhoods with a higher percentage of Caucasian residents (Meehan and Ponder 2002, 422). Specifically, "African Americans who travel in Sectors F and H, which are adjacent and contain the largest pockets of wealthier white neighborhoods, have query rates that are 325% and 383% greater than their number in the driver population" (Meehan and Ponder 2002, 17). "To achieve such high query rates," according to Meehan and Ponder, "officers must be 'hunting' for, or clearly noticing, African American drivers in these sectors" (Meehan and Ponder 2002, 17).

Meehan and Ponder (2002, 418) also examined the "hit rates" associated with the queries. That is, they looked at the proportion of queries that produced "information indicating legal problems with the vehicles or drivers"—comparing the rates for Caucasian and African American drivers. For this analysis they used a broader subset of queries than was used for the analyses described above. Specifically, for the analysis of hit rates the researchers included the queries used in the previous analyses and added queries that resulted in vehicle stops "to represent fairly all possible hits associated with first queries." When the data for all geographic subareas were analyzed together, the researchers found that the hit rates were higher for African American drivers. The difference, however, did not reach statistical significance. (*Lower* hit rates for African Americans would provide the red flag for biased policing.) When the data were analyzed within geographic subareas, the researchers found variation in their results depending on the extent to which the areas were comprised of African American versus Caucasian drivers. In sectors that bordered the high-minority city—areas with the highest proportion of African American drivers—the African American hit rates were higher than those for Caucasians. In the predominantly Caucasian areas away from the high-minority city, the queries of African American drivers produced hit rates that were lower than the queries of Caucasian drivers. In short, "the African American drivers in these whiter, nonborder sectors, who are subject to the higher levels of query surveillance, are the *least* likely to have legal problems (i.e., hits)" (Meehan and Ponder 2002, 420, emphasis in original).[49]

CONCLUSION

We have described researchers' use of crime data, crash data, transportation data, and survey data to benchmark police stops. Because these methods are still in the early stages of development and exploration, our coverage has been primarily descriptive rather than prescriptive. This chapter also has explained the use of Geographic Information System resources to facilitate the analysis of stop data and to produce descriptive information. The methods and analytical tools we have presented in this chapter hold promise for social science researchers measuring the existence or absence of racially biased policing. Social scientists working in this area are encouraged to develop them

---

[49] An additional finding of Meehan and Ponder comes from their analysis of the officers making the queries. They grouped officers into high, medium, and low users of MDTs. They report that high-MDT users, but not the low- and medium-MDT users, "disproportionately surveilled African Americans in both the border...and nonborder sectors" (Meehan and Ponder 2002, 421).

and other models that can be used by jurisdictions around the country to analyze their vehicle stop data. Following in the footsteps of Meehan and Ponder, social scientists also can continue to study police decisions outside of the context of vehicle stops. A more comprehensive assessment of racially biased policing will result.

Appendix A

USING CENSUS DATA FOR BENCHMARKING

Appendix A, written by Karen Parker of the University of Florida, has three parts: A.1, Summary Files Available from the 2000 Decennial Census; A.2, Definitions of the Geographic Units of Analysis Used by the 2000 Decennial Census and Summary Files with Data for Each Unit; and A.3, A Step-by-Step Guide to Accessing and Downloading Data from the U.S. Census Bureau Web Site.

APPENDIX A.1
SUMMARY FILES AVAILABLE FROM THE 2000 DECENNIAL CENSUS

For the four "summary files" available from the U.S. Census Bureau, we provide (1) a description by the Census Bureau of each file and (2) additional information that is relevant to the analyst conducting benchmarking with adjusted census data. Although all four files are described, note that it is Summary File 1 that will be of most value to the analyst.

Summary File 1

Summary File 1 (SF 1) contains the 100-percent data, which is the information compiled from the questions asked of all people and about every housing unit. Population items include sex, age, race, Hispanic or Latino, household relationship, and group quarters. Housing items include occupancy status, vacancy status, and tenure (owner occupied or renter occupied).

There is a total of 171 population tables (identified with a "P") and 56 housing tables (identified with an "H") shown down to the block level, and 59 population tables shown down to the census tract level (identified with a "PCT") for a total of 286 tables. There are 14 population tables and 4 housing tables shown down to the block level, and 4 population tables shown down to the census tract level that are repeated by major race and Hispanic or Latino groups.

The major race and Hispanic or Latino groups are: White alone; Black or African American alone; American Indian and Alaska Native alone; Asian alone; Native Hawaiian and Other Pacific Islander alone; Some other race alone; Two or more races; Hispanic or Latino; and White alone, not Hispanic or Latino.

SF 1 includes population and housing characteristics for the total population, population totals for an extensive list of race (American Indian and Alaska Native tribes, Asian, and Native Hawaiian and Other Pacific Islander) and Hispanic or Latino groups, and population and housing characteristics for a limited list of race and Hispanic or Latino groups. Population and housing items may be cross tabulated. Selected aggregates and medians also are provided. A complete listing of subjects in this file is found in the section, "Subject Locator."

    Source: U.S. Census Bureau, 2000 Census of Population and Housing, Summary File 1: Technical Documentation, 2001, p. 1-1. See www.census.gov.

As indicated above in the official description of SF 1 by the Census Bureau, this summary file contains basic tabulations of information collected on all people and housing units. It includes counts for many detailed race and Hispanic or Latino categories. This file will be the primary, if not sole, source of data for the analyst conducting adjusted census benchmarking.

Some (not all) of the information available in SF 1 is listed below. For a complete list of all person, household, family and housing unit characteristics, see "Data Sets" at http://factfinder.census.gov.

Person Characteristics:
    Total Population
    Urban and Rural
    Race
    Hispanic or Latino
        By Race
    Race for the population 18 years and over
    Hispanic or Latino
        By Race for the population 18 years and over
    Sex
        By Age
        By Race
        By Hispanic or Latino
    Median Age
        By Sex
        By Race
        By Hispanic or Latino
    Households
        By Race
        By Hispanic or Latino

Household Characteristics:
   Population in Households
      By Race
      By Hispanic or Latino
   Average Household Size
      By Race
      By Hispanic or Latino

Family Characteristics:
   Families
      By Race
      By Hispanic or Latino
   Population in Families
      By Race
      By Hispanic or Latino
   Average Family Size
      By Race
      By Hispanic or Latino

Housing Unit Characteristics:
   Housing Units
   Urban and Rural
   Occupancy Status
   Tenure
   Vacancy Status
   Race of Householder
      By Hispanic or Latino
   Total Population in Occupied Housing Units
      By Tenure
      By Race
      By Hispanic or Latino
   Average Household Size of Occupied Housing Units
      By Tenure
      By Race
      By Hispanic or Latino

Summary File 2

Summary File 2 (SF 2) contains the 100-percent data (the information compiled from the questions asked of all people and about every housing unit). Population items include sex, age, race, Hispanic or Latino, household relationship, and group quarters. Housing items include occupancy status, vacancy status, and tenure (owner occupied or renter occupied).

SF 2 includes population characteristics, such as sex by age, average household size, household type, relationship by household type (including living alone), unmarried-partner households, nonrelatives by household type, and own children under 18 years by family type and age. The file includes housing characteristics, such as tenure, tenure by age of householder, and tenure by household size for occupied housing units. Selected aggregates and medians also are provided. . . .

These 100-percent data are presented in 36 population tables (matrices) and 11 housing tables, identified with "PCT" and "HCT," respectively. Each table is iterated for 250 population groups: the total population, 132 race groups, 78 American Indian and Alaska Native tribe categories (reflecting 39 individual tribes), and 39 Hispanic or Latino groups. The presentation of SF 2 tables for any of the 250 population groups is subject to a population threshold of 100 or more people. That is, if there are fewer than 100 people in a specific population group in a specific geographic area, their population and housing characteristics data are not available for that geographic area in SF 2. . . .

Source: U.S. Census Bureau, 2000 Census of Population and Housing, Summary File 2: Technical Documentation, 2001, p. 1-1. See www.census.gov.

Summary File 2 will be of limited use to analysts conducting census benchmarking. It contains information on many of the same variables included in SF 1, but the presentation of race/ethnicity data in SF 1 is superior to that in SF 2.

Some (not all) of the subjects covered in SF 2 are listed below. For a complete listing, see "Data Sets" at http://factfinder.census.gov.

Person Characteristics:
    Total Population
    Urban and Rural
    Sex By Age
    Median Age By Sex
    Households

Household Characteristics:
    Population in Households
    Average Household Size

Family Characteristics:
    Families
    Population in Families
    Average Family Size

Housing Unit Characteristics:
    Housing Units
    Urban and Rural
    Occupancy Status
    Tenure
    Vacancy Status
    Total Population in Occupied Housing Units
    Average Household Size of Occupied Housing Units

Summary File 3

Summary File 3 (SF 3) contains the sample data, which is the information compiled from the questions asked of a sample of all people and housing units. Population items include basic population totals; urban and rural; households and families; marital status; grandparents as caregivers; language and ability to speak English; ancestry; place of birth, citizenship status, and year of entry; migration; place of work; journey to work (commuting); school enrollment and educational attainment; veteran status; disability; employment status; industry, occupation, and class of worker; income; and poverty status. Housing items include basic housing totals; urban and rural; number of rooms; number of bedrooms; year moved into unit; household size and occupants per room; units in structure; year structure built; heating fuel; telephone service; plumbing and kitchen facilities; vehicles available; value of home; monthly rent; and shelter costs.

In Summary File 3, population tables are identified with a "P" and housing tables are identified with an "H" prefix, followed by a sequential number. The "P" and "H" tables are shown for the block group and higher levels of geography, while the "PCT" and "HCT" tables are shown for the census tract and higher levels of geography. There are 16 "P" tables, 15 "PCT" tables, and 20 "HCT" tables that bear an alphabetic suffix on the table number, indicating that they are repeated for nine major race and Hispanic or Latino groups.

The major race and Hispanic or Latino groups are: White alone; Black or African American alone; American Indian and Alaska Native alone; Asian alone; Native Hawaiian and Other Pacific Islander alone; Some other race alone; Two or more races; Hispanic or Latino; and White alone, not Hispanic or Latino.

Summary File 3 contains a total of 813 unique tables—484 population tables and 329 housing tables. SF 3 includes population and housing characteristics for the total population and for a limited list of race and Hispanic or Latino groups. Population and housing items may be cross tabulated. Selected aggregates and medians also are provided. . . .

Source: U.S. Census Bureau, 2000 Census of Population and Housing, Summary File 3: Technical Documentation, 2002, pp. 1-1 and 1-2. See www.census.gov.

Summary File 3 contains race, ethnicity, age, and gender information for some variables that are not included in SF 1, but these variables are not needed by the researcher benchmarking stop data. SF 3 contains data on social, economic, and housing characteristics compiled from a sample of approximately 19 million housing units (about 1 in 6 households) that received the Census 2000 long-form questionnaire.

Some information is repeated for these nine (race and Hispanic or Latino) groups: White alone; Black or African

American alone; American Indian and Alaska Native alone; Asian alone; Native Hawaiian and Other Pacific Islander alone; Some other race alone; Two or more races; Hispanic or Latino; and White alone, not Hispanic or Latino. Some information is repeated by sex (male/female), age groups, and/or a combination of these characteristics (for example, by sex and age).

Some (not all) of the available information is listed below. For a complete listing, see "Data Sets" at http://factfinder.census.gov.

Social Characteristics:
    Ancestry
    Citizenship Status
    Disability Status
        By Age
        By Sex
    Education Attainment (persons age 25 and older)
        By Sex
        By Race
        By Hispanic or Latino
    Grandparents as Caregivers
    Households and Families
        By Age
        By Race
        By Hispanic or Latino
    Language and Ability to Speak English
        By Age
    Marital Status (persons age 15 and older)
        By Age
        By Sex
    Migration
        By Race
        By Hispanic or Latino
    Nativity and Place of Birth
        By Race
        By Hispanic or Latino

Region of Birth of Foreign Born
School Enrollment
   By Age
   By Sex
   By Race
   By Hispanic or Latino
Urban and Rural
Veteran Status (persons age 18 and older)
   By Age
   By Sex
   By Race
   By Hispanic or Latino

Economic Characteristics:
   Class of Worker
      By Age
      By Sex
   Employment Status (persons age 16 and older)
      By Sex
      By Race
      By Hispanic or Latino
   Commuting to Work
   Income (persons age 16 and older)
      By Sex
      By Race
      By Hispanic or Latino
   Industry (persons age 16 and older)
      By Sex
      By Race
      By Hispanic or Latino
   Occupation (persons age 16 and older)
      By Sex
   Poverty Status
      By Age
      By Sex
      By Race
      By Hispanic or Latino

Housing Characteristics:
    Journey to Work (persons age 16 and older)
    Heating Fuel
    Household Size
    Occupants per Room
    Monthly Rent
    Number of Bedrooms
    Number of Rooms
    Plumbing and Kitchen Facilities
    Telephone Service
    Units in Structure
    Value of Home
    Vehicles Available (persons aged 16 plus)
    Year Householder Moved into Unit
    Year Structure Built

Summary File 4

Summary File 4 (SF 4) contains the sample data, which is the information compiled from the questions asked of a sample of all people and housing units. Population items include basic population totals; urban and rural; households and families; marital status; grandparents as caregivers; language and ability to speak English; ancestry; place of birth, citizenship status, and year of entry; migration; place of work; journey to work (commuting); school enrollment and educational attainment; veteran status; disability; employment status; industry, occupation, and class of worker; income; and poverty status. Housing items include basic housing totals; urban and rural; number of rooms; number of bedrooms; year moved into unit; household size and occupants per room; units in structure; year structure built; heating fuel; telephone service; plumbing and kitchen facilities; vehicles available; value of home; monthly rent; and shelter costs.

In Summary File 4, the sample data are presented in 213 population tables (matrices) and 110 housing tables, identified with "PCT" and "HCT," respectively. Each table is iterated for 336 population groups: the total population, 132 race groups, 78 American Indian and Alaska Native tribe categories (reflecting 39 individual tribes), 39 Hispanic or Latino groups, and 86 ancestry groups. The presentation of SF 4 tables for any of the 336 population groups is subject to a population threshold. That is, if there are fewer than 100 people (100 percent count) in a specific population group in a specific geographic area, and there are fewer than 50 unweighted cases, their population and housing characteristics data are not available for that geographic area in SF 4. . . .

Population and housing items may be cross tabulated. Selected aggregates and medians also are provided. . . .

Source: U.S. Census Bureau, 2000 Census of Population and Housing, Summary File 4: Technical Documentation, 2003, p. 1-1. See www.census.gov.

Summary File 4 is of limited value for adjusted census benchmarking. Like SF 3, it presents information on the population and housing data collected on a sample basis from the Census 2000. SF 4 is repeated or iterated for the total population and 335 additional population groups: 132 race groups, 78 American Indian and Alaska Native tribe categories, 39 Hispanic or Latino groups, and 86 ancestry groups.

Population and housing data for any of the above population groups will be shown only if there are at least 50 unweighted sample cases in a specific geographic area. This file presents data on the population and housing known as the "Sample Data" because they are obtained from questions asked of a sample (generally 1-in-6) of persons and housing units.

Some information is repeated by sex (male/female), age groups, and/or a combination of other characteristics (for example, by sex and age, by sex by age by place of birth). Some (not all) of the information in Summary File 4 is listed below. For a complete listing, see "Data Sets" at http://factfinder.census.gov.

Person Characteristics:
    Ancestry
        By Sex
        By Age

Citizenship Status
    By Sex
    By Age
    By Place of Birth
Disability
    By Sex
    By Age
    By Employment Status
Educational Attainment
Employment Status
Grandparents as Caregivers
Households and Families
Income in 1999
Industry, Occupation, and Class of Worker
    By Sex
Journey to Work (commuting)
Language and Ability to Speak English
Marital Status
Migration
Place of Birth
Place of Work
Poverty Status in 1999
    By Sex
    By Age
    By Educational Attainment
    By Public Assistance
    By Place of Birth
School Enrollment
    By Sex
    By Age
Veteran Status
Work Status in 1999
Year of Entry
    By Sex
    By Place of Birth

Housing Characteristics:
- Bedrooms
    - By Rent
- Heating Fuel
- Kitchen Facilities
- Mortgage Status
- Plumbing Facilities
    - By Age of Householder
    - By Tenure
- Real Estate Taxes
- Rooms
- Selected Monthly Owner Costs (utilities, insurance, fuel costs)
- Telephone Services
- Units in Structure
    - By Age of Householder
    - By Household Income
- Value of Home or Monthly Rent Paid
    - By Occupied Housing Status
    - By Tenure
- Vehicles Available
    - By Tenure
- Year Moved into Structure
- Year Structure Built
    - By Tenure
    - By Age of Householder

Subjects included in SF 4 but also covered in Summary Files 1, 2, and 3 are:
- Age
- Hispanic or Latino Origin
- Household Relationship
- Race
- Sex
- Tenure
- Vacancy Status

APPENDIX A.2
DEFINITIONS OF THE GEOGRAPHIC UNITS OF ANALYSIS USED BY THE 2000 DECENNIAL CENSUS AND SUMMARY FILES WITH DATA FOR EACH UNIT

Area name	Area definition	SF 1	SF 2	SF 3	SF 4
Nation	U.S. geographical boundary.	Y	Y	Y	Y
Region	Four groupings of states (Northeast, South, Midwest, and West).	Y	Y	Y	Y
Division	A grouping of states within a geographic region. Currently the census has defined nine divisions.	Y	Y	Y	Y
State	The primary legal subdivision of the United States.	Y	Y	Y	Y
Block	A subdivision of a census tract. A block is the smallest geographic unit for which the Census Bureau provides tabular data. Many blocks correspond to individual city blocks bounded by streets. Especially in rural areas, blocks may include many square miles and may have some boundaries that are not streets. Blocks are defined uniquely within a census tract by a four-digit number.	Y			
Block Group	A subdivision of a census tract. A block group consists of all the blocks within a census tract with the same beginning number.	Y		Y	
ZIP Codes	A ZIP Code tabulation area is a statistical geographic entity that approximates the delivery area for a U.S. Postal Service five-digit or three-digit ZIP Code.	Y		Y	
Census Tract	A small, relatively permanent statistical subdivision of a county. Census tract boundaries are always nested within counties and designed to be relatively homogeneous units with respect to characteristics; census tracts average about 4,000 inhabitants.	Y	Y	Y	Y

Central City	The largest city and, in some cases, one or more additional cities in a metropolitan area (MA). In a number of instances, only part of a city qualifies as central, because another part of the city extends beyond the MA boundary.	Y	Y	Y	Y
City/ Consolidated	A type of incorporated place in 49 states and the District of Columbia in which the functions of the place and its county or minor civil division have merged.	Y	Y	Y	Y
County	The primary legal subdivision in most states. In Louisiana, these subdivisions are known as parishes. In Alaska, which has no counties, the county equivalents are boroughs. In four states (Maryland, Missouri, Nevada and Virginia), there are one or more cities that are independent of any county and thus constitute primary subdivisions of the state.	Y	Y	Y	Y
Place	A concentration of population either legally defined as an incorporated place or defined for statistical purposes as a census designated place. Typically used by most researchers to identify "city" boundaries.	Y	Y	Y	Y

Source: U.S. Census Bureau, 2000 Census of Population and Housing, Geographic Terms and Concepts. For additional information, see http://www.census.gov/geo/www/reference.html.

APPENDIX A.3
STEP-BY-STEP GUIDE TO ACCESSING AND DOWNLOADING DATA FROM THE U.S. CENSUS WEB SITE

We explain step-by-step how researchers can accomplish four tasks: locating geographic areas or subareas of a jurisdiction, obtaining race and ethnicity information for various ages, obtaining information on vehicle-less households by race/ethnicity, and obtaining average household size by race/ethnicity.

Locating Geographic Areas or Subareas of a Jurisdiction

To help researchers learn how to access the census data they need, we present here the steps to follow for one particular example: obtaining vacancy status information for housing units in census tract 2.03 at the block group level in Miami-Dade County, Florida.

Step 1: Go to http://factfinder.census.gov

Step 2: Under "Data Sets," select the summary file (for instance, SF 1) that contains information you wish to obtain (see Appendix A.1 and Appendix A.2).

Because the vacancy status is available in Summary File 1 at the block group level, select "2000 Summary File 1" of the decennial census. From the options at the right side of the page, choose the "about this data set" option.

Step 3: To make a data request, click on "detailed tables." This option will allow you to specify the parameters and geographic areas of interest for the information you need.

At this point, factfinder provides a series of drop-down options.

Step 4: Leave "Choose a Selection Method" in the default option, which is "list." Specify the "geographic type" from the available drop-down list that includes "state," "census tract," "block group," and "block," among others. Choose "block group."

Factfinder will prompt the researcher to select the "state" of interest. Choose "Florida."

Factfinder will now prompt the researcher to enter in the "county" where the block groups of interest are located. In the drop-down window, choose "Miami-Dade."

Then specify census tract 2.03.

Step 5: Choose "all block groups" from the next drop-down window and then click "add."

Step 6: Once all the block groups appear in the bottom window, click "next," which will allow the researcher to specify the data tables of interest.

At the top of the new page, leave the "search" option in the default position, which is "show all tables." All the data tables available in Summary File 1 for the geographic type specified in earlier steps will appear in the next window. Scroll through the table options to find the table of interest (vacancy status).

Highlight "H5: Vacancy Status (Vacant Housing units)" and then "add" this highlighted table to the next window.

Step 7: Once all tables of interest are highlighted and listed in the bottom window, select "show table" by single clicking on the prompt.

A data table will appear that looks like Table A.3.1.

Step 8: Note that in the upper righthand corner of the screen, Factfinder gives the researcher the options to print or download the data table. If the researcher chooses to print, the information displayed on the screen will print as shown. If the researcher chooses to download, two options are available: download the tables in presentation ready format or save the tables into a data base. **Presentation ready format** preserves the

Table A.3.1. Vacancy Status by Housing Type for All Block Groups in Census Tract 2.03 in Miami-Dade County, Florida

	Block Group 1, Census Tract 2.03, Miami-Dade County, Florida	Block Group 2, Census Tract 2.03, Miami-Dade County, Florida	Block Group 3, Census Tract 2.03, Miami-Dade County, Florida	Block Group 4, Census Tract 2.03, Miami-Dade County, Florida	Block Group 4, Census Tract 2.03, Miami-Dade County, Florida	Block Group 6, Census Tract 2.03, Miami-Dade County, Florida
Total:	8	446	13	100	16	10
For rent	0	79	1	16	1	0
For sale only	3	27	4	9	4	4
Rented or sold, not occupied	3	27	3	9	3	1
For seasonal, recreational, or occasional use	2	278	3	59	1	4
For migrant workers	0	0	0	0	0	0
Other vacant	0	35	2	7	7	1

Source: U.S. Census Bureau, 2000 Census.

table format, title, head note, and footnote(s) exactly as shown on the screen. Use these file formats if you need to insert tables directly into other documents. In the **data base ready format,** *only* data rows are downloaded. The table format, title, head note or footnote(s) are *excluded* from the download. Use the data base file if you intend to manipulate the data.

Presentation ready format options include:
1. Comma delimited
2. Tab delimited
3. Rich text format

Comma delimited and Tab delimited file formats are .txt files. The **rich text file format** is a word processor ready format (.rtf). That is, this file type allows you to open the table in any word processor (Word, WP, etc.). You also have the option to transpose rows and columns using any of the three options.

NOTE: The census bureau recommends the rich text file format over the other options when downloading the tables. If the researcher's browser recognizes the .rtf format, it will open the file automatically in the same window.

Data base ready formats include:
1. Microsoft Excel – This is the spreadsheet ready file format (.xls file).
2. Comma delimited database – This file format is for downloading the data records in order to load them into database software for data manipulation (.txt file).

All data base ready download files are compressed into one file named **output.zip**. This compressed file contains:
- One or more **data file(s)** – The naming format and number of these files will vary by data set and/or by the number of tables you have selected.
- One **geographic identifier file** – This file allows you to link multiple data files.

- One **readme.txt file** – This file explains the naming and content of the downloaded files and how to link them together.
- One **data set specific readme.txt file** – This file explains any data set anomalies and the location of the specific technical documentation for the data set

After you make your selections, click "OK." Now save your file in the location of your choice. That is, you will have the option to save to diskette, save to your computer hard drive, or open the table in the format you requested (for example, Excel, Word, etc.).

If you want to produce additional tables, change to a different summary file (SF 1-4) or choose additional geographical areas, select "change selections" at the top of the screen.

Obtaining Race and Ethnicity Information for Various Ages

We present here the steps to follow for one particular example: obtaining the number of Black, White, and Hispanic residents between 15 and 24 years of age for all census tracts in Carroll County, Indiana. As explained in Chapter 5, researchers will need to determine if the proportion of residents between the legal driving age and 24 within each racial/ethnic group are equivalent. They will also need to determine the race/ethnic breakdown of the residential population for residents over the driving age to produce their census benchmark.

Steps 1 – 3: Follow the steps explained above. Factfinder will then prompt the researcher to select the geographical areas of interest through a series of drop-down options.

Steps 4 – 6: Specify the "geographic type" as "census tract," "select a state" as "Indiana" from the drop-down list, then "select a county" as "Carroll County." The next drop-down box (that is, "select one or more geographical areas and then click

'ADD'") will allow the researcher to add "all census tracts" from the list because all tracts located in Carroll County are of interest. Once all the census tracts are listed in the bottom box, click "next."

At the top of the new page, leave the "search" option in the default position, which is "show all tables." All the data tables available in summary file (SF) 1 for the geographic type specified will appear in the next window. Scroll through the table options to find the table of interest (age information for race and ethnic groups).

After scrolling through the tables, notice that the census provides detailed information on residents' age by sex in table "P12: Sex by Age (total population)." Furthermore, the Census Bureau provides a breakdown of sex by age information for each race and ethnic group in tables P12A-P12I.

Highlight "P12A: Sex by Age (White alone)," "P12B: Sex and Age (Black Alone)" and "P12H: Sex by Age (Hispanic or Latino)." Add each table to the next window.

Step 7: Once all tables of interested are highlighted and listed in the bottom window, select "show table" by single clicking on the prompt.

The three tables—P12A, P12B, and P12H—will appear. Only P12A is reproduced below. It shows population counts of "Whites" within the seven census tracts of Carroll County. P12B and P12H (not shown) convey the same information for people who identify as "Black or African American" and as "Hispanic or Latino," respectively.

Step 8: Print the tables as they appear on the screen or download the data for statistical manipulation or computational use. (See detailed instructions in Step 8 of the first example.)

Using this information provided in the tables, determine the number of White, Black, and Hispanic residents between the ages of 15 and 24 for each census tract located in Carroll County, Indiana. To obtain this information, add the different

Table P12A. Sex by Age (White Males) continued from previous page

	Census Tract 9593, Carroll County, IN	Census Tract 9594, Carroll County, IN	Census Tract 9595, Carroll County, IN	Census Tract 9596, Carroll County, IN	Census Tract 9597, Carroll County, IN	Census Tract 9598, Carroll County, IN	Census Tract 9599, Carroll County, IN
Total:	2,958	2,453	2,468	3,177	3,274	2,923	2,438
Male:	1,464	1,253	1,268	1,533	1,662	1,371	1,244
Under 5 years	95	69	54	110	141	90	90
5 to 9 years	122	118	79	118	133	106	90
10 to 14 years	119	105	85	134	140	119	100
15 to 17 years	67	56	38	68	80	62	62
18 and 19 years	24	31	32	40	50	42	36
20 years	4	15	13	15	18	12	11
21 years	12	10	16	15	17	9	6
22 to 24 years	44	40	28	49	55	48	32
25 to 29 years	90	79	72	102	117	90	61
30 to 34 years	90	82	74	130	107	84	83
35 to 39 years	140	100	101	107	121	107	96
40 to 44 years	136	118	100	122	138	115	107
45 to 49 years	102	120	115	114	137	85	94
50 to 54 years	93	91	101	76	121	79	92
55 to 59 years	76	75	97	79	78	76	75
60 and 61 years	28	15	34	22	19	22	29
62 to 64 years	46	24	49	40	36	24	36
65 and 66 years	11	17	28	19	15	16	24
67 to 69 years	30	16	43	27	27	22	30
70 to 74 years	46	36	47	52	46	53	37
75 to 79 years	39	25	37	46	30	54	21
80 to 84 years	31	10	15	28	25	33	20
85 years and over	19	1	10	20	11	23	12

Source: U.S. Census Bureau, 2000 Decennial Census. Data set: Census 2000 Summary File 1.

Table P12A. Sex by Age (White Females) continued on next page

	Census Tract 9593, Carroll County, IN	Census Tract 9594, Carroll County, IN	Census Tract 9595, Carroll County, IN	Census Tract 9596, Carroll County, IN	Census Tract 9597, Carroll County, IN	Census Tract 9598, Carroll County, IN	Census Tract 9599, Carroll County, IN
Total:	2,958	2,453	2,468	3,177	3,274	2,923	2,438
Female:	1,494	1,200	1,200	1,644	1,612	1,552	1,194
Under 5 years	111	70	72	105	131	97	61
5 to 9 years	100	77	69	108	128	106	82
10 to 14 years	115	107	63	107	140	101	90
15 to 17 years	67	57	44	77	84	57	56
18 and 19 years	30	36	22	38	52	31	24
20 years	13	8	12	14	19	20	15
21 years	8	4	15	9	13	18	8
22 to 24 years	43	35	42	53	53	47	32
25 to 29 years	106	71	59	110	94	85	57
30 to 34 years	87	81	73	108	107	94	80
35 to 39 years	127	97	85	121	131	94	98
40 to 44 years	112	117	106	109	129	111	106
45 to 49 years	92	108	89	95	122	113	84
50 to 54 years	99	80	107	80	98	65	88
55 to 59 years	78	62	85	75	72	78	79
60 and 61 years	24	19	40	20	24	26	35
62 to 64 years	35	30	51	43	39	36	40
65 and 66 years	18	16	29	30	18	35	18
67 to 69 years	25	26	30	36	46	33	26
70 to 74 years	75	49	45	84	41	83	40
75 to 79 years	57	25	29	87	32	87	34
80 to 84 years	45	11	25	79	22	66	25
85 years and over	27	14	8	56	17	69	16

Source: U.S. Census Bureau, 2000 Decennial Census. Data set: Census 2000 Summary File 1.

age categories together (15 to 17, 18 to 19, 20, 21, 22 to 24) for males and then for females. Combine the age information for males and females to get the total number of residents between the ages of 15 and 24 per census tract location. This step will be repeated for each race and ethnic group.

Obtaining Information on Vehicle-less Households by Race/Ethnicity

Chapter 5 describes how to adjust census data to account for households that have no vehicles. Here we describe where to locate relevant information to implement this adjustment.

Summary File 3, tables HCT33 A-I, shows the number of occupied housing units with "no vehicle available" and "1 or more vehicles available" for a selected geographic area (census tract) by race and ethnicity.

For purposes of illustration, we display this table for one racial group (White residents) at the census tract level (within Miami-Dade County). Here's the tabular information using the rich text file format option described above.

Table HCT33A. Vehicles Available (White Alone Householder)

	Census Tract 1.06, Miami-Dade County, Florida	Census Tract 1.08, Miami-Dade County, Florida	Census Tract 1.09, Miami-Dade County, Florida	Census Tract 1.10, Miami-Dade County, Florida
Total:	2,491	1,780	511	2,688
No vehicle available	203	357	74	213
1 or more vehicles available	2,288	1,423	437	2,475

Source: U.S. Census Bureau, 2000 Decennial Census. Data set: Census 2000 Summary File 3.

Average Household Size by Race/Ethnicity

As indicated in Chapter 5, a researcher who is adjusting census data for household vehicle ownership will need to transform the household-level information into individual-level information using information regarding the average number of individuals per household for each racial/ethnic group. This information is available in Summary File 1 in tables for "Average Household Size" that can be produced for each racial/ethnic group. For instance, see P17B "Average Household Size (Black or African American Alone Households)."

Appendix B

APPENDIX B.
TRANSFORMING TWO-VARIABLE CENSUS DATA INTO A SINGLE RACE/ETHNICITY VARIABLE

If a law enforcement agency's form for recording police-citizen contacts includes Hispanic within a single race/ethnicity category, its researchers will need to transform the census data on jurisdiction residents from a two-variable structure into a single-variable structure. The hypothetical data presented in Appendix Table B will help explain how.

As noted in Chapter 5, the U.S. Census Bureau treats race and Hispanic Origin (referred to here as "ethnicity") separately. Appendix Table B, Panel 1, presents the number of jurisdiction residents by the separate variables of race and ethnicity. The census also provides information on the combined race/ethnicity of jurisdiction residents (Panel 2). In this panel the different races in the jurisdiction are presented by Hispanic origin or Non-Hispanic origin.

Adjusted census benchmarking requires that the census data and law enforcement agency data be comparable in structure. The result of the transformation to accomplish this is shown in Panel 3. First, jurisdiction residents that self-identify as being of Hispanic origin in Panel 2 would be subtracted from their respective race categories in Panel 1 to produce a new, lower tally for each race. Second, the 25,000 Caucasian-Hispanics,

3,000 African American-Hispanics, 600 Asian-Hispanics, and 50 Other Race-Hispanics would be added to produce a new "Hispanics" category shown in Panel 3.

Table B: Using Census Information Shown in Panels 1 and 2 to Produce Transformed Data in Panel 3, Hypothetical Data

PANEL 1	
Race	**Number**
Caucasian	75,000
African American	13,000
Asian	3,600
Other	300
TOTAL	91,900
Ethnicity	**Number**
Hispanic Origin	28,650
Non-Hispanic Origin	63,250
TOTAL	91,900
PANEL 2	
Race by Ethnicity	**Number**
Caucasian, Non-Hispanic	50,000
Caucasian, Hispanic	25,000
African American, Non-Hispanic	10,000
African American, Hispanic	3,000
Asian, Non-Hispanic	3,000
Asian, Hispanic	600
Other, Non-Hispanic	250
Other, Hispanic	50
TOTAL	91,900
PANEL 3	
Race/Ethnicity	**Number**
Caucasian	50,000
African American	10,000
Asian	3,000
Other	250
Hispanic	28,650
TOTAL	91,900

Appendix C

APPENDIX C
TRANSFORMING AGENCY DATA OR DMV DATA
TO PRODUCE COMPARABLE MEASURES OF RACE
AND ETHNICITY

Benchmarking to assess racially biased policing in a jurisdiction requires comparable stop data and benchmark data. In several benchmarking methods (for example, benchmarking with DMV data, described in Chapter 6, and benchmarking with data from "blind" enforcement mechanisms, described in Chapter 7), law enforcement agencies compare stop data and data from a state's Department of Motor Vehicles. Stop data and DMV data can vary in six ways. In four of them, a transformation is possible to make the data comparable:

1. If the state's DMV provides information on race alone and not on ethnicity, and if race and ethnicity are treated separately on the law enforcement agency's police-citizen contact data form, then analyses can be conducted to assess potential bias based on race only. The law enforcement agency would compare the racial profile of drivers stopped by police to the racial profile of people with a driver's license. The separate ethnicity variable must be ignored because no benchmark for it exists.

2. Conversely, if the DMV in the state has separate race and ethnicity variables but the agency form requests information on race only, the analyst would have to ignore the DMV's ethnicity information because she or he would not have the corresponding information in the stop data.
3. If the DMV has race/ethnicity in one variable, and if the agency's stop forms have race and ethnicity as separate variables, the analyst would transform the stop data to match the DMV data.[1] Appendix B explains how this can be accomplished. Note that in the transformation explained in Appendix B, the race by ethnicity information was available in the census data. In benchmarking that relies on DMV data with a single race/ethnicity variable, the race by ethnicity information is available in the stop data.
4. If the DMV has race/ethnicity combined into one variable, and if the agency's stop forms request information on race only, the analyst can use U.S. Census information to estimate the race data for the Hispanics in the data set. That is, the analyst can determine for the jurisdiction population of driving age the races of the Hispanic population based on the census data and then use that information to estimate the races of the Hispanics with a driver's license. For instance, if the census data indicate that 20 percent of the Hispanics of driving age are Caucasian, the analyst can reasonably estimate that 20 percent of the Hispanics with a driver's license are Caucasian, and so forth for each race category.

The appendix table below describes the four combinations of race and ethnicity measurements we have presented thus far and the transformations required. It also describes other possi-

---

[1] With census benchmarking, the opposite occurs: the census data are transformed to match the stop data.

ble combinations. In two cases, as the table shows, the incompatibility of the DMV data and the agency data cannot be overcome unless Hispanics comprise a very small percentage (for example, less than 5 percent) of the people stopped by police and of the people in the jurisdiction with a driver's license.

Appendix C Table
Measures of Race and/or Ethnicity, by DMV Data and Stop Data

STOP DATA	DMV Data on Registered Vehicle Owner		
	VARIABLE FOR RACE ONLY	SEPARATE VARIABLES FOR RACE AND ETHNICITY	RACE/ETHNICITY COMBINED IN ONE VARIABLE
VARIABLE FOR RACE ONLY	Measurements are matched; can proceed.	Can analyze data using race information only.	Can produce single race variable, using census data, by estimating the race of Hispanics who have a driver's license.
SEPARATE VARIABLES FOR RACE AND ETHNICITY	Can analyze data using race information only.	Measurements are matched; can proceed.	Transform separate variables in the stop data into single combined variable.
RACE/ETHNICITY COMBINED IN ONE VARIABLE	Cannot proceed with this method unless Hispanic groups in both the stop data and DMV data are small.	Cannot proceed with this method unless Hispanic groups in both the stop data and DMV data are small.	Measurements are matched; can proceed.

5. If the DMV has information only on race, and if the agency includes ethnicity in a single race/ethnicity variable on its form, the agency cannot use this benchmarking method. The only exception is if the Hispanic population is very small in both data sets. Then the analyst would exclude Hispanics from the numerator (stop data) and calculate the racial profile using only the remaining stops.
6. If the DMV has race and ethnicity separated into two variables, and if the agency has race and ethnicity combined into one variable, the agency also cannot use this benchmarking method. Again, the only exception is if the Hispanic population is very small in both data sets. Then the analyst would exclude Hispanics from the numerator (stop data) and benchmark the race of people stopped against the race of people with a driver's license; the analyst would ignore the DMV information on ethnicity.

In situations 5 and 6, the jurisdiction is, quite unfortunately, reducing the scope of its assessment of racially biased policing; the analyst is able to test only for racial bias and not for bias based on ethnicity.

Appendix D

**APPENDIX D
MAKING THE CASE FOR MEASURING "WHO IS DRIVING" INSTEAD OF "WHO IS VIOLATING"**

By John Lamberth, David Harris, Jack McDevitt, and Deborah Ramirez

One question facing those attempting to analyze traffic stop data involves the selection of the most appropriate benchmark to use for comparison. A number of measures have been used in the research to date and an open question remains as to whether using estimates of the population violating traffic laws (hereafter referred to as "violators") is an improvement over estimates of drivers operating on a community's roadways (hereafter referred to as "traffic"). Some early court decisions (including the *Soto* and *Wilkins* decisions)[1] originally held that the appropriate benchmark was a profile of violators, but then quickly changed their focus when it became obvious that the two groups–violators and traffic–were virtually synonymous populations. That is, these two courts and others have held that

---

[1] *State v. Pedro Soto*, 734 A.2d 350 (N.J. Super. Ct. Law Div. 1996); *Wilkins v. Maryland State Police*, Settlement Agreement, Civil No. MJG-93-468 (D. Md. 1995).

an appropriate benchmark would characterize the traffic on the relevant roadways.

Court decisions uniformly support the notion that any motorist violating a traffic law is subject to being stopped by police and thus motorists are the appropriate group to use in formulating a benchmark. Empirical evidence strongly supports the contention that traffic and violators are synonymous, and in *Soto* the court essentially considered them equivalent.

In the earliest scientific attempts to develop benchmarks for police stops, the research team (headed by the first author of this piece) determined both the proportion of Black motorists in the traffic stream and among those violating at least one traffic law (*New Jersey v. Soto*, et al.).[2] That is, the team developed both profiles. The results of that analysis, and subsequent analyses, determined that the two populations are virtually synonymous. First, in the research conducted for the cases of *Soto* and in *Wilkins v. Maryland State Police* (MSP) virtually every motorist was speeding (98.3 percent in *Soto* and 93.3 percent in *Wilkins*). More recently, Lamberth[3] reported a study in which police officers were given five minutes to determine whether randomly selected cars were violating some traffic law. The study concluded that fully 94 percent of the drivers were violating some law, and it took a mean of 28 seconds for the officers to spot the violation.

The empirical results presented above strongly support the contention that traffic and violators are essentially synonymous. Having made the case that everyone can be legally stopped, the important issue becomes which motorists are stopped and how their racial/ethnic makeup compares to those motorists driving.

---

[2] Lamberth, J. (1994) Revised statistical analysis of the incidence of police stops and arrests of black drivers/travelers on the New Jersey Turnpike between interchanges 1 and 3 from the years 1988 through 1991. Report submitted in *State v. Pedro Soto*, 734A. 2d 350 (N.J. Super. Ct. Law Div. 1996).

[3] Lamberth, John, "Measuring the racial/ethnic make up of traffic: The how, what and why." Paper presented at *Confronting Racial Profiling in the 21st Century: Implications for Racial Justice*. Boston, March, 2003.

We turn next to the issue of whether all violations are equally subject to enforcement by police. We consider two interrelated suggestions: (1) the police primarily stop egregious traffic violators, and (2) minority drivers are stopped more often than non-minorities because they fall in this egregious violator category.

While it is probably true that drivers engaged in the most egregious traffic violations are most likely to be stopped by the police, it remains an open question if those egregious violators vary by race of the driver. Police make the decision on which vehicles to stop for a wide variety of reasons including the impact of the stop on the other traffic proceeding along the roadway. Supporting the argument that police do not stop only egregious traffic violators is information pertaining to the proportion of stops by law enforcement that do not result in citations. Data on vehicle stops from a number of departments (for instance, Arizona Department of Public Safety, New Jersey State Police, Maryland State Police, Washtenaw County Sheriff's Department) indicate that approximately one-third to two-thirds or more stops do not result in citations. Furthermore, even though speeding is often the most cited infraction, substantially less than half of drivers who are speeding are going sufficiently over the speed limit to qualify as an egregious violator. For example, in a recent study of nine departments in Nevada[4], which accounted for 400,000 stops, only about 35 percent of the stops recorded were considered egregious. This means that approximately two-thirds of the stops were made of drivers who were not egregiously violating traffic laws.

Secondly, those who argue that minorities are more often in the group of egregious violators have scant empirical evidence to support their position. Some researchers have suggested that Blacks violate at least some traffic laws more egregiously than non-Blacks and therefore are more likely to be included in those motorists most likely to be stopped by police. This claim, made by the state's expert in *Soto*, was soundly rejected by the Court

---

[4] McCorkle, R.C., *A.B. 500 Traffic Stop Data Collection Study*. Report submitted to Attorney General of Nevada, Jan., 2003.

because the expert could not provide empirical support for his contention. Countering this expert's argument were five troopers and a police expert who testified that Blacks and non-Blacks could not be distinguished on the basis of their driving behavior.

One study (Lange, Blackman and Johnson, 2001) suggests that there are more Black than White egregious speeders (speeding more than 15 miles over the limit) on the New Jersey Turnpike when the speed limit is 65 miles per hour, but not when the speed limit was 55 miles per hour. This study, which has been soundly criticized, does not engender great confidence because of the difficulty in obtaining data from the study to perform independent analysis to confirm (or disconfirm) the original results. One methodological limitation of the study was that the race of about a third of the motorists could not be agreed upon by two of three coders. No information has yet been obtained on what it would be for a more scientifically defensible three of three coders, but it is safe to assume that there would be more motorists whose race/ethnicity could not be determined. Furthermore, the ambiguous finding concerning the 65- versus 55-miles per hour speed limits is unexplained.

Other evidence on speeding contradicts the assertion that minorities are more likely to be egregious speeding violators. The Nevada study cited above indicates that Blacks (32 percent) and Hispanics (30 percent) are less likely to be in the egregious violator category than are other race/ethnicity groups. Over all racial/ethnic groups, 35 percent were in the egregious violator category.

Finally, if minorities were those who egregiously violated traffic laws, they would be more frequently cited than nonminority drivers. In four jurisdictions where we have the data detailed enough to make comparisons, Blacks in all four jurisdictions and Hispanics in three are cited less frequently than are nonminorities.

An important argument against trying to measure "who is violating" is the fact that there are literally hundreds of traffic violations for which a motorist can be legally stopped. These range from the serious violations (excessive speeding, running a red light, dangerously weaving in and out of traffic, etc.) to a large number that reflect relatively minor equipment violations. And, as we have seen, non-egregious violations are the ones that generate a majority of stops.

Also related to the difficulty of measuring violations is the fact that, except for speeding, most violations are subjective, either in their definition or their enforcement. As one example, consider the violation of following too closely. There are at least two different methods for making this determination. The first is measuring the distance between a motorist and the vehicle ahead of that motorist by timing it. If the following vehicle passes a stationary point in less than 1.5 to 2 seconds after the leading car passes it, some officers call it following too closely. While we do know of some officers who carry stopwatches to make this call, the violation is more often determined on a less accurate basis of counting or other estimation. The second method is to estimate the number of car lengths between the leading and following car, with the assumption being that there should be one car length for each 10 miles of speed. Therefore at 50 miles per hour, there should be five car lengths. Only officers can tell us what they actually do to "measure" following too closely.

Finally, in the realm of measurement challenges, detecting the vast majority of traffic violations for which a motorist can be stopped from a stationary point or even from a moving vehicle is either not possible or prohibitively time consuming. That is, while many of the violations are always present (equipment violations), they may not be obvious until the vehicle is observed from several angles. Stationary observations do not allow the necessary views, and moving observations can take several minutes per vehicle to see the vehicle from all angles. Furthermore, categorizing hundreds of possible violations is an insurmountable task. Most importantly, the crucial information needed is not what traffic laws motorists are violating, but which violations officers are noting and using as a basis for stopping them. To know that motorists are violating several traffic laws is unimportant for our purposes; rather, we need to know to which violations officers attend.

Officers take a large number of factors into consideration when deciding to make a traffic stop. One important consideration is the severity of the violation but officers also legitimately take into consideration such things as the traffic flow at the time, any potential dangers to the traffic by making the stop, the priorities of the agency, the officers' attitudes about traffic enforcement in general and specific violations in particular, the time of day, and weather conditions. All of these factors and others influence the decision of an individual officer to stop a particular vehicle. No road survey or other social science measurement technique can adequately model this decision-making process.

Data from police stops (i.e., the actual people that officers do stop as opposed to those they can theoretically stop) is the more appropriate data source from which to determine who does get stopped and for which violations they are stopped. The motorists that officers actually stop is a more reliable measure of officer behavior than theoretically determining the violations for which officers could stop motorists.

For all of these reasons, we argue that the appropriate data to use in determining the race/ethnicity violation matrix are the stop data from police departments in comparison to the refined estimates (benchmarks) of the driving population. From these data we know what violations draw the attention of police, and we know the violations for which drivers are stopped. And as we have noted, the vast majority of drivers are subject to being stopped due to one violation or another. It is true that traffic stop analyses should account for variations in more egregious driving behavior (e.g., speeding more than 15 miles over the posted limit) and that separate analyses for these different levels of violation should be conducted. We believe that it is not necessary or possible to develop a benchmark that adequately measures the factors that influence a police officer to stop a particular vehicle.

Appendix E

**APPENDIX E
A SUMMARY OF ARGUMENTS PERTAINING TO
WHETHER ANALYSTS SHOULD MEASURE
"WHO IS DRIVING" OR "WHO IS VIOLATING" FOR THE
BENCHMARK POPULATION**

Question	Measure "Who is Driving" (Arguments from Appendix D)	Measure "Who is Violating" (Arguments from this report)
What is the appropriate benchmark?	The appropriate benchmark is the driving population. All drivers are subject to being stopped by police.	The appropriate benchmark is the violating population. Conceptually, the benchmark is the population of drivers at risk of being stopped by police, assuming no bias. Some drivers are at greater risk than others of being stopped by police for legitimate reasons. The frequency and seriousness of their violations increase their risk of being stopped. We instruct police to make stopping decisions based on driver-violating behavior; as such, we must include this factor in our studies of their decisions.
Does the population of drivers differ from the population of violators in a meaningful way?	No. The population of drivers is the same as the population of violators because most—if not all—drivers violate traffic laws to some extent. That is, all drivers are legally subject to stops by police.	Yes. While it is, indeed, likely that all drivers engage in violations, the drivers who engage in serious violations or violate most frequently are likely at greater risk of being stopped by police. This fact makes driving quality relevant in any analysis of officers' decisions to stop drivers.

Question	Measure "Who is Driving" (Arguments from Appendix D)	Measure "Who is Violating" (Arguments from this report)
Are the egregious violators the ones stopped by police? Are the egregious violators more at risk of being stopped by police?	No. Officers do not "primarily stop egregious violators." But, yes, it may be that "drivers engaged in the most egregious violations are (the drivers) most likely to be stopped by police."	Agree with Appendix D on both points: answers are "no" and "yes," respectively. Police do not stop only egregious violators, but it is likely that the most egregious violators are most likely to be stopped by police. It is precisely because the most egregious violators are most likely to be stopped by police, that driving quality must be a factor encompassed in the research design.
What have the courts said about the benchmarks?	Some lower court decisions have held that "who is driving" is a legitimate benchmark because the "who is driving" population is essentially the same as the "who is violating" population. Again, this is because most drivers violate traffic laws to some extent.	The few decisions by lower courts have not said it was wrong to measure "who is violating," only that it is not necessary to do so. These decisions are not the last, definitive word. Other courts with other expert witnesses might conclude differently.
Should social scientists adopt court standards?	Yes. "In heavily contested litigation, there is actually more criticism (and scrutiny) of (research) results than (occurs in the context of) scientific review" (Lamberth, 2003).	No. The social science standards found acceptable by the courts are sometimes deemed unacceptable by social scientists.

Question	Measure "Who is Driving" (Arguments from Appendix D)	Measure "Who is Violating" (Arguments from this report)
Is there evidence that racial minorities violate traffic laws at a greater rate than do nonminorities?	No. There is no clear evidence that racial minorities violate traffic laws at a greater rate than nonminorities.	No. There is no clear evidence that racial minorities violate traffic laws at a greater rate than nonminorities. As Lamberth et al. indicated in Appendix D, research has not shown definitively that one group violates more frequently or more egregiously than another. Neither has research shown definitively that there are no differences between groups. It is because researchers can't rule out the possibility of differences in driving quality across racial/ethnic groups, that researchers must consider driving quality in their analysis. It may be that nonminorities violate more frequently or more egregiously than minorities. If this is true and our analyses don't encompass this possibility by considering driving quality, we will not be able to conduct a viable assessment of the existence of racially biased policing.

Appendix E

Question	Measure "Who is Driving" (Arguments from Appendix D)	Measure "Who is Violating" (Arguments from this report)
Which population—drivers or violators—can be measured most reliably?	The population of drivers can be measured more reliably than the population of violators. Measuring the population of drivers who are violating the many and varied traffic laws is virtually impossible. There are hundreds of violation types and most measures (except for measures of speeding) would be subjective.	Agreed: the population of all drivers can be measured more reliably than the population of all violators. Lamberth et al. are correct that researchers cannot reliably produce a profile of the drivers who violate any of the many traffic laws. To develop a benchmark based on "who is violating" requires the researcher to select specific types of violations (such as speeding) that are most amenable to measurement. The assessment that is conducted with this benchmark is arguably more valid than one that does not consider the impact of driving quality on police decisions. However, the scope of the assessment is limited—providing only a "spot check" of racially biased policing. Further, it is possible that the "spot check" does not encompass the officers, areas, or violations that manifest racially biased policing. The "costs" of this reduced scope are offset by the benefits of a more valid analysis of the factors that affect officers' stopping decisions.

References

Alpert, Geoffrey P. 2002. Personal email communication, October.

———. 2003a. Personal verbal communication, February.

———. 2003b. Personal email communication, August.

Alpert, Geoffrey P., Michael R. Smith, and Roger G. Dunham. 2003. "Toward a Better Benchmark: Assessing the Utility of Not-at-Fault Traffic Crash Data in Racial Profiling Research." Paper presented at the conference "Confronting Racial Profiling in the Twenty-first Century: Implications for Racial Justice," sponsored by the Northeastern University Institute on Race and Justice, Boston, Massachusetts, March 8-9.

The Alpert Group. 2003. *Miami-Dade Racial Profiling Study.* Draft of the methods section of the report to be submitted to the Miami-Dade County (Florida) Police Department.

Ayres, Ian. 2001. *Pervasive Prejudice? Unconventional Evidence of Race and Gender Discrimination.* Chicago, Ill.: The University of Chicago Press.

Bickman, Leonard, Debra J. Rog, and Terry E. Hedrick. 1998. "Applied Research Design: A Practical Approach." In *Handbook of Applied Social Research Methods*, edited by Leonard Bickman and Debra J. Rog, 5-37. Thousand Oaks, Calif.: Sage Publications.

Boniface, David. 2000. *Report on the Street Surveys Carried out for the Ethnic Monitoring Committee of Watford and Three Rivers Division of Hertfordshire Constabulary.* Unpublished manuscript, Statistics Group, University of Hertfordshire.

Braver, E. R. 2003. "Race, Hispanic Origin, and Socioeconomic Status in Relation to Motor Vehicle Occupant Death Rates and Risk Factors among Adults." *Accident Analysis and Prevention* 35(3): 295-309.

Calnon, Jennifer M., and Robin Shepard Engel. 2002. "Further Exploration of Base Rate Methodologies for Police Traffic Stops." Paper presented at the annual meeting of the American Society of Criminology, Chicago, Illinois, November 15.

Campbell DeLong Resources, Inc. 1999. "Public Perceptions of Stop Decisions by Oregon Police Officers." PowerPoint presentation prepared for the Oregon Criminal Justice Commission.

Canter, Phil. 2003. Personal phone communication with Phil Canter of the Analysis Unit of the Baltimore County Police Department, April 3.

Colon, I. 1992. "Race, Belief in Destiny, and Seat Belt Usage: A Pilot Study." *American Journal of Public Health* 82(6): 875-877.

Cordner, Gary, Brian Williams, and Alfredo Velasco. 2002. *Vehicle Stops in San Diego: 2001.* Report submitted to the San Diego Police Department.

Cordner, Gary, Brian Williams, and Maria Zuniga. 2001. *Vehicle Stops for the Year 2000: Annual Report.* Report submitted to the San Diego Police Department.

Cummings, P. 2002. "Association of Seat Belt Use with Death: A Comparison of Estimates Based on Data from Police and Estimates Based on Data from Trained Crash Investigators." *Injury Prevention* 8(4): 338-341.

Cummings, P., J. D. Wells, and F. P. Rivara. 2003. "Estimating Seat Belt Effectiveness Using Matched-Pair Cohort Methods." *Accident Analysis and Prevention* 35(1): 143-149.

Davis, Ron. 2001. *Racial Profiling: What Does the Data Mean?* Alexandria, Va.: National Organization of Law Enforcement Executives.

Decker, Scott. 2002. Personal written communication, October.

Decker, Scott, and Jeff Rojek. 2002. *Saint Louis Metropolitan Police Department Traffic Stop Patterns*. Report submitted by the University of Missouri, St. Louis to the St. Louis Police Department, January.

Deichert, Jerry. 2003. Personal written communication, June.

DeYoung, D.J., R. C. Peck, and C. J. Helander. 1997. "Estimating the Exposure and Fatal Crash Rates of Suspended/Revoked and Unlicensed Drivers in California." *Crash Analysis and Prevention* 29(1): 17-23.

Eck, John E., Lin Liu, and Lisa Growette Bostaph. 2003. Police Vehicle Stops in Cincinnati: July 1 – December 31, 2001. Report of Parties to Collaborative Agreement to the Monitor of that Agreement.

Edwards, Terry D., Elizabeth L. Grossi, Gennaro F. Vito, and Angela D. West. 2002a. *Traffic Stop Practices of the Louisville Police Department: January 15 - December 31, 2001.* Report submitted to the Louisville Division of Police.

———. 2002b. *Traffic Stop Practices of the Iowa City Police Department: April 1 - December 31, 2001.* Report submitted to the Iowa City Police Department.

Engel, Robin Shepard, and Jennifer M. Calnon. 2003. Personal email and verbal communications, January/February.

———. forthcoming. "Comparing Benchmark Methodologies for Police-Citizen Contacts: Traffic Stop Data Collection for the Pennsylvania State Police." *Police Quarterly*.

Engel, Robin Shepard, Jennifer M. Calnon, and Joshua R. Dutill. 2003. *Project on Police-Citizen Contacts, Six-Month Report*. Report prepared for the Office of the Commissioner of the Pennsylvania State Police by the Population Research Institute of the Pennsylvania State University.

Farmer, J. 2001. "Monitors' Quarterly and Training Evaluation Reports Track State Police Progress: Attorney General Releases

Traffic Survey and Semiannual Data on Statewide State Police Traffic Enforcement and Trooper Conduct." Trenton, N.J.: New Jersey Department of Law and Public Safety.

Farrell, Amy. 2003a. "Auditing Municipal Traffic Stop Data: Implications for Racial Profiling Analysis." PowerPoint presentation at "Confronting Racial Profiling in the Twenty-first Century: Implications for Racial Justice," conference sponsored by Northeastern University's Institute on Race and Justice, Boston, Massachusetts, March 8-9.

——. 2003b. Personal email communication, March.

Farrell, Amy, Jack McDevitt, Shea Cronin, and Erica Pierce. 2003. *Rhode Island Traffic Stop Statistics Act: Final Report*. Report submitted to the state of Rhode Island by the Northeastern University Institute on Race and Justice, June 30.

Farrell, Amy, Jack McDevitt, and Michael E. Buerger 2002. "Moving Police and Community Dialogues Forward through Data Collection Task Forces." *Police Quarterly* 5(3): 359-379.

Feest, J. 1968. "Compliance with Legal Regulations: Observation of Stop Sign Behavior." *Law and Society Review* II: 447-461.

Friday, Steve. 2002. "Data Collection: Ohio State Highway Patrol Model." Paper presented at the conference entitled "Bias-Based Policing: Where Are We Now?" sponsored by the Ohio Association of Chiefs of Police, Columbus, Ohio, September 25.

Fridell, Lorie. 2004. *Understanding Race Data from Vehicle Stops: A Stakeholder's Guide*. Washington, D.C.: Police Executive Research Forum.

Fridell, Lorie, Robert Lunney, Dre Diamond, and Bruce Kubu with Michael Scott and Colleen Lang. 2001. *Racially Biased Policing: A Principled Response*. Washington, D.C.: Police Executive Research Forum.

Gaines, Larry K. 2002. *An Analysis of Traffic Stop Data in the City of Riverside (California)*. Report submitted to the City of Riverside.

The Gallup Organization. 1999. "Racial Profiling Is Seen as Widespread, Particularly among Young Black Men." Available online at http://www.gallup.com/poll/releases/pr991209.asp.

——. 2001. "Gallup Social Audit on Black/White Relations in the U.S." Available online at http://www.gallup.com/poll/releases/pr010711.asp.

Glassbrenner, Donna. 2002. *Safety Belt and Helmet Use in 2002: Overall Results.* National Highway Traffic Safety Administration Technical Report, DOT HS 809 500, September.

——. 2003. Safety Belt Use in 2002: Demographic Characteristics. A National Highway Traffic Safety Administration Research Note, DOT HS 809 557, March.

Greenwald, Howard P. 2001. *Final Report: Police Vehicle Stops in Sacramento California.* Report to the Sacramento Police Department, October 31.

Hagan, Frank E. 1993. *Research Methods in Criminal Justice and Criminology*, 3d ed. Ontario: Macmillan Publishing Company.

Harris, David. 1999. "The Stories, the Statistics, and the Law: Why 'Driving while Black' Matters." *Minnesota Law Review* 84: 101-162.

Harris, David. 2002. *Profiles in Injustice: Why Racial Profiling Cannot Work.* New York, New York: The New Press.

Institute on Race and Poverty. 2003. *Minnesota Statewide Racial Profiling Report: All Participating Jurisdictions.* Report to the Minnesota Legislature, September 22.

Kirk, A., and N. Stamatiadis. 2001. *Evaluation of the Quasi-induced Exposure: Final Report.* Lexington, Ky.: University of Kentucky, Department of Civil Engineering.

Koornstra, M. J. 1973. "A Model for Estimation of Collective Exposure and Proneness from Crash Data." *Crash Analysis and Prevention* 5: 157-173.

Lamberth, John. 1996a. *Revised Statistical Analysis of the Incidence of Police Stops and Arrests of Black Drivers/Travelers on the New Jersey Turnpike between Interchanges 1 and 3 from the Years 1988 through 1991.*

Report of defendant's expert in *State* v. *Pedro Soto*, 734 A. 2d 350 (N.J. Super. Ct. Law. Div. 1996).

———. 1996b. Report of plaintiff's expert in *Wilkins* v. *Maryland State Police et al.*, Civil No. MJG-93-468 (D. Md. 1996).

———. 2001. *A Study of Biased Police Practices: Data Collection and Evaluation of the Washtenaw County Sheriff's Department.* Report submitted to the Washtenaw County (Michigan) Sheriff's Department, September.

———. 2002. Personal email communication, December.

———. 2003. Personal phone and email communications, July and August.

Lamberth, John, Karl Lamberth, and Jerry Clayton. 2003. Phone conversation, February.

Langan, Patrick A., Lawrence A. Greenfeld, Steven K. Smith, Matthew R. Durose, and David J. Levin. 2001. *Contacts between Police and the Public: Findings from the 1999 National Survey.* Report NCJ 184957. Washington, D.C.: U.S. Department of Justice.

Lange, James E., Kenneth O. Blackman, and Mark B. Johnson. 2001. *Speed Violation Survey of the New Jersey Turnpike: Final Report.* Report submitted by the Pacific Institute for Research and Evaluation to the Office of the Attorney General, State of New Jersey, December 13.

Lawson, Catherine. 2003. Personal email, October 5, from Catherine Lawson, assistant professor in the Geography and Planning Department, the University at Albany.

Lundman, Richard, and Robert L. Kaufman. 2003. "Driving while Black: Effects of Race, Ethnicity, and Gender on Citizen Self-Reports of Traffic Stops and Police Actions." *Criminology* 41(1): 195-220.

Lyles, R.W., P. Stamatiadis, and D. R. Lighthizer. 1991. "Quasi-induced Exposure Revisited." *Crash Analysis and Prevention* 23: 275-285.

Mastrofski, Stephen D., and Roger B. Parks. 1990. "Improving Observational Studies of Police." *Criminology* 28(August): 475-496.

Mastrofski, Stephen D., Roger B. Parks, Albert J. Reiss, Jr., Robert E. Worden, Christina DeJong, Jeffrey B. Snipes, and William Terrill. 1998. *Systematic Observation of Public Police: Applying Field Research Methods to Policy Issues.* Report NCJ 172859. Washington, D.C.: National Institute of Justice.

MVA and Joel Miller. 2000. "Profiling populations available for stops and searches." Police Research Series Paper 131. London: Home Office.

McConnell, Elizabeth H., and Amie R. Scheidegger. 2001. "Race and Speeding Citations: Comparing Speeding Citations Issued by Air Traffic Officers with Those Issued by Ground Traffic Officers." Paper presented at the annual meeting of the Academy of Criminal Justice Sciences, Washington, D.C., April 4-8.

McDevitt, Jack 2003. Personal email communication with Jack McDevitt, director, Institute on Race and Justice, Northeastern University, February.

McMahon, Joyce, Joel Garner, Ron Davis, and Amanda Kraus. 2002. *How to Correctly Collect and Analyze Racial Profiling Data: Your Reputation Depends on It! Final Report for Racial Profiling–Data Collection and Analysis.* Washington, D.C.: Government Printing Office. Available online at http://www.cops.usdoj.gov/Default.asp?Open=True&Item=770.

Meehan, Albert J., and Michael C. Ponder. 2002. "Race and Place: The Ecology of Racial Profiling African American Motorists." *Justice Quarterly* 19(3): 399-430.

Montgomery County (MD) Department of Police. 2002. *Traffic Stop Data Collection Analysis*, 3d report.

Moswoswe, Shamiso. 2003. Personal email communication, August, with Shamiso Moswoswe, program assistant of the Texas Criminal Justice Reform Coalition.

National Center for Statistics and Analysis (NCSA). 2002. *Annual Assessment of Motor Vehicle Crashes, Safety Belts.* Washington, D.C.: National Highway Traffic Safety Administration. Available at http://www-nrd.nhtsa.dot.gov/pdf/nrd-30/NCSA/Rpts/2003/Assess02.pdf (pages 51-54).

Norusis, Marija J. (n.d.). *SPSS 6.1 Guide to Data Analysis*. Englewood Cliffs, N.J.: Prentice Hall.

Novak, Kenneth. forthcoming. "Disparity and Racial Profiling in Traffic Enforcement." *Police Quarterly*.

Pierchala, Carl E., and Jyoti Surti. 1999. *Control Charts as a Tool in Data Quality Improvement*. Technical report of the U.S. Department of Transportation, National Highway Traffic Safety Administration, No. DOT HS 809 005.

Pisarski, Alan E. 1996. *Commuting in America II: The Second National Report on Commuting Patterns and Trends*. Lansdowne, Va.: Eno Transportation Foundation, Inc.

Posner, Mark A. 2002. Letter from Mark Posner, attorney with the Special Litigation Section of the Civil Rights Division of the U.S. Department of Justice, to Anthony Cowell, deputy attorney general, acting director of State Police Affairs in New Jersey, January 8.

Ramirez, D., J. McDevitt, and A. Farrell. 2000. *A Resource Guide on Racial Profiling Data Collection Systems: Promising Practices and Lessons Learned*. Washington, D.C.: U.S. Department of Justice.

Reichardt, Charles S., and Melvin M. Mark. 1998. "Quasi-experimentation." In *Handbook of Applied Social Research Methods*, edited by Leonard Bickman and Debra J. Rog, 193-228. Thousand Oaks, Calif.: Sage Publications.

Reiss, Albert J., Jr. 1967. *The Police and the Public*. New Haven, Conn.: Yale University Press.

———. 1968. "Stuff and Nonsense about Social Surveys and Observation." In *Institutions and the Person: Papers Presented to C. Everett Hughes*, edited by Howard S. Becker, Blanche Greer, David Riesman, and Robert S. Weiss. Chicago: Aldine Publishing Company.

———. 1971. "Systematic Observation of Natural Social Phenomena." In *Sociological Methodology*, ed. Herbert L. Costner, 3-33. San Francisco: Jossey-Bass.

Ridgeway, Greg. 2003. *Analysis of Racial Profiling in the Urban Environment*. Report for the Police Executive Research

Forum by the RAND Corporation, October.

Rojek, Jeff, Richard Rosenfeld, and Scott Decker. 2002. "The Influence of Driver's Race on Traffic Stops in Missouri." Unpublished document, University of Missouri, St. Louis.

Scales, Robert. 2001. "Racial Profiling: Seattle's Community Involved Approach." Presentation at the 2001 International Problem Oriented Policing Conference sponsored by the Police Executive Research Forum, San Diego, December.

Schafer, Joseph A., David L. Carter, and Andra Katz-Bannister. forthcoming. "Studying Traffic Stop Encounters. *Journal of Criminal Justice.*

Schmitt, Erica Leah, Patrick A. Langan, and Matthew R. Durose. 2002. *Characteristics of Drivers Stopped by Police, 1999.* NCJ 191548. Washington, DC: Bureau of Justice Statistics, U.S. Department of Justice.

Smith, Michael R. 2000. *The Traffic Stop Practices of the Richmond, Virginia, Police Department.* Final report submitted to the Richmond Police Department, November 1.

Smith, Michael R., and Geoffrey P. Alpert. 2003. "Searching for Direction: Courts, Social Science, and the Adjudication of Racial Profiling Claims." *Justice Quarterly* 19(4): 673-703.

Smith, M., and M. Petrocelli. 2001. "Racial Profiling? A Multivariate Analysis of Police Traffic Stop Data." *Police Quarterly* 4: 4-27.

Smith, Terry. 2003. "Review, Critique and Recommendations for Improving Racial Profiling Studies." Document developed by the Service Improvement Analyst of the City of Eugene Police Department.

Smith, William R., Donald Tomaskovic-Derey, Matthew T. Zingraff, H. Marcinda Mason, Patricia Y. Warren, and Cynthia Pfaff Wright. 2003. *The North Carolina Highway Traffic Study*. Final report submitted to the National Institute of Justice, Grant No. 1999-MU-CX-0022. Washington, D.C.: National Institute of Justice.

Spitzer, Eliot. 1999. *The New York City Police Department's "Stop and Frisk" Practices: A Report to the People of the State of New*

York from the Office of the Attorney General. Civil Rights Bureau, Attorney General of the State of New York, December 1. http://www.oag.state.ny.us/press/reports/stop_frisk/stop_frisk.html

Stamatiadis, N., and J. A. Deacon. 1997. "Quasi-induced Exposure: Methodology and Insight." *Crash Analysis and Prevention* 29(1): 37-52.

State v. Pedro Soto 734 A. 2d 350 (N.J. Super.Ct. Law. Div. 1996).

Thomas, Deborah. 2001. *Preliminary Summary Report: Denver Police Department Contact Card Data, June 1, 2001 through August 31, 2001.* Report provided to the Denver Police Department. http://admin.denvergov.org/police/template/9843.asp.

———. 2002. *First Annual Report, Denver Police Department Contact Card Data Analysis, June 1, 2001 through May 31, 2002.* Report provided to the Denver Police Department, October. http://admin.denvergov.org.

Tomaskovic-Devey, Donald, Cynthia Pfaff Wright, and Ronald Czaja. 2003. "Self-Reports of Police Speeding Stops by Race: Results from the North Carolina Reverse Record Check Survey." Unpublished manuscript, Department of Sociology and Anthropology, North Carolina State University.

U.S. Department of Transportation, Federal Highway Administration. 1995. *Nationwide Personal Transportation Survey*, Microdata Files CD-ROM. Washington, D.C.: U.S. Department of Transportation.

U.S. Department of Transportation, Bureau of Transportation Statistics, *Transportation Statistics Annual Report 2000*, BTS01-02 (Washington, D.C.: 2001). See http://www.bts.gov/publications/tsar.

Walker, Samuel. 2001. Searching for the denominator: Problems with police traffic stop data and an early warning system solution. Justice Research and Policy, Vol. 3(2): 63-95.

———. 2002. "The Citizen's Guide to Interpreting Traffic Stop Data: Unraveling the Racial Profiling Controversy." Unpublished.

———. 2003. Internal benchmarking for traffic stop data: An early intervention system approach. Discussion paper available at http://www.policeforum.org.

Walker, S., and G. Alpert. 2000. *Early Warning Systems: Concept, History, and Issues*. IQ Service Report, No. 8, August. Washington, D.C.: International City Management Association.

Wilkins v. Maryland State Police, Settlement Agreement, Civil No. MJG-93-468 (D. Md. 1995).

Zingraff, Matthew T. 2003a. Personal email communication, March.

———.2003b. Personal phone communication, August.

Zingraff, Matthew T., H. Marcinda Mason, William R. Smith, Donald Tomaskovic-Devey, Patricia Warren, Harvey L. McMurray, and C. Robert Fenlon. 2000. *Evaluating North Carolina State Highway Patrol Data: Citations, Warnings and Searches in 1998*. Report submitted to the North Carolina Department of Crime Control and Public Safety and North Carolina State Highway Patrol. Available online at http://www.nccrimecontrol.org/shp/ncshpreport.htm.

About the Author

Dr. Lorie Fridell is Director of Research for the Police Executive Research Forum (PERF) and a social scientist by training. Prior to joining PERF in 1999, she was a tenured associate professor of criminology and criminal justice first at the University of Nebraska and then at Florida State University. She has been conducting research on law enforcement for more than 15 years and is a national expert on racial profiling. The lead author of *Racially Biased Policing: A Principled Response* (PERF 2001), Fridell also has written extensively on such topics as police use of force, citizen complaints, police pursuits, and problem-oriented policing.

About the Office of Community Oriented Policing Services (COPS) U.S. Department of Justice

The Office of Community Oriented Policing Services (COPS) was created in 1994 and has the unique mission to directly serve the needs of state and local law enforcement. The COPS Office has been the driving force in advancing the concept of community policing, and is responsible for one of the greatest infusions of resources into state and local law enforcement in our nation's history.

Since 1994, COPS has invested $10.6 billion to add community policing officers to the nation's streets, enhance crime fighting technology, support crime prevention initiatives, and provide training and technical assistance to help advance community policing. COPS funding has furthered the advancement of community policing through community policing innovation conferences, the development of best practices, pilot community policing programs, and applied research and evaluation initiatives. COPS has also positioned itself to respond directly to emerging law enforcement needs. Examples include working in partnership with departments to enhance police integrity, promoting safe schools, and combating the methamphetamine drug problem.

The COPS Office has made substantial investments in law enforcement training. COPS created a national network of Regional Community Policing Institutes that are available to state and local law enforcement, elected officials and community leaders for training opportunities on a wide range of community policing topics. COPS also supports the advancement of community policing strategies through the Community Policing Consortium. Additionally, COPS has made a major investment in applied research which makes possible the growing body of substantive knowledge covering all aspects of community policing.

These substantial investments have produced a significant national community policing infrastructure, as evidenced by the fact that at the present time, approximately 86% of the nation's population is served by law enforcement agencies practicing community policing. The COPS Office continues to respond proactively by providing critical resources, training, and technical assistance to help state and local law enforcement implement innovative and effective community policing strategies.

About PERF

The Police Executive Research Forum (PERF) is a national professional association of chief executives of large city, county and state law enforcement agencies. PERF's objective is to improve the delivery of police services and the effectiveness of crime control through several means:

- the exercise of strong national leadership,
- the public debate of police and criminal justice issues,
- the development of research and policy, and
- the provision of vital management and leadership services to police agencies.

PERF members are selected on the basis of their commitment to PERF's objectives and principles. PERF operates under the following tenets:

- Research, experimentation and exchange of ideas through public discussion and debate are paths for the development of a comprehensive body of knowledge about policing.
- Substantial and purposeful academic study is a prerequisite for acquiring, understanding and adding to that body of knowledge.
- Maintenance of the highest standards of ethics and integrity is imperative in the improvement of policing.
- The police must, within the limits of the law, be responsible and accountable to citizens as the ultimate source of police authority.
- The principles embodied in the Constitution are the foundation of policing.

Related PERF Titles

And Justice for All: Understanding and Controlling Police Abuse of Force

Citizen Involvement: How Community Factors Affect Progressive Policing

Citizen Review Resource Manual

Crime Analysis Through Computer Mapping

Crime Mapping Case Studies: Successes in the Field (Volumes 1 and 2)

Deadly Force: What We Know(A Practitioner's Desk Reference on Police Involved Shootings

Drug Enforcement in Minority Communities: The Minneapolis Police Department, 1985-1990

Force Factor: Measuring Police Use of Force Relative to Suspect Resistance

Information Management and Crime Analysis: Practitioner's Recipes for Success Mapping Across Boundaries: Regional Crime Analysis

Police Education and Minority Recruitment: The Impact of a College Requirement

Police Interactions with Racial and Ethnic Minorities: Resolving the Contradictions Between Allegations and Evidence

Policing a Multicultural Community

Racially Biased Policing: A Principled Response

Using Research: A Primer for Law Enforcement Managers

Why Police Organizations Change: A Study of Community-Oriented Policing

PERF also has many publications on community problem solving, evaluating police agencies and practices and other materials used for promotion exams, training and university classes. For a free catalog or more information, call toll-free to 1-888-202-4563. PERF's online bookstore and free download documents can be found at www.policeforum.org.

www.ingramcontent.com/pod-product-compliance
Lightning Source LLC
Chambersburg PA
CBHW080234180526
45167CB00006B/2271